126 FAMOUS PEOPLE TELL OF THE
TEACHERS WHO MADE A DIFFERENCE

andi Toksvig Andrew Motion Emma Thomps   Oldfield Julian Cla
lonty Don Martin Bell John Mortimer Fiona Bruce Peter Hillary Mic
osen David Atten   ker Alan Titchn
Quentin Blake A   n Widdecor
onnie O'Sull   stinov Sue
hnston Al   remy Clar
hris Bonir   Helena
ennedy S   on Call
lalcolm F   Steve
edgrave   Nettles
larissa Di   Jeremy
ue Leith   bson Sian
hillips Olive   er Jennie E
lichael Fish J   man Baker
usannah York   ven Berkoff Sc
lis-Bextor Ran   John Inverdale A
homas Ellis Rog   y John Humphr
om Parker Bowle   el Eavis Bear Gryll
imothy Spall Kir   ner Gaby Logan Mich
spel Lynne   Rego Joe Royle Candi
vcett Green Deborah Meaden Peter Snow Josephine Cox Mark Rampr
enny Vincenzi Nigel Planer Carol Smillie Gordon Ramsay Toyah Willc
cEwan Zoë Wanamaker Clare Balding Steve Redgrave Michael Winner H

My Favourite Teacher

First Published 2012

Printed in England

For more information visit:
www.ovolobooks.co.uk

Aspect is an imprint of Ovolo Books Ltd

**These interviews were previously published
in the Times Educational Supplement**

126 celebrities tell tales of the teachers who inspired them

Sandi Toksvig	Geri Halliwell	Tom Parker Bowles
Andrew Motion	Tim Waterstone	Marsha Hunt
Emma Thompson	Betty Boothroyd	Anna Massey
Bruce Oldfield	Steve Redgrave	Michael Eavis
Julian Clary	Helen Mirren	Bear Grylls
Monty Don	Brendan Barber	Timothy Spall
Martin Bell	Howard Jacobson	Kirsty Wark
John Mortimer	John Nettles	Denis Healey
Fiona Bruce	Clarissa Dixon Wright	Connie Fisher
Peter Hillary	Anna Ford	Gaby Logan
Michael Rosen	Brian Blessed	Michael Aspel
David Attenborough	Matthew Parris	Lynne Truss
Gary Rhodes	Jeremy Vine	Leslie Thomas
Zoe Wanamaker	Prue Leith	Aled Jones
Alan Titchmarsh	Patrick Moore	Paula Rego
Quentin Blake	Maeve Binchy	Joe Royle
Angela Huth	Antony Worrall Thompson	Candida Lycett Green
Nick Robinson	Sian Phillips	Deborah Meaden
Wayne Sleep	Oliver Sacks	Peter Snow
Ann Widdecombe	Mariella Frostrup	Josephine Cox
Ronnie O'Sullivan	Nigel Havers	Mark Ramprakash
Jilly Cooper	Frank Skinner	Penny Vincenzi
John Birt	Jennie Bond	Nigel Planer
Jasper Conran	Michael Fish	Carol Smillie
Peter Ustinov	Joanne Harris	Rasshied Din
Sue Johnston	Benedict Allen	Helen Boaden
Alan Sugar	Vanessa-Mae	Ian McEwan
Joanna Trollope	Norman Baker	Rhona Cameron
Clive James	Susannah York	Dickie Bird
Hazel Irvine	Frank Gardner	Beryl Bainbridge
Jeremy Clarkson	Duchess of Devonshire	Susie Dent
Chris Bonington	Steven Berkoff	Michael Holroyd
Gordon Ramsay	Sophie Ellis-Bextor	Jill Paton Walsh
Toyah Willcox	Ranulph Fiennes	Sam Torrance
James Dyson	Diane Abbott	Wendy Holden
Helena Kennedy	Ned Sherrin	Roger Graef
Steve Jones	John Inverdale	Tony Hawks
Clare Balding	Alice Thomas Ellis	Colleen McCullough
Michael Winner	Roger McGough	Philip Gould
Betty Jackson	Edward Heath	Max Clifford
Simon Callow	Sarah Beeny	Michael Bond
Malcolm Rifkind	John Humphrys	Joan Sims

CLIVE JAMES
journalist

Jazz Aked taught English as if it was carpentry. He taught us how to parse a sentence. He taught us the parts of speech. He taught us the art of composition. And if your composition was regarded as good, he would get you to read it out and the result is the foundation of what I laughingly call my career.

We called him Jazz because he loved jazz and talked about it. I was 13 or 14 when I first met him, and his great influence on my life was when I was between 14 and 15.

The only thing at school I was really good at was English. I gradually got worse at everything else but stayed good at English, mainly because of his influence. He was very patient with the people who didn't have a knack for the subject. I was inevitably one of his pets because I got it quite quickly. He would have a spelling bee at the end of class and the boy who got most right got off early and was the first down to the sweet shop to get a frozen lolly on a stick. I won often enough to become very unpopular until I learned the knack of losing occasionally.

I was in the wrong school. Sydney Technical High School was a very mathematical school and I had a reverse gift for mathematics. I should have gone to Sydney High. I had a scholarship to go there but didn't want to go because my friends from primary school were going to Sydney Tec. I was absolutely no good with my hands - as was soon proved in the woodworking and metalworking classes. I produced an 89 degree set square and made a breadboard from four pieces of wood which I planed so much eventually they were size of chopsticks, and I ended up with a breadboard you couldn't have cut a baguette on.

It occurred to me in later years that perhaps Jazz Aked was in the wrong school, too. He should have been working with pupils who had more of a knack for what he was teaching. But he was dedicated. He was full of suspicion when the new kind of teaching started to come in and pupils were encouraged to do projects and paste things onto pieces of cardboard and so on. He did his duty and carried out the new curriculum, but he thought it was time wasted from what we should have been doing, which was learning to construct an English sentence.

Reading out my compositions in class came easy to me. It was pretty hard to stop me; I was a natural performer. I can remember reading out an essay I wrote about being in primary school when it was caught in a bush fire. Some of the episodes I wrote about I eventually put into my autobiography.

Jazz Aked had a good appreciation of the Australian landscape. If you wrote about a tree he'd get you to say what kind it was. He was very good on building vocabulary. We did lots of tests on similes and antonyms, creative exercises that stocked my memory. He was a natural sub-editor. He was very good at going through a sentence and explaining where you had said something twice, or not said enough. He didn't write creatively himself, but he wrote a very elegant sentence in a very clear hand.

He was wonderfully uninterested in school sports. He would turn us loose on the football field and go off and read a book. He looked on with sympathy as my marks in other classes withered away so I barely got my leaving certificate. I'm not so sure he thought I'd get to university at the rate I was going, but he suggested that as I was good at reading and writing I should do something with that. I studied English among other subjects at Sydney University, but I majored in psychology, and eventually came to England and read English at Cambridge.

I saw Jazz again 20 years later when I went back to Australia. He hadn't changed a bit. He is one of those men who looks permanently young and fit. He had followed my work, which was extremely flattering, and I think he'd noted his influence in my correctly constructed sentences.

SANDI TOKSVIG
broadcaster, writer and comedienne

It was quite by chance I ended up in Duke Schirmer's English class. My father was a foreign correspondent for Danish television and I spent my formative years in New York. When I joined Mamaroneck High School as a freshman in the 9th grade, aged 13, I was offered a wide choice of classes. Duke Schirmer taught creative writing and I was attracted by his name. To be honest, I thought he was going to be black – I was very "right on".

My first sight of him was standing on his head in the corner of the room as I walked in.

Mamaroneck was an enormous school. There were 2,600 students and I knew no one. It was a public school – what we'd call a state school – and at first I was terrified by its size. I'd been to many schools before – indeed, I'd been thrown out of a couple – but never anywhere so large. In the American system you have a home room where you gather at the beginning of the day to say the pledge of allegiance, and then you all go off to different classes and you may never see your classmates again for the rest of the day.

When I was there in 1971 all the male teachers wore suits, but Duke Schirmer dressed in jeans and a T-shirt and this was considered a little weird. He was a very intense man with very thick glasses and the fact that he taught a lot of his classes standing on his head was also seen as extremely peculiar.

I never found out the reason he stood on his head. I think it helped him to think more clearly – or so he claimed. I tried it myself without success; I'm not physically adept, I can't even do a forward roll.

He taught me for one year and it was probably one of the most creative years of my life. He didn't believe in giving marks for grammar or punctuation; he implied that the mechanics of writing were not important if you had something to say. When I wrote a short story for him called "Army", he simply wrote across the bottom: "Keep writing like a fiend". My story was about a soldier who goes out to Vietnam thinking he is fighting for freedom and realises all he is doing is killing women and children. The Vietnam War was a very big topic at the time, but it was something about which I could have known nothing whatsoever at the age of 13.

Those few words of encouragement had a fantastic effect on me in terms of wanting to write and be involved in writing. When I came to England the following year to go to boarding school to do my O and A- levels I was incensed by being made to read books and take them apart grammatically and look at structure all the time.

Duke Schirmer had an energy and a love of teaching and a love of his subject that I don't think I came across again until I went to university. We called him Duke, which was pretty far out, and for many of his lessons we would sit on the floor with our legs crossed which seemed very cool and hip.

His teaching method was to write a word on the board and you would have to say what immediately sprung into your mind – a technique I use now if I get stuck when I'm writing. For a long while I had a blackboard and a piece of chalk in my office and would write trigger words for myself if I came to a complete stop. It's much the same technique as is used in improvisation. Duke Schirmer was interested in unlocking your creativity and I suspect that's why he didn't wear a jacket and tie and why we called him Duke and why lessons were very relaxed. We were allowed to be free in what we were thinking.

I have kept in touch with a group of friends from those high school days and curiously enough quite a lot of us were interested in the creative arts and went into the theatre. I think he had a huge impact on many people.

I want to find him again. I want to say to him: "Thank you so much. Thank you for what you did for me".

EMMA THOMPSON
actress and screenwriter

On the first day of the school year at Beckford Primary we all sat cross-legged on the floor in the school hall waiting to be told which form we'd be going into and those of us who were lucky enough to be picked to go into Mr Ray's class cheered. He was a remarkable teacher, and popular with everyone.

He was Indian, a handsome man who always wore dark trousers and a newly-pressed and laundered crisp white shirt. He was probably under 30 then because he's still teaching now – he's a headmaster – and I invited him to the premiere of my film, *Nanny McPhee*.

What made Mr Ray so special was that his lessons were consistently interesting and he seemed genuinely interested in us kids. We were a very mixed bag. It was a state school of multiple ethnicity and many different levels of capability and commitment and he managed to turn the whole class into a cohesive group.

He also kept discipline in an original way. I remember once, at the time of one of the moon landings, we had all made Apollo rockets out of the usual *Blue Peter* materials and had them proudly displayed around the classroom. We had acted up and Mr Ray decided to punish the entire class. He got a big black bin liner and one by one put all our models into the bag. He did it very carefully, so I knew he wasn't really going to throw them away, but I was only seven or eight and have never forgotten the silence in which this terrible task was performed.

At home my mother said I was so full of energy bringing me up was like being flattened by a steam roller, but I was law-abiding at school.

I had some great teachers at my secondary school, Camden School For Girls. Terry Buckley, who taught classics, was enormous fun. He was very enthused and he managed to enthuse us too. So did Anne Spratling, another Latin teacher I loved. Both of them brought humour and wit to their teaching. I was good at Latin, French, English and biology. I was not good at physics or chemistry or geography or history and was rubbish at games. In the main the teachers I liked were those who taught the subjects I enjoyed. Had I got on better with my history teacher I think I would have enjoyed it more because history is now something that fascinates me.

It was a pretty academic school, but more artsy academic than sciencey academic. We didn't do much in the way of theatrical productions though I remember playing the part of a man in *Lady Audley's Secret*.

We had some wonderful English teachers including Mrs Strickland, who was heaven. She would stare into space, above our heads, and talk about a book or a passage in a kind of incandescent way. Mrs Kellaway was also an enthused and loving teacher. We did *Macbeth* and I was profoundly in love with that play and its dark, sticky, bloody language. And one must not forget Mrs Popplewell, who taught biology. Biology was the one science I liked and I did it for a year along with French, Latin and English until I found I couldn't manage four A-levels. Mrs Popplewell was a lot of fun.

But if I had to choose the one teacher who influenced me more than any other it would be Mr Ray because when I was very young he made me believe in myself. He was good at giving praise where it was due and he was judicious. He didn't have favourites. I loved the fact that he made us all feel equal and that we all belonged.

I was lucky with my tutors at Cambridge, too. Jean Gooder who interviewed me for a place was fantastic. She actually listened to what I had to say about Charlotte Brontë and seemed genuinely interested. She had the same quality that Mr Ray had. She made me feel that I had something worth saying – that's a remarkable quality that is not necessarily present in all teachers, even the good ones.

9

BRUCE OLDFIELD
fashion designer

I enjoyed my time at school much more than the time I spent in the Dr Barnardo's Home where I lived. The food and the whole environment were better and I had some good teachers. Looking back I realise that I veered towards the women teachers – probably because I was looking for a mother figure.

Edith Allison was the most inspirational teacher I ever had. She taught English literature and had a profound effect on me because of her passion for the poetry of Gerard Manley Hopkins. We all thought she was 60, but she was probably only in her early forties, a spinster with a rather cruel mouth and black hair flecked with grey. As teenagers we could see smut in anything but when she explained the quotation: "Yields tender as a pushed peach" from *The Bugler's First Communion* we showed her respect. She knew what she was talking about and took no truck from anybody. She had a presence. When she walked into the room everyone was quiet.

Because of Miss Allison, the work of Gerard Manley Hopkins made such an impression on me that I asked to be given an anthology of his poems instead of the traditional Bible when I left Barnardo's. I still dip into it often. A few years ago, after she'd died, somebody found her actual copy with all her annotations in a junk shop and sent it to me. It's a treasured possession.

Another favourite teacher was Constance Gilbey with whom I am still in touch. She was headmistress at Ripon Grammar School and also ran the girls' boarding house (the school was part day and part boarding). She taught Latin and French. Petite, with spectacles and a billowing black gown, there was a motherly side to her, though she could be formidable when checking the girls' skirt length. I found her very understanding when I joined the school late without having done any Latin and had to start from scratch in the third year.

I was bewitched by Miss Houston, who looked like a movie star. I always sat on the front row in her classes. She taught French, which I was good at, and was elegant rather than sexy — more Deborah Kerr than Gina Lollobrigida — dressed in beautiful suits and co-ordinated from head to toe. I remember her handbags and shoes being always perfectly matched and she had lots of different attachments to her spectacles to tone in with her outfits.

I had a crush on Miss Hurd, who taught art and craft. She was young and slightly hippie. She had very long straight hair with a fringe and looked a bit like Sandie Shaw with shoes. To me she seemed the embodiment of chic. I remember making two three-sided pots in her class which were turned into lamp bases. I got on very well with Tony Smith, too, who taught art. He never once commented on the fact that every picture I drew was of women in dresses with high heels, usually bar scenes or in discotheques. I failed O-level art the first time round and took it again.

I doodled in most lessons, which got me into trouble sometimes. I was good at subjects I was interested in and very poor at the rest. I didn't get on at all well with the woodwork teacher or the gym master but enjoyed biology because it was well taught by a man whose name I cannot now remember.

The headmaster, Mr Atkinson, known by his initials RA, was an intimidating figure in his academic gown, but he was kindly towards me and I made great friends with his daughter, Susan, who was gorgeous and very bright. His parting shot on my final report was: "He expects a lot from life. We shall miss him."

Constance Gilbey left Ripon to go to Sheffield City College and I followed her and took a teacher training course there. I finished the course, but never taught. I knew I'd make a lousy teacher so I went to art college and set about realising my ambition of becoming a fashion designer.

JULIAN CLARY
comedian and novelist

When I was 14 or 15 I quite enjoyed the celebrity status of being the school poof. It had a bit of glamour about it. My friend, Nick, and I wandered around with colour-rinsed hair, certain we were going to be famous, and the teachers turned a blind eye. We were quite subversive, though never did anything we could get into trouble for. We would wear odd socks and too much aftershave, which weren't beatable offences.

My early school days were happy. I wasn't very bright and couldn't read or write until long after I should have been able to – I used to do mirror writing – but I had a number of teachers at Sacred Heart Primary who helped me, Mrs Lang in particular. She was petite and energetic and had red hair. She took a lot of time with me and was ever so pleased when I got something right because it didn't happen very often. We're still in touch. She lives in Manchester now and comes to see me when I'm touring and brings her daughter.

When I was about 10 I suddenly caught up enough to get me through the 11-plus and the entrance exam to St Benedict's, the junior school of Ealing Abbey. I was a well-mannered, charming little boy and I think I charmed the monks at my interview. I was very chatty and a good Catholic. I was an altar boy and tended the priests' garden. I remember telling the monks how to tell the sex of a baby guinea pig which no doubt swung things at the interview.

To me the monks seemed very glamorous in their flowing long black robes with hoods, swanning along the corridors and I liked the chanting and the vestments and the incense. The headmaster, Father G, and I took to each other immediately. He was gentle and kind, in his late 40s, tall with a ruddy complexion and big yellow teeth. His eyes twinkled with wit and warmth. Whenever he asked a question in class I always put up my hand just because I liked having a banter with him.

Then, one Wednesday, I forgot my swimming kit – an offence that led to Father G punishing me by beating me with a leather strap about a foot long and half an inch thick. What shocked me most wasn't the humiliation of being flogged for a minor matter of forgetfulness, but the terrifying transformation of Father G from paternal holy priest to furious strap wielding monster. I never willingly spoke to him again. My father being a policeman and my mother a probation officer, I had a very strong sense of right and wrong and justice and was outraged.

Most of my teachers were monks, but some were real people. One of my favourites was John Moore who taught English and drama. He was young, tall and languid and a bit fey and wore flared trousers. He introduced me to something called "exciting writing." He staged a drama once where one of the naughty boys from another class burst in and started shouting and swearing and we were asked to write down what we felt during the experience. I was good at writing stories and Mr Moore taught me to trust my imagination and to go with the flow.

I remember Mr Klepacz who was my form master in Upper 4, too. He looked a bit like Marc Bolan with lots of curly hair and a moustache. I didn't particularly bond with him – he was a bit blokey – and he taught physics with chemistry which was a mystery to me. My least favourite teacher was Father Kasimir. He was quite fearsome and smelly and grubby and walked with a purposeful strut as if he knew he was just about to discover some wrongdoing round the next corner. My best teacher of all, my own Jean Brodie, was Frances Hanley who also taught English. She was glamorous, young and beautiful with flowing red hair. Her classes were a joy and she inspired us all. She let me exercise my imagination and was full of encouragement. On one end of term report she wrote of me: "The sky's his limit." When she left to have children I was devastated.

FIONA BRUCE
TV newsreader and broadcaster

When I was 10 my father's job took him to Italy and I went to the International School of Milan which was a melting pot of children from all over the world. The teachers came from all over the world too and they were an anarchic bunch.

One of my favourites was Mrs McKay, who taught English. She was a rigorous grammar teacher in a way that I never came across at any other point in my education. She was obsessed with the minutiae of grammar: sub-clauses, subjunctives and all that. But she livened up what could have been rather dry, boring lessons by suddenly taking off her wig at dull moments. She had dark auburn hair and one day it would be short and the next long, but it took us a while to suspect that she wore a wig. Eventually someone plucked up the courage to ask and after that she would whip it off just to liven things up.

There was another English teacher at the school I liked called John Ward. He had long blond hair and a big moustache and we all thought he was groovy. His trick when a class got boring was to do a handstand. We would all be sitting with heads down writing and if he thought things were getting a bit serious he'd do a handstand – just for the hell of it. He was fantastic. He was in his 30s I should think, a really funky guy who wore jeans and tank tops which were very trendy in the 1970s.

I was one of the few in the class for whom English was a first language and while the others were doing basic stuff, which I finished quickly, he would call me to his desk. We would discuss literature, read poetry and he'd show me pictures of Goya paintings. He was particularly interested in the Spanish Civil War. We talked about things that weren't always strictly related to English, but were part of his aim of expanding my horizons. I learned from him to appreciate creative writing and to think critically.

If the headmaster had walked in while Mr Ward was doing one of his handstands he wouldn't have cared two hoots. Although education was taken seriously, it was a very relaxed school. There was no uniform and the curriculum was pretty flexible.

Madame Vassallo, who taught French, didn't do handstands, but she had a unique style. From the moment she walked in the classroom she spoke nothing but French and we were only allowed to speak French. At first we couldn't understand a word as she chattered away, but gradually it began to sink in. Even if we put up our hand to go to the loo, or to ask what something meant, we would have to say it in French. We were completely baffled to begin with but my goodness, her technique worked.

When I came to England at 14 and went to Haberdashers Aske's in south-east London it was quite a shock. It was an all-girls school with a structured curriculum. Everyone wore uniform and the pupils seemed very sophisticated. A lot of them wore make up and smoked.

There were a number of fantastic teachers at Aske's, including Miss Doris Griffin, who taught music. The school was known for its music and its reputation was all down to her. She taught us music at O-level and A-level. She organised choirs, put on musicals and even operas. I can remember singing a duet with a girl called Cherry. Miss Griffin was one of those teachers with a passion for what she did which she couldn't help but communicate to others. Even unmusical girls came out of that school with some love of music. She was inspirational, dedicated and a lovely woman with a mischievous sense of fun.

A few years ago when I went back for a reunion I saw her for the first time since I left. She hadn't changed a bit. She asked me to call her Doris, but I just couldn't bring myself to.

I enjoyed my schooldays enormously. Italy was fun. Aske's was different, but the teachers were good and caring. I made the best friends of my life at school.

MONTY DON

TV gardener

I was kicked out of primary school for putting nettles down girls' knickers and getting more black marks in a term than anyone had in their entire school career. So at the age of eight I became a boarder a little earlier than planned. I went to an all-boys school, which no longer exists, with the spectacular name of Bigshotte. The headmaster had been a boy at the school in the 1920s and it really hadn't changed from his day. The curriculum was based on Latin, Greek, French, maths, English, history, geography and divinity and that was it. We didn't get any science at all. Everything was geared towards Common Entrance and classes were small. The biggest, I think, was 12 and it wasn't unusual to be in a group of eight. We were kept busy from morning till night. It was a harsh regime; we were always hungry and always cold. But we had 60 acres of woods to play in.

Ian McWhinnie, who taught English and drama, was different from the other teachers. He brought a tape recorder into class and we listened to plays he had recorded from the radio. He'd put on a piece of music and get us paint a picture of the music and then write a poem about the picture. I took to his teaching style and Mr McWhinnie nurtured and encouraged me. I wrote poetry and entered national competitions and won them. He put on a play every term and I took part. We did T.S. Eliot's *Murder in the Cathedral* and I was Beckett.

With hindsight, Mr McWhinnie wasn't a particularly nice man. He had a terrible temper and could be a bully, screaming and shouting at little boys, reducing them to tears. He didn't do it to me because I was his favourite. But he was incredibly involved and passionate and his great gift as a teacher was that he took us all seriously. He asked what you thought about things and gave the impression that he really wanted to know. If you did a painting he'd put it on the wall and bring in people to look at it. His lessons were great fun and he got very good results. He was the first person to teach me that expressing yourself through writing, music, acting or painting was something to be really treasured.

I went next to Malvern, which I loathed from day one. Jeremy Paxman went there too and I know that he hated it as well. I never engaged with the school and the school never engaged with me. I stayed for seven terms and then by mutual agreement, left. I got seven O-levels despite them and went to sixth-form college to do my A-levels. My results were appalling. I hitchhiked through France with my guitar and round about Marseilles decided to go back and re-take English, entirely for my own pride. I worked on a building site by day and studied in the evening. I got an A grade and an S level and then went off to France again.

While I was in France I decided I'd like to go to Cambridge, sent off for past papers and got into Magdalen College where I was taught by a wonderful man called Arthur Sale. I was 21 and he was 70 and I adored him. Arthur was an old-fashioned bohemian from a working-class background in Nottingham. He was a poet, loved paintings, was funny and iconoclastic. He'd met Eliot, corresponded with DH Lawrence and seemed to know many leading literary figures, but he never boasted. He was the most modest man I'd ever met.

Arthur's standards were astonishingly high. If there was one tiny error of punctuation or grammar, he'd pounce. He wouldn't allow any sloppiness. I used to sit writing my essays for Arthur with sweat pouring off me. When I read him my work he'd somehow manage to make me feel wonderful while at the same time that my essay had just scratched the surface and there was much more to learn, a lot of which he would tell me and the rest I would be inspired to go to find out.

Arthur and I shared a love of wild flowers, the countryside and walking as well as poetry and music. I left university planning to write fiction and probably work on a farm to finance it. He thought that was great.

DAVID ATTENBOROUGH
naturalist, broadcaster and author

Horace Lacey taught biology with gusto in the sixth form at Wyggeston Grammar School for Boys in Leicester when I was there in the 1940s. His enthusiasm for his subject spilled over. He was a stocky man who walked like a gamecock with his head turned to one side, and he had wiry frizzy hair. He had enormous brio.

Until I reached the sixth form I didn't enjoy my schooldays much. There was so much rote learning – I can still say, *"Amo, amas, amat, amamus, amatis, amant"* but God knows what that has done for me. I wasn't interested in most of the subjects we had to study. I defy anybody to be interested in Latin declensions or French irregular verbs. My reports said: "Good work, spoilt by silly behaviour." I played up, tried to create some kind of diversion. It wasn't until I was in the science sixth and was studying a subject I really enjoyed that I had a good time.

To come into Horace Lacey's class, where you were treated as a thinking human being who might have interests and enthusiasms was so refreshing. He was a good teacher who conveyed his delight and fascination for the natural world and I was very grateful to him.

As well as being a good naturalist, I remember he was also passionate about steam engines and would talk to us about Sir Nigel Gresley, the great engineer who designed and built locomotives for the Great Western Railway. I'm not in the least interested in steam engines, but his sheer infectious enthusiasm made me seem delighted by it all.

I'd been keen on natural history since I was very young and by the age of seven had my own "museum" at home in which I displayed my collection of butterflies, birds' eggs, abandoned nests, conkers, the shed skin of a grass snake and fossils. What I was most interested in was geology and palaeontology. Fossils have fascinated me for as long as I can remember. As a boy I spent much of my free time collecting the ammonites which are abundant in the Jurassic limestone in the countryside around Leicester. The excitement of hitting a block of stone with a hammer and seeing it fall apart to reveal a beautiful coiled shell 50 million years old is as exiting to me today as it was when I was a small boy.

The school had no provision for geology, but my father, who was principal of the city's University College, discovered that one of the masters had read the subject at university. His name was J.R. Cottrill and he was teaching physics at the time, but he saw me after school and guided my interest and advised me which books to read, which was very helpful.

I was at Wyggeston Grammar during the War and everybody of military age was in the services, so most of the teachers were elderly. I was astonished even then how much time all the teachers devoted to us kids, giving up their evenings to help us. The school had a very good amateur dramatic society organised by Mr Russell in which I was involved – though not to the degree that my brother Richard was – and we spent day after day rehearsing. We did a lot of Gilbert and Sullivan. I can still sing the whole of the first act of *HMS Pinafore*, playing all the parts, without taking breath.

When Horace Lacey retired I was invited to the school prize day. I'd read natural sciences at Cambridge and by that stage was on television and had a public reputation and I think he was pleased by what I had done. It was my first opportunity to say thank you to him. I started off on a eulogy of dear old Horace, going on about how good he was, but was suddenly completely thrown when I glanced at him across the school hall and saw he was so moved that his shoulders were wracked with sobs.

GARY RHODES
celebrity chef

I did OK at school, but by the time I was 14 I'd decided I wanted to become a chef so I left at 16 to go to technical college to do a three-year catering course. That was where I met Peter Barratt, a brilliant tutor who became a close friend.

I had already taken over cooking the Sunday lunch at home and was obsessed with food. Graham Kerr was my hero. He was the TV chef known as the Galloping Gourmet who first put entertainment into food. I was also a great fan of Marguerite Patten, an amazing lady now in her eighties with whom I have since worked several times. It was Marguerite's recipe for lemon sponge pudding that really decided my fate. The look on my family's face when I turned the pudding out of the bowl and poured over the luscious lemon sauce was worth all the effort I'd put into making it.

Peter Barratt was one of the senior tutors at Thanet Technical College and he had an aura about him that commanded respect. He'd been a chef all his life, working in Switzerland and France before deciding he wanted to teach. Every time you went to one of his lessons you knew you were going to learn something special. He taught us more than cooking; he explained why different ingredients were put together and what he was trying to achieve. You could tell by the tone of his voice that he loved what he was doing. We had a lot of good teachers, but Peter stood out.

He was a big chap, tall with broad shoulders, always dressed in full chef's whites with the tall hat and checked trousers – and his shoes were always sparklingly clean. He never raised his voice because he didn't need to. I wouldn't leave him alone. I was always asking questions, always wanting to do something more, try something different and I was very competitive. (I was named student of the year and chef of the year while I was there).

Peter emphasised the importance of the natural taste of food and the need to avoid overwhelming the flavour of the basic ingredient. He taught us that success came from consistency, being able to cook classic dishes just right over and over again.

I was very lucky. I was at college when there was no shortage of money and we were supplied with the very best ingredients. In my final year in Peter's advanced cookery classes I remember walking in to see a whole venison hanging up, still in fur, which Peter showed us how to skin and gut and butcher as well as cook.

He never panicked in the kitchen – and he taught his pupils to stay calm even when things went wrong. We had a college restaurant which was open to the public and now and again we would get a bit behind and start running around. Peter would call us over and slow us down. If things went wrong he wouldn't take over, he would show us how to put matters right. When someone overcooked the green beans he showed us how to add cream and shallots and turn them into a delicious sauce sprinkled with toasted flaked almonds.

Like everyone, I had my share of disasters. I remember making a sauce hollandaise, which was thick and creamy, and I was really pleased with it until Peter came round and tasted it and found it was so salty he had to call for a glass of water.

I met my wife Jenny at college – she was in the third year advanced cookery class – and she and I have stayed friends with Peter and his wife.

Occasionally he invites us to his home and cooks us lunch. He's just dynamite in the kitchen: a culinary genius with an extraordinary range and superb palette. Last time we went over with our two sons, Peter made us fabulous hors d'oeuvres followed by lobster, cooked absolutely to perfection, and then barbecued lamb. It was a banquet, but it was easy alfresco eating and the meal lasted all day. I'm a little apprehensive about cooking for him. Even now, well over 20 years after I left college, I want to impress him. I want him to be proud that I was one of his boys in his kitchen. When he visits, I open a bottle of champagne and then take him out to a nearby restaurant.

NICK ROBINSON
BBC political editor

Peter Bullock proved that science wasn't for boring geeks and made physics enormous fun. In every lesson he would produce one of those classwork sheets in purple ink that smelled fresh from the machine. We relished them being handed out because every sheet contained a poem, a classical reference or a joke. I've kept them all to show to my own children. There was one poem in particular that's stayed in my memory, which went:

"In early days Man measured Time
By sunrise and sunset sublime;
Then came the French, who gave us next
Metres, kilogrammes and secs.
But then the stream of Time we saw
Discharge through a capacitor:
I second now's the 'Farad-Ohm'
Which floats upon the stream as 'fohm'
In which, like seed within the bud,

We find the 'microfohm' or 'Sud';
So that in lower sixth it's known
A million Suds make up 1 Fohm…

As well as being able to turn physics into poetry, Peter Bullock had energy and enthusiasm and conveyed the sense that science was part of the world around you and not a dull boring academic discipline. He was also the man who founded the debate club at Cheadle Hulme School in Cheshire and encouraged me to take part and sound off in a way that I've been doing ever since – and getting paid for it. As a schoolboy I was naturally gobby.

What made Peter an exciting teacher was that you could never predict how he would present the lesson. I'm sure he was sticking pretty much to the standard topics – waves and electricity and so on – but he managed to convert everything into a joke or a story and did so with wit. You got the sense that every lesson was a challenge for him as to how he could make it exciting.

Peter Bullock taught me throughout my secondary schooling and I took physics, chemistry and maths at A-level. He was young in spirit, probably in his mid to late 30s, neatly dressed in a jacket and tie. He was a quiet man, almost shy, the sort of person who if it hadn't been for the personality he put into teaching, would have been the sort of teacher kids would have taken the mickey out of. But because of the huge verve he brought to his teaching, they didn't. Everyone in his class was an enthusiast. He was inspiring. He turned me onto the idea that the things you enthuse about that might on the surface seem dull, you can enthuse others about. For instance, when I tell people I'm interested in politics they may think: "How boring." I suspect being a physics teacher is much the same. Peter showed me that what matters is how you convey your own enthusiasm so you excite other people.

As well as science, my passion at school was for drama and the other teacher who had a big influence on me was Paul Allan, who taught English. He involved me in the school drama society and I still have the school report that says: "Nicholas gave a commanding and most convincing portrayal of Commissar Amos in *The Queen and the Rebels*."

Part of the reason I ended up in journalism was that the school put on a careers fair at which parents came in and chatted with you about their jobs. One parent was well known in radio and I told him I was interested in going to the BBC. "That's easy," he said. "You just need to get to Oxford, get a first and get a blue and you'll have no problem." I didn't get a blue or a first but I did get to Oxford.

ALAN SUGAR

entrepreneur

My business career began at school. From the age of 12 I was flogging stuff to the other kids. I'd buy massive rolls of 35mm film from the Army surplus store which was past its sell by date, but still suitable for amateur work, cut it into bits and put them into little canisters and sell them at half the price you'd pay for a new film. I also sold transistor bits and radio bits. By the time I was 15 I earned more money at school than my dad was earning going to work five days a week. The school thought I was very enterprising and when they needed something selling, like the school magazine or raffle tickets, they got me to do it.

I enjoyed my schooldays. I went to Joseph Priestley in Clapton, which later became Brooke House Comprehensive, and I had some good teachers, although none of them could be described as a mentor. I liked science, particularly chemistry, and Victor Pollard was a professional pharmacist as well as my chemistry teacher, form teacher and house master. He really knew his stuff. I remember learning how to make gunpowder from iron filings, saltpetre and sulphur and demonstrating how it ignites in a special flameproof chamber. Later on I enjoyed what was called "spots" where you were given an unknown compound and had to work out what it was made from using a series of experiments and tests.

I liked lessons in which there was something to see and do. In Mr Brown's physics lessons I remember learning a bit of electrics, Ohm's law and all that stuff, the Archimedes principle and getting metal balls to move side to side on lumps of string. I also enjoyed engineering and woodwork and technical drawing, though I can't now remember the names of the masters who taught them.

I remember Mr Grant, the maths master, because even though he gave up on me, I managed to pass my O-level. He was a real eccentric. We used to call him Theta Grant because he made us laugh when he wrote the Greek sign theta on the blackboard. He was accident-prone. From time to time he'd come into school with his face smashed in or a broken arm. There were all sorts of rumours going round the school, but we never found out the cause of his injuries.

When I discovered that the maths O-level syllabus involved something called calculus, which was supposed to be really difficult, I was fascinated. I've always enjoyed a challenge. I'm a quick learner and have a photographic memory. Within three or four weeks I became the whiz- kid of calculus, which got me through the exam. Theta Grant couldn't believe it.

Although I was in the top stream right through school, if I wasn't interested in a lesson I daydreamed. I regret now looking out of the bloody window, watching people playing football instead of concentrating on things like French. I keep telling my grandchildren to accept that you have to go to school until the age of 16 and while you're there take what you're offered and absorb it.

I was made a prefect and then a senior prefect, passed seven O-levels and went on to do chemistry, physics and maths at A-level, but I didn't complete them. I wanted to get out of school, go to work and buy a car. For a year and a half I worked for other people and then set up on my own. When I started out I was a small- time trader. The only other person in my family in business was my Uncle John who had a corner shop. I helped out in the shop and watched how he did things and very quickly I had a much bigger business than he had. Then I got into the electronics wholesale business and there was another person I looked up to and watched how he operated. And so on, through my career.

I've never had a mentor in the sense of someone I would go to for advice, but there have been a number of people I have admired, particularly Arnold Weinstock [founder of GEC] and Rupert Murdoch [with whom he was involved in the launch of Sky television].

ZOE WANAMAKER
actress

My earliest school memory is of custard – horrible, thick, lumpy custard which was served at my first little primary school somewhere off the Finchley Road in north London. It put me off custard for life. Then, when I was seven or eight my very liberal parents sent me to King Alfred's, a co-educational school in London which was based on the Summerhill philosophy that if you treat children like adults they will integrate smoothly into society. I don't remember if the school dinners at King Alfred's were any better – my whole memory of school is vague – but I do remember spending much of my time there gazing out of the window, daydreaming.

I was a bossy, boisterous child and I had a gang. I'm the middle one of three girls. The others were smarter than me. My elder sister went to a grammar school and then to Dartington and became a speech therapist and the younger one was at the Lycée Français, has a PhD in Chinese and became a lawyer.

Being a progressive school, there was no uniform at King Alfred's and we called our teachers by their first names. Deciding what to wear became a big deal. Sometimes I'd put on three things — a pair of trousers and two frocks — and choose on the way to school, stuffing the rejects into my satchel.

I was very good at art and English, although my grammar is appalling. But I'm numerically dyslexic which is why I adored my maths teacher Roy Greenfield who said there was no point in me doing it any more and allowed me to drop it. He was a benevolent, bald-headed, kind man who realised that for me maths was torture.

My English teacher at King Alfred's was great too. She was small with glasses and I think her name was Elizabeth. She taught a subject I was interested in and found fascinating. I loved reading aloud in class and of course I was part of the school drama group. I remember playing Rosalind in *As You Like It* and I was damned fine. My boyfriend played Orlando, which helped.

It was a fantastic school. I was in a class of 20 and was treated as an individual. We had music lessons and an open-air theatre. The school was run by the pupils and once I was the class councillor. Even so, I was miserable. The premise of King Alfred's was that it was left to your conscience to work and I had a very bad conscience. I think I needed parameters, something to kick against, and I didn't have them at school, so I kicked against my parents instead. I was a real troublemaker.

Next, I was packed off to a Quaker boarding school in Somerset to get my A-levels. There was a wonderful history master there who had a gammy finger so as he wrote on the blackboard he would rub out bits of the line above he'd just written. He used to wear his pyjamas underneath his trousers. Sometimes his flies were slightly undone and you could see his pyjamas peeking through. I was very homesick and was only there for a year.

Acting was in my blood. Despite being born Jewish, I flirted briefly with the idea of becoming a nun, attracted by the romance of the black gown and the celibacy and the quiet and the singing. I also considered becoming an artist. But by the time I was 10 I knew I'd act. My parents tried to dissuade me because I'm not very good at rejection, which is what this business is all about. With their encouragement I went to art school and also took a secretarial course.

Eventually I went to drama school where I had a fantastic teacher by the name of Litz Pisk, an extraordinary woman who taught movement, with a kind of magic. I used to think education had been wasted on me but it really came to the fore when I began acting and then I was totally motivated when researching the parts I play.

JASPER CONRAN
designer

I got on best with women teachers, and those I remember most clearly were not only good teachers, they also all had style.

There was certain naughtiness about Miss Watson, who taught piano at Port Regis, the prep school for Bryanston in Dorset. She was great. I loved her. She had lots of different outfits, mostly tailored tweeds, and marvellous pearlised handbags with shoes to match. She used to play the piano every morning in assembly and as she played, she wiggled her bottom. We were all mesmerised.

I can remember playing my Chopin and telling her that what I really wanted to learn was syncopated beat because I wanted to be able to play Elvis Presley songs, and she broke off in the middle of the lesson and started playing Elvis. She did it well and obviously enjoyed it. But the Latin master came flying out of the room next door complaining that it wasn't the sort of music you expected to hear in a public school.

I was a shy and portly child and Mrs Baker, who taught art, took me under her wing and encouraged me. You expect teachers to encourage you, but I found that many of them took away my self-confidence. I didn't like boarding, but I didn't have a choice. Nobody asked me if I wanted to go away to school, I was just following in the footsteps of my father and older brother, both of whom had been happy at Bryanston.

When I got to the senior school my favourite teacher was Dr Mash, whom we called Hot Lips because of her very, very red lipstick. She was gorgeous. She had marvellous Renoir-like hair and used to wear low cut T-shirts and circular skirts with cinched waists and very high heels. She taught biology, which I was absolutely hopeless at, despite her excellent teaching.

Dr Mash's lessons were marvellous. We dissected frogs and cut up worms and best of all was sex education, which she taught with some aplomb, despite our doing all we could to make her blush. It is a great sadness that, despite her best endeavours, and being really interested in the subject, I failed my biology O-level. I was much more into art, history, history of art, English and languages. And I always came top of the class in religious studies which infuriated my father who was highly atheist.

Luckily, I have an ability to absorb information and do other things at the same time because I was always doodling. From the age of 13 onwards I was drawing outfits all the time, whatever the lesson. Dr Mash believed in me and encouraged me and she and I came to an arrangement. Because I was no good at football, I was allowed to miss games and do all the diagrammatic drawings for biology lessons instead, with another boy who also hated sport. But we used to colour in the diagrams at will so there must be generations of boys coming out of Bryanston who think that photosynthesis takes place in pink.

We kept in touch, but I didn't see Dr Mash for many years after I left school until one day we had a marvellous lunch together and caught up with all the gossip.

I went from Bryanston to study art in New York where my draping teacher Mrs Gepetta, a very strict, big Italian lady, taught me how to create on a stand. She had worked for Captain Molyneux, the couturier, in Paris, so was steeped in couture and although we grumbled because we had to hand stitch everything, all I learned from her has proven to be incredibly useful.

The best days of my life were as a student in New York. I was not a happy schoolboy. I didn't have a lot in common with my fellow pupils. I was bored and I didn't want to be in Dorset while my family was in London. For me school was like prison, but luckily these ladies made it bearable.

JEREMY CLARKSON
TV presenter and journalist

I enjoyed my schooldays hugely. I had a wonderful time. It was like one long party. I knew a mortgage and children and all those things were coming and I made the most of this period of no responsibility. I went to Repton in Derbyshire and no-one seemed to be bothered that I spent a lot of my time at the local girls' school and in the pubs around Burton-on-Trent (the brewing capital of the world) which was about four miles away. The first two years were a bit tough, I suppose. Fagging was brutal and I got bullied horribly, but it wasn't the end of the world. I got beaten up and my belongings thrown in the swimming pool. It was par for the course then. Everybody was bullied; I just accepted it. Nobody complained. They would now. We're becoming a nation of weaklings.

Public school instilled in me that you never rat on your peers. I learned to be rebellious at school, too. When the careers master asked me what I wanted to do I said: "I don't care as long as I don't have to wear a suit" – for which I got a detention. We used to do these career tests and I would put that I wanted to be an astronaut or a king and get detention again and again. The goal of the school was to produce 100 estate agents and stockbrokers a year.

I owe a great debt of gratitude to my housemaster for the last three years, Tony Price. I suspect he saw that I might do something that didn't require a suit because he protected me from other masters who were determined to get me. There were a lot of teachers who didn't like me because I pushed the rules all the time. I didn't do anything seriously bad, but I would refuse to do up my top button or wear slightly the wrong colour jacket, and training shoes. Tony Price would say: "You're in trouble with so and so, but I shouldn't worry too much about it."

He was an immensely likeable man. He taught me chemistry lower down the school and I didn't understand the first thing. I wasn't really good at anything. I managed to get nine O-levels, but it took years. Economics bored me; I couldn't see the point of history (though now I wish I had). I knew the names of all the capital cities and that was about it. I sat and read *Melody Maker* throughout my French O-level in an attempt to look cool and got naught per cent. My English was mediocre. Nobody ever said: "Ooh, that's good" about an essay I wrote. I didn't win any prizes and I was never made a prefect. I was useless at games. You have no idea how unco-ordinated I am. I once took a penalty in a game of football and the nearest the ball got to the goalmouth was when it was on the spot.

Tony Price was my ally and a sort of father figure. All I did at school was try to make people laugh and I have a sneaking suspicion that he quite liked that. He wasn't at all strict. Although smoking was banned he'd walk into my study full of smoke and say nothing. He didn't catch me drinking in the pub because he didn't look.

When I was in the sixth form I managed to convince him that I should have a car so I could drive home at weekends because my father was ill. I actually had no intention of going home, but he agreed as long as it was parked in his driveway and he kept the keys. The car was an Audi and I gave him an old set of Fiat keys but he didn't seem to notice. I regularly took the car out in the evening and he turned a blind eye.

He had the right attitude because if I'd had one of the more authoritarian housemasters I would never have lasted at the school as long as I did. They threw me out 10 weeks before my A-levels. I could have gone back to sit the exams, but by then I'd got a job.

All through my schooldays my reports were greeted with tears and recriminations at home, but after I'd tipped off Tony Price that one boy who was being bullied really wasn't up for it he praised my "streak of goodness". His parting words, as I left, were: "When you get sent to borstal, try to make it the one nearby so we can come and visit you." But he said it with a glint in his eye.

HELEN MIRREN
actress

Everyone loved Miss Welding, my English teacher at St Bernard's Convent, Westcliff-on-Sea, Essex. She was one of those teachers who has the ability to fire your imagination and to entertain.

What is funny is that she didn't do it with huge wit or great performance. She was actually rather a modest woman and quite quiet. Perhaps it was simply that she enjoyed the material she worked with so much herself that she communicated that, or maybe she was simply a natural teacher, I don't know. All I know is that she was very sensitive to people and everyone who was lucky enough to be taught by her, loved her.

She taught me between the ages of 13 and 17 and was instrumental in me becoming an actress. She knew I was interested in acting, but it wasn't a professional choice in my world. My father was a driving examiner and I wasn't exposed to acting as a career. We had no television in our house, I never went to the cinema and we didn't go to the theatre, not because of a lack of interest, but because my parents couldn't afford to take us.

My older sister became a teacher and I trained first as a speech and drama teacher. It was a simple question of economics. It was a way of perpetuating my education and being able to get a grant for doing so.

It was Miss Welding who told me about the National Youth Theatre, which was an organisation I wasn't aware of. She suggested I should look into it and think about going there. She wasn't really into drama herself; she didn't put on the school productions. They were organised by Miss Angel, who taught us elocution, but was really a drama teacher.

It was my love of Shakespeare that drew me into wanting to become an actress. The school had a Shakespeare club in which the pupils cast parts and rehearsed themselves. I remember being absolutely fired up by the stories and the characters and the magic of the world Shakespeare created – but whether it was Miss Welding who fired me up, or I got fired up all on my own I have no idea.

Miss Welding reminded me of a little sparrow. In appearance she was very ladylike, always very nicely dressed and her hair neat.

My other special teacher, Miss O'Shaunessy, was a very different kettle of fish. She also looked like a bird – but like a hawk. She would swoop around the school in her black academic gown and had greying black, out-of-control hair. I thought she was fabulous. She was very fierce and grumpy, but also very charismatic. She had a sharp tongue and terrorised the students. I think she was probably very brilliant.

She taught geography, a subject I absolutely loved, and I still enjoy studying maps. I loved Miss O'Shaunessy because she was funny and she was interesting. It is almost impossible to extricate whether it was the teachers or their subjects that attracted me most, but I think probably the teacher came first, then the subject.

About 10 years after I left school, when I was with the Royal Shakespeare Company and playing fairly high profile parts, I got a letter from Miss Welding saying she was following my career with interest, but as far as I know she never came to see me perform. She certainly never came to see me backstage.

STEVE REDGRAVE
Olympic rowing gold medallist

If it hadn't have been for my English master, Francis Smith, I would never have got into a boat. He started an after-school rowing club at Great Marlow Comprehensive School and invited pupils with big hands and feet to join. He had this theory that if he picked people with big hands and feet the chances were they were going to grow into big people. I fitted the criteria so I was asked to give it a go and I thought it sounded like fun.

I have always loved sport and was a good all rounder at school. I was OK at rugby and cricket and a good sprinter and threw the shot and ran for the district. On sports days another guy and I won the school cup in alternate years. Academically, I didn't do particularly well. We still had the 11-plus in Marlow and I knew I wasn't going to pass, but it was never a big issue to me. At primary school I came bottom of the class in tests, but it didn't worry me. I'm dyslexic and have had problems with reading all my life. I'd had extra lessons with Mrs Cloak, the headmistress of Burford Primary, and when I went to the comprehensive, I was taken out of French to do extra English.

Francis Smith was head of English and took the top stream and only taught me for one year. He seemed very strict; but people weren't scared of him, they admired him. He was cross-eyed and we learned very early on that if you were causing mischief in the class and he looked directly at you, he couldn't see you – but if he put his head to one side you were going to be in trouble.

The punishment was usually being made to kneel in the front of the classroom and hold a heavy stool out in front of you by its legs. Francis's two loves were rugby and rowing and he helped with a number of sporting activities and was hugely enthusiastic and wanted us all to enjoy what we did.

I was about 13 when I began rowing. At first there were 12 of us but very soon we were down to four in the under-14 group. After two or three months of rowing up and down the river Francis asked us if we would like to take part in a race and we competed in the Avon schools' regatta and won. We entered seven events in our first season and won them all. We thought we were God's gift to rowing. I was the biggest and the strongest so was in the stroke seat, but I never saw myself as captain. We were all in it together.

We trained every day after school and sometimes at lunchtime in school as well, doing weights and stuff like that. Francis made it all seem like fun; it was never a chore. He was cunning. Sometimes when we had to do a round run we didn't always go the full distance. He knew what was going on but never said anything. Instead, next time he'd take us in his car and drop us off somewhere so we had no alternative but to run all the way back to school or the rowing club. Afterwards he always dropped us off at our homes so we could get our homework done ready for the next school day.

The reason we did so well, I later discovered, was that we did more training than any of the other competitors. We rowed every weekday, had Saturdays off and then rowed on Sunday mornings. During the winter we went training with Marlow Rowing Club on Tuesday and Thursday evenings. Francis Smith taught us discipline. People like doing things they are good at and that are fun, and the professional way he organised things to make it easy for us, and enjoyable, was impressive. In the coaching I do now I hope I come across in the same way, trying to get people to achieve their potential without flogging them so they hate it and never want to come back to sport once they've finished school.

Francis Smith and I became friends and are still in touch. He's a great guy. He's been retired for some time now but he doesn't look any different from when I started rowing in '76.

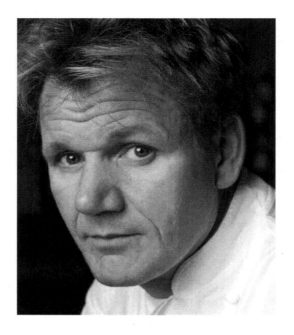

GORDON RAMSAY
chef and restaurateur

When I failed my 11-plus miserably, Dickie Vale, my sports master at Stratford-upon-Avon High School, was delighted. It meant I stayed in the school football team and he was able to nurture my talent so that a few years later I was spotted by a Glasgow Rangers scout and became a professional, until injury forced me to change careers.

Dickie was an amazing guy, an inspirational coach with incredible vision. Although I wanted to play centre-forward, Dickie saw immediately that I was a natural left-footer and he nursed me as a left back. He stopped me playing rugby, which I couldn't stand anyway, in case I picked up an injury. Thanks to him, the school football team won all the inter-school competitions in and around Warwickshire, and one month he coached six or seven players from our team to represent the county. He'd been a professional himself, but we never found out what team he played for. We knew very little about him. He'd drive us to matches in an old Transit van but never talked about anything except football.

Like 95 per cent of young guys, I dreamed of becoming a professional footballer – I had pictures of Kenny Dalglish and Graeme Souness on my bedroom wall – and Dickie Vale made me believe it was possible. My dad was a sports teacher, too. He'd been a PE teacher at Strathclyde University and taught in the sports centre in Stratford-upon-Avon, but his big thing was swimming.

One of the advantages of being good at sport was that if we were playing in a match, I'd get off school early. I wasn't very academic. I was bloody good at maths and I liked human biology, but I was never any good at English. My reports were mixed. I remember the RE teacher suggesting I was disruptive, but Dickie Vale always gave me an A-plus and said I was a great team leader and an inspiration.

As a boy, my aggression was channelled into my feet. I never got into trouble for bad behaviour at school. Honestly. I've made up for it since, though these days I'm not manic, just obsessive. I have always been a perfectionist.

Home economics was compulsory at Stratford High and I was a disaster at cookery, which was taught by a pretty, sexy young lady called Miss Baisley. She definitely didn't spot any talent in me. We made boring things like steamed jam roly-poly, flapjacks and spotted dick, which I always ate before I got home because I was so hungry. Miss Baisley was lovely, but she didn't inspire me to become a chef.

I've had some very good teachers as an adult. Marco Pierre White was an exciting guy who taught me a massive amount about finesse, great execution on a plate, balance and understanding flavours. Albert Roux showed me how to make something plain into something stunning. He's also a very clever businessman. With Marco you would use just the white part of a leek, with Albert not only would you use the dark green and the white parts, you'd use the root as well.

I met Lenny Henry when he came in for a meal when I was at the Gavroche. He does a lot for Comic Relief and asked me to go out to Tanzania with him to cook for the street children there for a film to raise money. I wasn't prepared for the harshness, rawness and emotional trauma involved. I was moved to tears when I saw how these kids live, and I learned a lot from Lenny about controlling emotions and having fun with the children.

I once went back to my old school but sadly didn't see Dickie Vale. We lost touch after I left. I'd like to see him again. He's welcome at any of my restaurants any time as my guest.

TOYAH WILLCOX
singer and actress

The day I left school Miss Joyce, the headmistress, shook my hand and said she was very pleased I was never coming back.

Edgbaston Church of England College For Girls in Birmingham was a very strict academic fee-paying public school and I loathed every minute I was there – with the exception of art and music lessons. Even the uniform was horrible. We wore brown skirts, cream shirts and tomato-coloured cardigans.

I really was a handful, though I didn't do anything very terrible by today's standards. I just did my own thing and didn't fit in. My parents were constantly being called up to the school. I loathed the fact that it was an all girls' school. I loathed the fact that if you were academic you sat at the front and if not, you sat at the back.

I was dyslexic. I was disabled – I lost a year of schooling through having some bones straightened and ended up with one leg longer than the other – and I had a lisp. They just didn't reckon on me at all and I was treated like a lost cause. I was disruptive. I talked in lessons, didn't do as I was told, didn't do my homework. I was badly behaved in every lesson except art.

It was a school for young ladies and I wasn't interested in the feminine ideal they wanted us to be. I was there in the Seventies, a time when women were starting to break free of middle-class chauvinistic confines, and I felt school was holding me back big time.

Karen Howell, the art teacher was my saviour. She was petite, wore make-up and was independent and a reflection of what we wanted to be when we were grown up. She was also young – probably only about five years older than we were – and because of that she had a particularly good understanding of our growing pains. We spent a lot of time in class talking about things we really wanted to talk about such as make-up, boys and rock music and because of that she got the best results out of us. She was like one of us, more of an older sister than a teacher. We even called her Karen, which was unusual then, and if anyone had heard us we'd have been lynched.

I already knew I wanted to act and sing when I left school and she was probably the only person who didn't scoff at my ambition. She was into the same music I was into: Marc Bolan, Alice Cooper, David Bowie and Roxy Music. One night after school I went off to see T-Rex at the Birmingham Odeon wearing satin trousers and glitter drops on my cheeks and there was Karen Howell in the audience similarly turned out with sparkle on her face.

Eventually I was banned from art lessons, and music, which was the only other subject I enjoyed, as punishment for not working well in other areas. Karen was very diplomatic about it and we stayed friends and are still in touch, correspond and meet up from time to time.

The music teacher, Miss Nelson, was lovely, too. She gave us an incredible love of classical music. I remember her playing Holst's *Planet Suite* and allowing us to move around the room to the music. Both she and Miss Howell gave us a lot of physical freedom in a school where everything else was cerebral. They understood our need to be young and enthusiastic. Art and music lessons were the only two places where we could be ourselves.

I took music theory at O-level and passed but I failed all my other nine O-levels. I left the school under a cloud at 16, having been there from four and a half, and went to drama school. Absolutely nothing I learned at school had any relevance to what I did and who I am today.

JAMES DYSON
inventor and businessman

Because my family were all classicists – my father taught classics and I had a very clever elder brother who was a classics scholar – it was assumed I was a classicist too, or at the very least an academic. I wasn't. I found Greek and Latin pointless and boring and slept through most of the lessons. CDT didn't exist when I was at school at Gresham's in Norfolk. I could turn out coffee tables in the woodshed or go into the art department, but it was only after I left school that I discovered engineering and practical design and technology.

I arrived at the Royal College of Art aged 20 to study furniture design but transferred to the architectural school because I found dealing with big structures and space more interesting, and that was where I came across Tony Hunt.

I saw very quickly that structures are the most interesting aspect of architecture, particularly modern architecture, and was fascinated to learn how buildings stay up and how they can be made to stay up differently. It was a particularly interesting time; the large concrete structures of the Sixties were beginning to be replaced by tensile structures. In America, Buckminster

Fuller was creating buildings with large span aluminium framed roofs and here, Norman Foster and Richard Rogers were heavily into anything other than steel and concrete.

Tony Hunt came to college once a week to teach structural engineering. He had his own engineering practice, working for architects such as Foster and Rogers and had designed the international terminal at Waterloo station. He was considered to be the most influential experimental and ambitious structural engineer for the past 30 years. What made him such a good teacher was that he was a designer as well as an engineer. He could talk with equal enthusiasm both about how structures worked and the aesthetics of structures.

He would sketch on the blackboard good simple drawings explaining how structures worked, which even with O-level maths I could follow. He was able to synthesise quite a complex thing into simple equations and simple logic.

He was an inspirational teacher. As well as giving lectures, he would come round the studio to discuss individual projects and his enthusiasm and fascination for what you were trying to create was infectious. He didn't just look at your project as an engineer to see whether it would stay up or not, he was excited about how you could make it stay up in the unusual or particularly crazy way you wanted to do it.

I produced a strange structure in the shape of a giant mushroom made out of light aluminium tubes for Joan Littlewood, the theatrical impresario. She wanted to build a children's theatre which could be open in the summer and tented in winter. It was huge – about 60 ft across – and Tony helped me, breaking down the project into simple components. We made a model and got planning permission, but we couldn't raise the money to build it.

He was the first teacher to really enthuse me. I didn't enjoy my schooldays much, mainly because I was studying the wrong things. I did no science at all and had a kind of mental block against technology until Tony showed me that engineering could be creative. I had planned to become an architect until he got me interested in engineering. He really changed the direction of my life. I saw that engineering could be the driving force of a building or a product and its whole *raison d'être*.

I went off into industry, at first to work on military boats and then I invented the Ballbarrow. Over 25 years later when I needed a factory to produce my dual cyclone vacuum cleaner I asked Tony Hart to design one for me. We have become great friends. I gave him one of my vacuum cleaners as a thank you for being such an inspirational teacher.

CLARE BALDING
sports journalist and television presenter

nglish was the only thing, apart from riding, I was really good at and Miss Healy, who taught me at Downe House, the girls' boarding school in Berkshire, was the first teacher to make me realise it. She taught me at A-level and introduced me to Robert Browning, with whom I had an instant rapport. I loved his collection, *Men and Women* and particular the poem "In a Year", which he wrote in a female voice. I think it is one of the most brilliant examples of female bitterness written by a man. It is so full of hurt and real anger and lack of understanding of why this guy could possibly leave her.

I enjoy a challenge, and Miss Healy made me feel I had to prove myself which was good, because otherwise I could be quite idle. She encouraged me in terms of the breadth of my reading and to think differently. I don't think I had realised until then that having an opinion wasn't enough – you had to be able to substantiate it.

I was a mixture of confidence (in playing sport and I had already achieved quite a lot in riding) and uncertainty (academically). I was a bit younger than everyone else in the class right through the school and always seemed to be chasing to keep up.

Miss Healy was good at getting people to speak up in lessons and to give their opinions. She had a dry sense of humour. If you said something outrageous she would laugh, she wouldn't put you down. She was much younger than the other teachers. She probably hadn't been long out of university. She'd been to Oxford and gave the impression of having had a great time there. I remember thinking I had never met anyone so clever in my life. I enjoyed English lessons so much that when classes sometimes began at 1.50pm instead of two o'clock I even missed the end of *Neighbours* on television to make sure I wasn't late, and got teased by the other girls.

I left Downe intending to become a barrister, but didn't get a university place. So I had two years out and, inspired by Miss Healy, tried for English at Cambridge. Very early on I'd been asked by the headmistress what I wanted to do when I left school and I said I wanted to be an eventer (meaning riding in three-day events). She misheard me and said: "Really, how exciting. What do you want to invent?" They were very good at school about my riding, but it was never considered to be a career option.

I re-took my history A-level to get it up to an A, went to the Sorbonne in Paris to do a diploma in French civilisation, taught youngsters to ride at Pony Club camp, took a secretarial course — and rode in a lot of races.

I'd done a lot of public speaking at school. I was head girl and quite often had to stand up and say something. Everybody had to take a turn at reading in chapel, and there was a lot of reading aloud in class and plenty of opportunities to appear in school plays. I was always happy speaking in public and at Cambridge I did a lot of debating and became president of the Union

I was competing in one-day events and show-jumping when I was at school, and started racing when I left. My first week at Cambridge coincided with the race that made me champion amateur jockey. Luckily my director of studies, Jean Gooder, believed it was good to encourage students who had other interests to pursue them. She allowed me to take a day off to ride at Chepstow on condition I explained the racing page to her. Mrs Gooder was a big Henry James fan and I got very into American literature through her. We are still in touch.

Dr Sue Manning took over where Miss Healy had left off in developing my essay-writing skills. Writing against the clock was always my problem and Dr Manning helped me get things down on paper within the period of an exam. We lost touch but I think she went on to be head of English at Edinburgh. I don't know what became of Miss Healy, but I will always be grateful to her, especially for encouraging me to think for myself and have the confidence to put my point across.

43

SIMON CALLOW
actor, director and writer

Nic Fizelle was a sophisticated Frenchman who taught me French initially and then history at the London Oratory School, which in those days was a primitive place. It had been used as a prisoner of war camp and still had bars at the windows. Many of the staff were poorly equipped and piety seemed to be the main qualification for being a teacher there.

So it was extraordinary to find this exceptional, intellectual man, who was independent and not part of the teaching establishment, in their midst. He was quite slight and somewhat deaf, and he wore the kind of spectacles that act as hearing aids. He was mercilessly mocked by the pupils, who were very unruly and rather savagely disciplined by the other teachers.

Nic sort of imposed order, but he wasn't very interested in discipline, and boys would shout and throw bits of chalk around in lessons. He was interested in engaging his pupils and having a proper intellectual exchange. He treated them like adults who would be interested in the facts of either the French language or history. It was he who first introduced me to history as a question of cause and effect, instead of an unrelenting recitation of facts which you had to learn to pass an examination.

He taught me to "look outside the box" as they say now, to question history, never to assume that things happened because they were inevitable. The essays I wrote for him were pretty good because he taught me so well. His methods were alien to many, but those of us who responded were remarkably well educated as a result.

He talked fearlessly to 13 and 14-year-olds about Marx and hardcore political exposition of the way history had been shaped. He was very interesting in lots of ways.

We would discuss all kinds of things and eventually – probably rather dangerously at the time – he invited me to his house. We would have a bottle of wine and he introduced me to French music, particularly Debussy and Ravel, and the poems of Baudelaire and the whole world of French culture. He'd been in the Resistance in France during the War and won various medals. But the thing that struck me most was that on VE day, because of the stress, all his hair fell out and then grew back again half white and half black.

He lived in a small house off the King's Road in Chelsea, which was full of beautiful objects of an exquisiteness I hadn't encountered before. When he gave me an edition of Baudelaire's *Les Fleurs du Mal* there was no ulterior motive; he was just delighted to find somebody who was interested in the things that interested him.

I would have said he was gay, but he was not practising because he was a strong and sophisticated Catholic. He became a confidant. My parents had separated and I was brought up by my mother and grandmother, so he filled a gap because there was no man in my life at that time.

Nic was like a godfather to me, or a wonderful older brother, or a young uncle. We kept in touch after I left school and went to the opera together. When I started working in the theatre – in the box office at the Old Vic – I'd get him tickets for things and we'd go, and analyse them carefully afterwards. He stayed on teaching at the Oratory until he died quite young in the early 1970s. I was still at drama school, so he never saw me on stage.

VANESSA-MAE
violinist

Mrs Anderson, my headmistress at Francis Holland School in Sloane Square, was really understanding about me taking time off for my music. It was an academic school, but Mrs Anderson was musically inclined and broad thinking. She saw that I had potential and to realise that potential I had to work on it early in life.

It was thanks to Mr Cleveland, my piano teacher at Francis Holland from the age of four, that my musical talent was spotted so early. He suggested to my parents that I had potential and needed special training. I took up the violin when I was about five and when I was eight I went to China for six months' intensive tuition. Mrs Anderson was really cool about letting me go.

I studied with a big panda of a man called Professor Lin at Beijing Conservatoire. He concentrated on technique and making sure even if I was playing something difficult, I looked relaxed. The problem was that Professor Lin didn't speak English. My mother was with me for the first three months and she speaks very good Mandarin and was able to translate, but for the next three months my grandmother was with me and she speaks only basic English, so I had to learn Chinese very quickly.

By the time I was eight I was only going to school for half a day and spending the rest of the time concentrating on my violin. I started to tour when I was 12 and then spent about one week in every month at school because the rest of the time I was recording or rehearsing or travelling. I made my first crossover album when I was 14 and by 16 I was touring non-stop.

When I was there, I loved school. I loved the social aspect of it, but by the age of 14 it was really just somewhere I went to hang out with my friends when I wasn't working. I found it very frustrating to get really hooked on a subject and then have to go on tour and catch up by taking notes from my friends.

Eventually, of course, I had to knuckle down to GCSEs, and because of my bizarre schedule I had private tutors who taught me in a spare room on the top floor of our house in Kensington. It's amazing how much you can achieve in six months one to one with private tutors. I took seven GCSEs and passed them all, but unfortunately I got a couple of B grades – I was hoping for straight As.

Chris Kubiak was my favourite tutor. He was an American, of east European descent, living in London. He taught me English, which was my favourite subject because I loved my teacher. He was about 35 then with messy blond hair, sneakers and his shirt always half tucked in and half out.

Chris's classes would go on and on (at no extra cost). We both became so engrossed the time fled and sometimes lessons which were supposed to last an hour, would go on for two, three or even four hours. He was an inspirational teacher. He encouraged me to ask questions, which I liked. Being an only child and spending so much time in the adult world of professional music, I felt at ease in adult company. He'd taken a PhD but couldn't find a job that rewarded him appropriately for his expertise. After I'd finished my exams he hung around for a couple of years and then went back to the United States to study law. We kept in touch and met up when I went on tour in the US.

I started to do A-levels but was travelling so much I could never fit in the lessons. I missed out on a lot because my music career began so early and I wish now I'd had a tutor with me on the road. I was passionate about music, but I would like to have had the option of more study. I didn't even get around to taking my driving test until I was 23.

FRANK SKINNER

comedian

Mrs McGee, who taught me at St Hubert's Roman Catholic Junior School in Oldbury, near Birmingham, was the first teacher to cotton on to the fact that I was a bit of a joker. One day when she had to leave the classroom for a few minutes, she asked me to get up and tell one or two jokes in her absence. It was my first stand-up gig. It was only three or four minutes, but it went down well. I was about ten at the time.

Most teachers thought of me as a quiet kid, but in the company of friends I'd been the class comedian since I started school at Moat Farm Infants at the age of five. After three years my Dad decided I'd spent quite enough time among the Protestants and moved me to St Hubert's which was a three-halfpenny bus ride away. Some of the teachers were nuns and I remember them as being quite ferocious.

Mother Mary Adrian, the headmistress, once caught me and a friend singing in the corridor and we were absolutely terrified. Being a nun, Mother Mary had the power and authority of God as well as that of a headmistress as far as we were concerned. Mother Mary Adrian must have been in her early sixties, but the younger nuns were just as hard. Smacking was a normal activity – usually across the legs, so tempting when kids have short trousers on. I got no sympathy at home. Dad believed that if a teacher hit you it must have been for a good reason.

Mrs McGee was one of those teachers whose authority you felt before you walked into the room. She never raised her voice. She was a very thin, frail-looking woman, but she had warmth. She thought I was capable of getting into King Edward's, which was the top grammar school in the area, but I didn't want to go to a school with a lot of snobby kids and persuaded my parents to send me to Oldbury Tech – not because I was handy, but if you didn't want to go to grammar school and you weren't thick there was nowhere else. I remember two teachers there: Norman Hughes, who taught art, and Ray Wilcockson, who taught English. They were the only subjects I passed at O-level out of the eight I took.

Norman Hughes was a bluff Yorkshireman who, when we reached the fourth form, encouraged us to call him Norm. I could draw and paint a bit, but he inspired me to try a lot harder.

Mr Wilcockson got me to realise that it was OK to be interested in things like Shakespeare that might in working-class circles be regarded as slightly poncy. He would talk about the Rolling Stones and various film actresses he fancied and it started to dawn on me that some teachers were actually human beings. With a few friends I formed a pop group called Olde English and Mr Wilcockson compared us with the Howlin Wolf blues band, which was incredibly flattering.

I was only in the sixth form for six weeks before I got expelled. I'd been picking up used dinner tickets and re-selling them. I'd been on a last warning for truancy and various other things and I think the headmaster, Mr Lardner, felt he had to make an example of me. I don't bear him any ill will: he gave me more chances than many would have done. I thought my future lay in pop music, but I got chucked out of the group for drinking too much cider. So I worked in a factory for a couple of years.

Dad, who was a great believer in second chances, then subsidised me while I went to Warley College of Technology to do my O-levels again. Then I did A-levels and went to Birmingham Polytechnic to train to be a teacher. I failed everything except English in which I got an A – and thanks to two teachers, Marilyn Young and Marjorie Birtwistle – I was allowed to transfer to study for an English degree. I got a 2:1 and did an MA.

Eventually, I got a job as a lecturer at Halesowen College. For a while I was a comedian by night and a teacher by day, but gradually the comedy took over. People say that stand-up comedy is tough – but teaching's tougher.

TIMOTHY SPALL
actor

If it hadn't been for Helena Mietz I'd probably have joined the Army. I wanted to be a tank driver till Miss Mietz, who did my make up as the Cowardly Lion in the school production of *The Wizard of Oz*, suggested I could make a career as an actor. She told me about the National Youth Theatre, which I'd never heard of, and helped me apply. I got in and then she advised me about drama schools. She was unequivocal and gave me the confidence to believe I could make a living from acting, which until then had never occurred to me.

She was one of those modern teachers who allowed you to call her by her first name. She taught drama at Battersea Secondary Modern and was young and pretty and I was 16 and of course I fell in love with her. She was probably only about ten years older than me and we became friends.

Apart from drama, English and art I didn't do very well at school. I didn't shine at anything. I failed all my GCSEs, except art. I was regarded basically as just an oaf who sat at the back of the class and was disruptive, talking and being generally annoying. My reports said I was lazy, didn't bother and was more interested in fooling about than learning. It was a school where most kids left at 15 and during my entire time there I think only three or four people went to university. Much to everyone's surprise I decided to stay on and do my O-levels and take art at A-level. I remember the maths master saying:"What's the point? Why don't you just leave?"

All of a sudden things changed then and I had four very good teachers, one of whom was Helena Mietz. Keith Kimberley was another. He was head of English and directed the school plays. He was a nice man and a good teacher. He was known as Catweazel, after the TV character, because he had a beard and long hair. I suddenly began taking an interest. I asked questions in class and read a lot. Keith was inspirational in the classroom, very encouraging. And he cast me in the school production of *The Wizard of Oz*.

There were a couple of art teachers I liked too. Norman Barratt was a groovy bloke, a bit older than Keith and Helena and quite posh. His hair was long and he would swear in class now and again. He saw I could draw and thought I should go to art college and learn to be a draughtsman. Linda Marshall was more of a free expressionist, but they were both free-thinking and experimental. I remember making a sculpture with Norman's help called "My Mum in Hospital". My art was very individual. Once I stuck pubic hair on apples and nailed them up around the school.

Both teachers gave me great encouragement and I briefly thought that if I didn't join the Army I might go to art school. I used to go off on my own to the Tate Gallery. But once I'd decided to follow Helena's advice and become an actor, there were no second thoughts.

My father worked for the Post Office and my mother was a hairdresser but I had an inkling she would have liked to have gone to drama school herself, though years ago if you came from a working class family it was just a pipe dream. My grandfather, who was a rep for *The Times*, used to have a song and dance comedy music hall act with his friend Billy.

I first trod the boards at junior school in a play written by the headmaster, Mr Gray, called *The Witches' Convention*. I was given the part of a bumbling old gentleman. Right from the beginning, I was into character acting.

I haven't seen Helena since I left school. She moved away and we lost touch. She was one of the most influential people in my life and I tried to reach her through Friends Reunited without success. I'd like to say thank you to all these teachers, but particularly Helena because I wouldn't have become an actor without her support and encouragement.

MAX CLIFFORD
publicist

I was a "disruptive influence" at school. I was not remotely academic and spent as little time as possible in the classroom. I was good at sport, so I often escaped lessons because I'd be off representing the school at cricket, football, swimming and so on. When I was in class I would grasp the basics of what we were meant to be learning in the first five minutes and then my concentration would drift away and I'd spend the rest of the time mucking about. I was easily bored. I often got sent out for taking the Mickey out of one of the kids or flicking someone. The headmaster would see me standing outside the classroom door and say: "Oh, it's you again, Clifford."

The teachers did their best. I have no-one to blame but myself for my lack of academic achievement. If my teachers remember me at all it is probably as somebody who had too much confidence for his own good. I was always fighting. Being the youngest of four and having two elder brothers I was used to scrapping with people stronger and bigger than me. I was always in the thick of things and very competitive. I still am. I got away with a lot, but sometimes I was caught and was given the cane and if Mum found out she'd give me a clip round the ear as well. I left school as soon as I could, at 15, with no formal qualifications.

I got my confidence from Mum and Dad and from Dad I also inherited a love of music. He was a classical pianist and from an early age I was listening to Chopin and Rachmaninov, though I also liked pop music. When I got a job on the local paper as a trainee reporter I started a record column just to get free records so I could open a disco

I was 19 when I went to work for the person who, apart from my parents, has taught me most. Syd Gillingham was chief press officer at the record company, EMI. He is a very straight and honest man and you don't meet many of those. He is also very perceptive and doesn't suffer fools, which is a quality I admire, particularly in the entertainment industry which is full of much to do about nothing. Syd realised that I work best on my own, doing my own thing my own way. He didn't tell me what to do, it was just: "Off you go". The first act I handled was The Beatles.

Syd was calm and authoritative in his dealings with stars. He knew what he was doing. His philosophy was that they might be famous actors or singers but they don't know our game; and we do, and they need us. He led by example and stood out because most press officers in record companies in those days were sycophants. Syd was never like that and people respected him for it. I've never sucked up to anyone either. I'm not capable. I go to the other extreme. I was never star struck. Within a few weeks of meeting John Lennon, he and I had a fist fight. He took a pop at me over something silly and one thing led to another. He was as good as gold to work with after that. John was the Beatle I most admired. We shared a similar sense of humour.

It was a roller coaster time in pop music. People like Cliff Richard and Adam Faith were coming through and we also had Motown on the label. I never had to work with anyone I didn't like. Syd let me have the pick of the bunch of the acts and when he left to set up his own company I went with him. We worked together for two years before I launched out on my own.

As well as giving me opportunities, Syd taught me the importance of looking after contacts and making time for people. I regularly have students coming to me wanting help with their dissertations. I run a happy office and that's down to Syd, too. His was a happy office with no threats, no bullying, no shouting. Syd is about 15 years older than me and has retired now but we are still great friends and regularly go for a fish and chip supper together.

FRANK GARDNER
BBC security correspondent

It was my English master, John Osborne, who set me on the road to the Middle East. He was a very inspiring teacher of English literature, but he also took an extracurricular sixth form class at Marlborough on Islamic culture. He'd spent some time in Iran and studied the architecture there and showed us superb photographs he'd taken of Isfahan and Shiraz. I was fascinated to hear him talk about mosques and caravanserais and how the irrigation systems worked. Back then, in the Seventies, nobody in Britain knew anything about Islam or the Islamic world. They were about to, because the Iranian revolution was nearly upon us. These were the last months of the Shah's regime.

My interest in the Arab world had begun when I was 16 and met Sir Wilfred Thesiger, the veteran Arabian explorer and author. But he wasn't as inspiring as John Osborne who talked about the Middle East as a fascinating place with wonderful friendly people and an amazing culture and civilisation. He encouraged us to do some research and to give mini-talks on the art of the mosque and the minaret and later at university when I went on to read

Arabic and Islamic studies, my dissertation on Islamic art in north Africa was inspired by John Osborne.

Deciding to read Arabic at university was the only sensible decision I took as a teenager. I liked languages and thought here was a language not many Britons speak. It's the lingua franca in 22 countries and most important, many of those countries have oil, so I reasoned that there should always be a job. It didn't quite work out as simply as that. I soon learnt I had to graft the Arabic onto an additional skill, and drifted into banking.

At school I remember John Osborne as a rather pinched sallow unhealthy looking chap which is why I didn't recognise him when I saw him just after he retired. Now he is fit and tanned and looks much younger than his years. He is still leading tours to various parts of the world, including Iran. Then, he appeared bookish, was bald and reminded me of a singer of the time called Eno. His personality shone through though and his passion for books was infectious. He wasn't teaching because it was a job, he was teaching because he loved literature and that rubbed off on us, like his love of Islam did. John Osborne also stands out because he was a good listener. A lot of teachers preach at you. His classes were interactive.

However, Oliver Ramsbotham who taught late medieval history at O-level and was my personal tutor, is probably the best teacher I had. He was an immensely kind person with glasses, long straight sandy hair and a pale freckled skin. He was of the era of corduroy jackets with leather elbow patches. He is now at Bradford University in the peace studies department. Like John Osborne, he was passionate about his subject. His descriptions of the conquest of South America were so vivid we could imagine ourselves wearing suits of armour. He also taught us a lot about writing essays. I remember being told not to be afraid of using semi-colons.

I was not a star pupil. I got an exhibition to Marlborough but once I was there didn't shine academically. I never made it to prefect and wasn't particularly well-behaved. It was quite extraordinary, therefore, to read John Osborne's review of my book, *Blood and Sand*, in the school magazine, "The Old Marlburian". To have a teacher of nearly 30 years ago praising my punctuation and use of grammar when I never really excelled in those things at school was great. I was really chuffed about that.

MARIELLA FROSTRUP
broadcaster, writer and critic

went to about ten schools because my parents kept moving house and although I was not a Catholic, most of the schools I attended were convent schools. The standard of State education in Ireland then (the 1970s) was high, but also very old-fashioned in approach. There was a lot of learning by rote, an awful lot of corporal punishment and large chunks of the day were devoted to religion.

But St Laurence's College, county Dublin, although affiliated to the church, was radical and enlightened. It was co-educational and we had a mixture of lay teachers and Brothers, although none of the Brothers wore robes. I was only there for two years, but during that time I encountered the two teachers who had the biggest influence on my entire school career.

The teacher who influenced me most, and who inspired my lifelong love of language, was Mr Murtagh the English master. He was small and dynamic and I met him at a time in my life when, although I was quite precocious, I was also quite confused. My parents had recently split up and I was going through archetypal teenage rebellion. Mr Murtagh's inspirational teaching and constant emphasis on encouraging me to explain what I was feeling and write about it gave me confidence that writing was something I could do well. I thought he was fantastic.

I was really committed to academia. I found school a place where I could escape to another world. Mr Murtagh encouraged debate and had a unique ability to find each pupil's strength and turn an English class into a forum for expression. We read what was on the syllabus, but he took things further all the time. If you said you'd enjoyed a book he would suggest other books by the same author. He even brought Greek plays to life and made them vivid. He once cast me as a prostitute in some Greek comedy that was really very funny. He encouraged me to write poetry and I won a prize. I owe him a huge debt also for encouraging me to read literature that was perhaps slightly beyond my understanding at the time. Mr Murtagh taught me to read properly, to not skip a sentence – though professionally what I need now is a speed reading course.

My other special teacher at St Laurence's was Brother Jim, who taught maths. He was special because I was madly in love with him, I don't know why – though it may have been because of his twinkly blue eyes. He was also an inspirational teacher and made clear a subject I'd never excelled in before or since. In the year I was in his class I tried extra hard and got an A grade – but that was a one off.

After St Laurence's I moved schools again and left as soon as I could. The moment I was 16 I caught the ferry and came to London.

I got an email from Brother Jim recently out of the blue. He said he had this terrible memory of a pupil in his class who he'd once made sit with a piece of chalk in her mouth because she wouldn't stop talking, and he'd never been able to forgive himself for it. That was me and I've never been able to forget the humiliation. But I deserved the punishment. My way of getting him to notice me was to be disruptive and talk incessantly.

JOHN HUMPHRYS
broadcaster

I was a semi-detached pupil. School was something I went through but had very little interest in. I got eight or nine O-levels from Cardiff High, which probably helped me get my first job on the *Penarth Times*, but otherwise the school did absolutely nothing for me and I never felt I belonged.

I was a working-class kid brought up in what nowadays I suppose would be considered a slum area – Splott in Cardiff – and I was the first in the family to pass the 11-plus to go to what was considered the best grammar school in the city. Cardiff High was absurdly conscious of its status. It had a terrific academic record, an awful lot of the boys won scholarships and went on to the best universities, and it excelled at sport.

When I arrived I remember an enormous feeling of isolation and inhibition. I didn't know a soul. At primary school I was a gang leader and confident; all of us came from the same sort of background. When I got to grammar school I was very conscious that most of the boys there had parents who were pretty well off.

It hadn't occurred to me before that my family was any worse off than anyone else's because I'd lived in the same area all my life. It took a bit of getting used to, being aware that I was slightly different. My father was a French polisher, and I was the third of five children. It was quite a struggle for my parents to pay for my uniform.

One of the few teachers I remember was a chap called Salter, who was my form master and French teacher. He was youngish and I got on well with him because I found French very easy and was the best in the class. He was a small, slight, bespectacled man, timid compared with some of the staff.

I was pretty good at English, too, but average at everything else and absolutely hopeless at all games. I made an effort at cross-country running but was useless at team sports, and the school attached huge importance to games. It was a grammar school that thought it was a public school.

The headmaster, George Diamond, was an autocrat and a strict disciplinarian. He caned routinely. I remember being sent to him for being late. I had three paper rounds: one in the morning, one in the evening and one on Sundays. The paper rounds were important because we needed the money, but I don't think the school approved. One morning the papers were late being delivered to the shop, so I was late for school. Mr Diamond clearly had no understanding of why one of his boys should be doing something so grubby as delivering papers. He said it was no kind of excuse for being late. He was probably right, but a good head should recognise that children have other concerns outside school.

George Diamond was regarded as a great headmaster. He did run a highly successful school, but looked at from my perspective my time at Cardiff High was unmemorable. I wish I had enjoyed what are probably the five most formative years of one's life. Maybe I'm blaming the school for my own deficiencies, but it seems to me that the whole point of a good school is that it should be able to get hold of boys like me and get them involved, and make them feel they belong.

I left school at 15 and started work the next week. In fairness to George Diamond, he did say I should do A-levels and go to university, but because of the financial situation at home, and because I was obsessed with the idea of being a journalist and was convinced I had to start on a local paper as soon as possible, there was never any question of staying on. For years I regretted that I didn't go to university, but I certainly can't blame the school.

George Diamond retired soon after I left and I went to interview him for the local paper. It was strange to see the man who had been such a remote, magisterial figure in a gown, sitting in his arm chair, wearing slippers, and with a glass of whisky at his side.

SUE JOHNSTON
actress

Being taught by Nora Potter was the best thing that happened to me. She changed my life by making me see what was possible and it was because of her I became an actress. I tried for years to track her down without success to say thank you, but it wasn't until the National Teaching Awards ceremony one year that we met up again.

She had wanted to become an actress herself but hadn't had the courage and instead became a teacher of English and drama. She gave me a part in the school production of *The Tinderbox* and there was a moment on stage when I did something and everybody laughed and I felt so at home, so right in my skin. I knew then that I wanted to be an actress and she recognised it too.

It was hard for people from our background in those days. In the North, you didn't even know that drama schools existed and nobody in my family had gone into the theatre. Miss Potter told me how it could be done. But my dad wouldn't have any of it. He had never had the opportunity to go to university and was longing for me to go.

I was in my second year at Prescot and Huyton Girls' Grammar School when Miss

Potter joined the staff. I remember the first day she came into class. She was very attractive, with short blonde hair and an hourglass figure and she took no nonsense. She was a terrific teacher and we all adored her. I remember reading a Keats poem for her in front of the class and she was so complimentary, she gave me great confidence. I was a happy, well-adjusted child, but I was a bit self-conscious.

Miss Potter started a spoken English competition, which I won. I remember practising for ages, reading to Mum and Dad every night. She took a school party to Stratford to see *Coriolanus*. Just before the play started they announced that Olivier had broken his leg and his understudy would be appearing instead. We all groaned, then out came Albert Finney and we all fell in love with him. I told him about this years later when I worked with him and he said: "Imagine what it was like to be in my dressing room when I heard you all groan."

We lived just outside Liverpool and I used to be taken to the Playhouse by my godmother, Lavinia, for my birthday treat. We would go and have lunch and then go on to a matinée. My mum took me to the ballet, which I adored, and when I was 12 I went with the school to Sadler's Wells to see *Tosca* and I remember being transfixed with the wonder of it all.

Miss Potter suggested I try to get into RADA and because my father was against it I rebelled. I stomped off and left school after one year in the sixth form and got a job in the tax office which was in Mathew Street, just near the Cavern in Liverpool. Then I got involved with the Liverpool music scene and worked for the Beatles' manager, Brian Epstein. I was also in an amateur drama company that entertained in old folks' homes, but it wasn't until a relationship I was in went badly wrong and the Beatles had gone to London that I started thinking again about acting professionally. I was nearly 22 when I went to the Webber Douglas drama school.

I'd lost touch with Miss Potter by then and couldn't find her to tell her. I even went to a school reunion, but nobody knew what had happened to her. She had married in my last year at school and I later discovered that she had moved to Yorkshire.

When we finally met up again I was thrilled to discover that she hadn't forgotten me. She had kept a diary of the time when I was at school and had written about me. She told me I am one of her favourite actresses and although she had always felt there was something familiar about me, she hadn't recognised me as the Susan Wright she used to teach.

We are great friends now, but at school there was always a distance between us. She never made me feel I was any more special than any of the other girls. I didn't even know her name was Nora.

JEREMY VINE
broadcaster

What made Neil Laing such a special teacher was that he was so cool. Because he was cool he could explain Shakespeare and Marlow and Webster and poetry to spotty teenagers who couldn't see the relevance of any of it and somehow engender great enthusiasm. We realised that you didn't have to be a wimp to enjoy things that were artistic and complicated.

He had a dog called Jack who sat passively in a basket under his desk throughout the lesson, never once causing any distraction. Jack was so respectful I think all of us potentially uproarious boys looked at the dog and thought if he's going to obey this guy, we certainly will. The dog was white with brown spots and long ears. Appropriately, being an English master's pet, I think he was an English setter.

Neil Laing was also cool because he was married to someone who worked for *The Times*. His wife was a sub-editor in the days before careers officers had heard of the media.

Nobody ever tried it on in Neil Laing's lessons, and they tried it on in lots of other classes. He was an accessible, likeable man and he took me through English

O and A-levels at Epsom College. He was about 6ft, lean with a very well trimmed moustache, a jutting brow and a slightly intense look. He had what Tom Wolfe would describe as a lantern jaw. He was the model of courtesy and very neat. He looked as though he had come out of a Thomas Hardy period drama.

He knew how to trigger boyhood interests by focussing on the sexual imagery in the texts we were studying. And when we were discussing *King Lear* I remember him saying we needed to understand the interiors and that what goes on inside people is more important than what is on the outside. Twenty years later I still vividly remember him telling us that physical illness is a picnic compared to mental illness.

He got us reading aloud in lessons and I liked that. There is some sort of actor gene in me: my brother is a comedian and my sister an actress. But he was very cross with me once when I read *Hamlet* in a silly accent. My school reports always said things like: "He is clearly interested in things other than the class he is doing."

English was the only subject that spurred me and which I wasn't doing just to pass exams. I still love poetry and it was quite an achievement to get adolescent boys not to think verse was sissy. Neil Laing would go off on flights of fancy and sometimes in a class which lasted an hour, he would spend 50 minutes talking about just one line in Shakespeare. I remember once asking him whether we were reading too much into these plays, which set off a discussion that lasted a double lesson.

I didn't enjoy school. I was very bad at sport, which was humiliating in a public school culture that was very sporty. Now, I realise of course that the people who were good at sport are working as clerks in pension firms or are middle managers so their lives ended when the school bell rang for the last time, which is hugely satisfying.

I was set on a career in the media from the age of 12. I saw myself on the radio and playing records. My heroes were people like Roger Scott and Kenny Everett. When we had a careers session at school and I said I wanted to go into the media there was real shock. But Neil Laing encouraged me. He invited me round to his house to meet his wife and have a chat about her work as a journalist. And when I started playing records on the radio station at the local psychiatric hospital in Banstead once a week he thought it was a great idea to get cracking early.

Neil Laing had absolutely the right balance as a teacher between the chummy and the personal and also the authoritative, which is a difficult balance to get. I owe him and never told him and this is a great opportunity to do so.

DIANE ABBOTT
the first black woman to be elected to the House of Commons

I was the only black girl at Harrow County Grammar School for Girls and I was completely counter-stereotype. I was very academic and terrible at sport. I was a plump child, always with my head in a book.

Right from being at infant school I had been good at writing essays. My work was always read out in class and pinned up for the others to read.

English was my favourite subject, and Miss Landry, who taught me at Harrow, was a very charismatic teacher. She was Welsh and glamorous, and was just passionate about literature and language. She conveyed that to her pupils. She wasn't a soft touch – she was quite spiky – but there was a star quality about her.

Miss Landry's approach contrasted sharply with that of my first English teacher at the school, Miss Peck, who was an austere woman. For our first lesson she set us an essay to write and the next lesson read out our marks. She began reading out the list, beginning with those who had got A+, then A, B+ and so on, working her way to the Cs and Ds. Being used to getting good marks, I was shocked not to hear my name as she went through the list. Finally, she had read out everyone's marks except mine. I put up my hand and asked what had happened to my essay and she said she would see me at the end of the lesson.

When the class was over I went to her desk and she pushed my essay towards me saying, "Where did you copy this from?" She couldn't believe that a black girl had written such a good essay. I was so shocked, I didn't defend myself and went away feeling humiliated. For the remainder of the year I deliberately didn't write as well as I could because I didn't want that humiliation again. Once Miss Peck stopped teaching me, I went back to my old high standard.

My parents, in common with many immigrants, were passionate about education. I can remember going home from school one night having come second in something and my father said:" It's no good being second. You always have to do better than white people."

It was quite a formal school and we had a uniform: a navy gym slip, cream blouse and navy and pink tie. In the winter we wore a navy felt hat and in the summer, a navy straw. That straw hat was always a problem – because I had so much curly hair it kept coming off. I lost it in my last term in the sixth form.

I got nine O-levels, but I wasn't made a prefect. I don't think the teachers saw me as school prefect material. And when I wanted to take the Oxbridge entrance exams they tried to dissuade me. I was determined enough to insist. We'd been on a school outing to Cambridge and I thought it was a wonderful place. I wanted to study history but my history teacher, Miss Buckley, said she didn't think I was up to it. I replied:"But I do." I got four As at A-level and, with one other girl, stayed on an extra term, tutored by Miss Buckley, to take the Cambridge entrance exam. We both passed.

My school ran a joint drama society with the local county boys' school and I remember making appearances in a production of *Macbeth* in which Michael Portillo played Macduff and I was Lady Macduff. Clive Anderson was in the same school drama group. So was Francis Matthews, who went on to become a professional actor.

I was very conscious of inequality when I was in my teens and twenties, and my ambition then was to become a politician. I wanted to be able to look in the mirror and say:" Well, at least you tried." I am very fortunate to have achieved my ambition and to have a job I really enjoy. Another ambition was to have children and I have a son, James. My one remaining ambition is to write a book. I am interested in history and I might write about the history of the Caribbean or slavery – but that may have to wait until I leave the House of Commons.

IAN McEWAN
author

I was sent back from Tripoli in North Africa where my father, who was in the Army, was stationed, to go to Woolverstone Hall in Norfolk at 11. It was a state boarding school and most of the pupils were bright working-class lads, often from split families, who were being given a crack at pseudo public school life.

I think as boarding schools went in the late Fifties it was probably kinder and more civilised than most, but I was very disoriented. I was 2,000 miles from home and very shy.

I found the lack of privacy quite devastating. It was noisy and the amount of pastoral care was minimal. There was one matron between 60 boys and her main concerns were with the laundry and dabbing iodine on cuts. She wasn't in any way a mother figure.

I sort of got through school. Until I got to the sixth form I'd been fairly mediocre. I had plenty of friends, but I hadn't shone in class, hadn't been trying particularly. Nobody encouraged me. Nobody really knew I was there.

Then in the sixth form I met Neil Clayton, my English teacher. It was a fortunate moment in my life, when I was suddenly hungry for the kinds of things he had to offer – an excitement about poetry and about literature in general.

I realise now how young he must have been – I guess in his late twenties. He was rather cool, not in the hip sense, but he seemed a little impatient with school-mastering. He never wore a gown, as many of the other teachers did. He was quick-witted and enjoyed repartee. He had a streak of cynicism, even scepticism, about the world which was very appealing to adolescents. I think there was a degree of hero worship. He was of medium height, fairly handsome, played golf and cricket, and had the ability, without a great deal of effort, to communicate a passion for reading widely.

He had been educated at Cambridge and brought us very much that priesthood sense of studying literature. We barely touched the A-level syllabus in the first four terms and prided ourselves on knowing our way round the canon.

His particular enthusiasms were first-generation romantic poets. I think one of the first things he took us through was TS Eliot's *The Waste Land*. He wasn't afraid of difficulty and I think he knew we would be proud of undertaking something different. He got things out of me that no one ever had. I was very keen to have his good opinion and worked furiously for that.

Neil Clayton encouraged me to go for a scholarship to King's College, Cambridge, but I did very little work and all sorts of emotional things got in the way and I fluffed the exam. I took a year off and did some travelling around Greece, worked as a dustman for Camden Council and then went to Sussex where I read English. I began writing while I was there. Then I went to East Anglia to do an MA. I never had any lecturers from Malcolm Bradbury, but I used to meet him in the pub and he and Angus Wilson encouraged me to write.

I sent Neil Clayton a copy of my first book and others I wrote in the early years. His reaction was always enthusiastic. After I left school our contact was only occasional. In that ruthless way one does, I moved on, and it is only as I get older I realise how lucky I was to have such a gifted teacher. It is always a matter of luck who walks into your life at a certain point and it was very fortunate for me, coming from a non-literary family, to meet Neil Clayton when I did.

He left teaching and now deals in antiquarian drawings and paintings. He once gave me a marvellous leather-bound book, published in 1803, containing the first mention in print of William Blake. It is something I really treasure.

HELENA KENNEDY
barrister

Mr Lavelle was the senior classics master at Holyrood School, Glasgow, a co-educational Catholic senior secondary school to which my three sisters and I all went. His name was John but he was known as Friend Lavelle because he used the term "friend" when addressing pupils. The tradition was that girls were called by their first names and boys by their surnames. Mr Lavelle was the only teacher who avoided impersonal surnames and called the boys Friend. He was a wonderful teacher and I suspect he had a great influence on many others as well as me.

Mr Lavelle made me feel special. I was only in my first or second year when he picked me for a school team taking part in a new Scottish television programme, a cross between *Top of the Form* and *University Challenge*. I was flattered. Being chosen is always a great means of inspiring a child's loyalty.

I had no personal experience of Mr Lavelle as a teacher at that stage, but I knew him because he had taught my elder sisters and occasionally he would meet my father in the pub. My father was rather bookish and very keen on education although he was unskilled. He worked as a bundle strangler [a dispatch hand] on the

Glasgow Daily Record. Mr Lavelle was about my father's age, or a little older. He had wavy, sandy-coloured hair, going grey, a lined face and twinkly eyes.

I really enjoyed learning Latin and when I was in my third year, because I liked Mr Lavelle so much, I asked him if I might start doing Greek. He was thrilled because very few others were interested. I explained that what appealed to me about Latin was that it was like a puzzle. I remember him saying that classical Greek was even more of a puzzle. I was the only one in my year studying Greek and Mr Lavelle juggled my timetable to fit the lessons in. We became good friends.

Part of his skill was that he made lessons interesting. He was never patronising, never had to raise his voice. He always wore a gown and sometimes he twirled his sleeve as he talked. He would walk up and down with his hands behind his back and say: "Let's be hearing from you Friend." He could be strict. If you didn't do your homework, he'd set twice as much next time.

Because I felt special and wanted to please him, I worked hard. My solo Greek lessons were like private tutorials. We discussed how classical stories affected our view of war and the way mythology from the classics feeds into today's literature.

Mr Lavelle ran the school debating society and encouraged me to get involved from the age of 14 or 15, even though the others taking part were sixth-formers. He taught me how to build up an argument and how to look at things from both sides. I soon began to love debating and took part in inter-school competitions. It was a great grounding for someone going to the Bar.

I have been a judge in the *Observer* Mace competition and one of the disappointing things is that independent sector schools are incredibly good at debating, but you rarely see state system pupils as confident and skilled. I think learning how to debate is essential in encouraging young people to think and to engage with issues. I'd like to see debating given emphasis in the state school system.

I talked about my future with Mr Lavelle and my first plan was to take an English degree. I had a place at Glasgow University but at the last minute came to England and went to the Council of Legal Education, the Inns of Court School of Law and then the Bar. Mr Lavelle approved of that. He was rather pleased that I'd decided to do what he felt I should have done all along.

I went back to see him after I'd left school and although I thanked him for his help, I don't think I expressed to him clearly enough how influential he was in my life. Many years later, after I'd presented *Heart of the Matter* on television, he wrote to me. By that time he was very ill and his handwriting was shaky. He said in the letter that he always thought of me as his Portia.

ALED JONES
broadcaster and former child singer

I led a double life as a schoolboy. From Monday to Friday I was in class and at the weekends and during the holidays I'd be performing and making records. Occasionally if I had to sing on a weekday or appear on a programme they'd fly me back to Wales by plane or helicopter so I didn't miss school the next day.

None of my classmates knew what was going on. I never talked about performing at school. And my mother, being a teacher, was particularly anxious that I missed as little schooling as possible and tried to arrange my professional life to fit in with the school curriculum. Eventually, of course, especially after *Walking in the Air*, people found out and I got ribbed a bit, but most of my friends didn't care a damn.

My mother taught the reception class at Llandegfan Primary near our home in Anglesey and when I was five she decided it would be best if I went to a different school. But I only lasted one morning. I sobbed the whole time because I wanted to be with my friends so Mam had a word with her boss, the headmaster, and I joined her class. That didn't mean I had an easy time, quite the opposite. My mother was harder on me than she was on the rest of the kids.

Lessons were taught in Welsh and singing played an important role in school life. When I was seven I began regularly taking part in eisteddfodau. Everybody did something: some kids played recorder, others recited poetry. I went for singing and a lovely gentle teacher, Nia Jones, coached me.

When a young progressive headmaster, Edward Morris Jones, joined the school we did more music and more competing. He played guitar in assembly and encouraged us all to take up a musical instrument. I wanted to learn to play Beatles tunes on the piano. Elsie Francis, who taught English and music, suggested I went to Bangor Cathedral and asked the choirmaster, Andrew Goodwin, to give me lessons. Meeting him changed my life. He agreed to teach me piano but he also asked me to sing a few scales. He spotted me as a potential chorister and I joined the cathedral choir.

By the time I went to David Hughes Comprehensive I had a bit of a reputation as a performer. I'd played Joseph in my primary school's production of *Joseph and the Technicolor Dreamcoat* and appeared on television in the Welsh equivalent of *Songs of Praise*. Then someone in the congregation at Bangor Cathedral asked a local record company to record one of my performances. Andrew Goodwin suggested I had extra coaching from Julie Wynne and Robert Wyn Roberts, who had just graduated from the Royal Northern College of Music.

Andrew taught me the basics, but everything else musically I learned from Robert and Julie and they were the biggest influence on my career as a boy soprano. They were great fun. I made an album. A BBC producer heard it and asked me to sing in Handel's oratorio *Jeptha*.

My fellow pupils still didn't know much about my professional life, even when the BBC made a documentary about me. The film crew came to school and said they were making a programme about maths teaching. The camera was on me most of the time, but only about half the kids guessed what was really going on.

When they saw me on television they weren't particularly bothered. I got a bit of ribbing when *Walking in the Air* became a hit. That was in 1985, when everything seemed to happen and I missed half of the school year, but I managed to get 10 O-levels. The headmaster, Dafydd Jones, was great about me taking time off. My main interest at school was football. I didn't concentrate in maths or science and occasionally got into trouble. I remember when we were dissecting a pig's heart I put a bit of it into a girl's pencil case and was banned from biology lessons for a week.

I gave up singing on my 16th birthday, not because my voice broke, but because it wasn't performing as well as I hoped. I went to the Royal Academy of Music, formed a pop group, became president of the students' union and had a good time.

GERI HALLIWELL
former Spice Girl turned author

I loved Mrs Flitt, my form teacher at junior school, because she was warm and kind and fair. I once went to her home for tea – I think we had beans on toast – because my mother was working and couldn't bring me back in time for the evening performance of the school play.

I was small for my age and when a horrible big butch girl threatened to throw me over the railway, Mrs Flitt intervened in a very gentle way and sorted out the problem without causing a drama.

I was so fond of her I put her in my first children's book. Recently I went back to the school to read to the pupils, but unfortunately Mrs Flitt had left. The school is now called Beechfield, but in my day it was Walter de Merton, Watford. I felt more nervous reading to the children than I ever did performing with the Spice Girls.

Mrs Medina, my English teacher at Watford Grammar School for Girls, also got a name check in one of my stories. She was a very elegant lady who looked a bit like Diana Rigg. I've always loved writing and reading and I enjoyed drama and Mrs Medina introduced me to Shakespeare. We studied *A Midsummer Night's Dream* and she took us to the open air theatre in Regent's Park to see it performed. She encouraged me to write and believed in my ability to perform. She often asked me to read in front of the class.

Because I liked Mrs Medina I wanted to please her and when I once forgot my lines in the school play I really felt I'd let her down. I was so upset, the next morning I hid under my desk and she looked at me half in dismay and half with humour. Then I got braces and started to lisp badly and she was rather disappointed by all the lisping and spitting when I read out loud.

I got a C in English and could have done much better if I hadn't spent so much time chatting at the back of the class. I always enjoyed the social aspect of school. I was talkative and cheeky, but always polite, and rarely got into serious trouble. I did bunk off once – but I got caught and put in detention. I dodged a music lesson because I didn't like the teacher.

It wasn't until I was 20 that I really got the most out of education. I went back to college to study English literature at A-level and by then I was old enough and mature enough to appreciate it.

Mrs White recognised that I was ready to learn and she helped me to access literature. I suddenly understood the wealth and power of words. We studied *Hamlet* and DH Lawrence's *Sons and Lovers* and for the first time I started getting great marks for my essays. Mrs White, who was a thin little bird-like woman, was passionate about her subject and I found her passion contagious. I started reading Oscar Wilde and joined book clubs. I asked questions in class and re-connected with my early enthusiasm for reading and writing. Mrs White took us to the Donmar theatre to see Alan Cummins in a great production of *Hamlet*.

Then one day I was pulled out of class to be told that my father had died. I was paralysed with grief, but Mrs White helped me through. I found comfort in words and read and wrote dark poetry that I was too shy to show to anyone.

Soon after, I went into the music business so my attention was distracted from my studies but when I was with the Spice Girls I always felt most comfortable and confident writing lyrics. According to mum writing is what I was meant to do.

LESLIE THOMAS
author

Maggie Hayes was a teacher at St Luke's Elementary School in Kingston-upon-Thames where I went when I was in the Barnardo's home after my parents both died within six months. It was wartime and when the flying bombs started all 150 boys in the home were evacuated to Norfolk. It was an idyllic summer and I'd never lived in the country before and thought it was great.

There was a small village school which wasn't big enough to take us all so we thought we'd never have to go to school again. That summer I really got into reading and there was a lake nearby where we went sailing in a boat made out of an old aircraft fuel tank.

Then one Sunday night in church we spotted Maggie Hayes. She'd come up from Kingston to teach us and it was arranged that half of us would go to school in the mornings and half in the afternoons. Maggie was a well-meaning woman, a typical 1940s unmarried schoolmistress with grey hair, which she wore in a bun, glasses, tweed skirts and wrinkled stockings.

There was a curtain down the middle of the classroom and we were on one side and the village children and their teacher were on the other. We were disgraceful. We behaved so badly that the village schoolteacher used to order her children out into the playground so they wouldn't be contaminated by our bad behaviour. It was the sugar beet season and we threw sugar beets at each other. We were rude. We were rowdy. As the year went on and it got colder and colder the poor village children would put their little faces to the window and beg us to calm down so they could come back into the warm.

Maggie tried so hard. She took us for walks in the countryside and tried to explain nature to us. She had an old sit-up-and-beg bicycle and we took the chain off it and let down her tyres. We used to lose her purposely on these nature walks and she'd be wheeling her bike across the fields shouting, "Where are you?" I'm ashamed now when I think about it. I realise how good she was and how forbearing.

Every morning one of us had to read a few verses from the Bible. I was a little swine. I'd hold the Bible upside down and knock the blackboard over – anything to get a few cheap laughs. But one day she gave me the "Song of Solomon" to read: "For the winter is past and over, the time of the singing of the birds is come and the voice of the turtle is heard in our land." It was a road to Damascus moment: I had a revelation of words for the first time. It's a wonderful poem and moves me even now. Right then I decided I wanted to be a writer.

Maggie added to my ambitions by taking us on a trip to Norfolk and the Barnardo's superintendent offered a prize of 2s 6d for the best essay about the trip. I won with a piece I called "Exertion to Norwich." Maggie said, "Don't you mean excursion?" and being a smart-arse I replied, "Well, it was very tiring."

We went back to Kingston and Maggie dropped out of my life so I was never able to thank her. I went to the local technical school to learn to be a bricklayer and then another influential person came into my life: Wally Brampton who was a housemaster at Barnardo's. We called him the Walrus because of his moustache. He was a soldier who had been invalided out of the War.

When I got chickenpox I was put into the billiard room because I was infectious and he came to see me. I wrote a story called Sleek the Otter, which owed a lot to Henry Williams' Tarka, and Mr Brampton read it and told me I was a good writer. He brought me a load of adventure stories and encouraged me to write more, and when I was 16 Barnardo's got me a job on the local paper and bought me a typewriter.

CAROL SMILLIE
TV presenter

If Miss Crockett could have seen me on *Changing Rooms* running up people's curtains without even tacking them she'd have laughed herself silly. She taught me how to use a sewing machine at Hutchesons' Grammar School in Glasgow, in her fabrics and fashion class and was a stickler for preparation.

I was never much good at sewing. I remember making some God-awful drawstring gym bag in yellow gingham with my name embroidered on the front, which kicked about the house for a long time. Miss Crockett insisted we did things properly, but on *Changing Rooms* we didn't have time for that.

She was a teacher of the old school. She had silver hair, was terribly polite, and we sat down and did as we were told in her lessons. Teaching was her life and she cared passionately about it. She was a kindly woman. I remember once taking in a favourite jumper which, shock-horror, had a cigarette burn on it (I didn't smoke, but my boyfriend did) and she darned it for me, which I thought was quite cool.

Hutchy (as we called it) was a school for young ladies then – it has since become co-ed. I loved my time there and did OK, but it was an academic school and I wasn't up there with the high achievers. Art was probably my best subject. My ambition was to be a fashion designer, but when I went to the careers office for advice I got the same response I'd get if I'd said I wanted to be a pop star. They didn't know what to do with me.

To gain the necessary qualifications to get into art school I went next to Cardonald College, a further education establishment in Glasgow, where I came across the teacher who had a huge influence on me.

Anna Sambucci was a friend as well as a teacher. She taught art and she was glamorous and fun and she made art lessons fun. She was very enthusiastic about my work, and very committed, and she was the first teacher to make me feel completely successful at what I was doing. I really felt she was on my side.

She was Scottish, married to an Italian who had a little restaurant/delicatessen and I often used to see her around Glasgow with her husband. She didn't look like you might expect an art teacher to look. She had long blonde hair and wore designer clothes and beautiful jewellery. Her nails were always polished and her hair perfectly brushed and styled and she had an air about her that I thought was attractive and interesting. I wanted to be like her.

I went on to Glasgow School of Art, but quickly realised that it wasn't for me and gave up after a year. While I was there I blagged my way into modelling, mostly photographic work because I'm a bit short for catwalks.

Changing Rooms was probably the best job of my career and the only part of my school education that helped me on the show was sewing. Nobody ever asked me if I could sew when I began presenting the programme, but it shocked me how few people even knew how to thread a sewing machine, never mind use one, so I just took it on. I got bored waiting around and I thought if I don't do it, nobody will.

My sewing has come on so much just from having a go with other people's bits and pieces. I've made some horrendous mistakes upholstering sofas up and down the country, but I'm quite good at it now. For my next birthday my husband is going to build me an arts studio where I can finish off all the sewing jobs and other projects I've started and abandoned. I want to finish everything off myself. I want it done properly. I wouldn't like anyone else giving my home a makeover.

MICHAEL ASPEL
radio and television presenter

I started school at two and a half and I remember my first teacher, Miss Bates, because we did this "King's Breakfast" routine. I had to slide down a table saying: "I do like a little bit of butter on my bread." It was my first performance.

I was with Miss Bates at Waldron Road School in Earlsfield in south-west London until I was seven and then I was evacuated to Chard in Somerset.

I remember the school in Chard mainly for being whacked with a cane by the headmaster, Mr Rose, for being cheeky to my "lady" – the foster parent I was staying with. I'd get a clip round the ear at home for various crimes I never quite understood and then I'd get punished at school as well, which I thought was unjust.

Mr Rose was my least favourite teacher. Once, half way through a beating I asked him to stop. Then when I went back into the class and showed the others the marks on my hand where he'd hit me, he told everyone, with a big smile, that I had begged for mercy. I hated him from then on.

There were two nice teachers at that school: Miss Guppy and Miss Wyler, young women who were acting as relief teachers while the men were away fighting in the War. Miss Guppy was particularly attractive. She had lovely legs. Many years later, when I was working at Alexandra Palace as a newsreader, I had a letter from her asking if I was the same Michael Aspel she had taught in Somerset, and she came to see me. Miss Guppy had the right personality for a teacher. She had authority, she had humour and she was perceptive. What I remember most about Miss Wyler is that she had a splendid bosom.

I returned to London and got a scholarship to Emanuel School in Wandsworth. I remember all the teachers at Emanuel. There was Taffy Neath who taught Latin and every day, holding a cricket bat, chanted: "Weary day after weary day, weary week after weary week, monotonous month after monotonous month – and you still don't know anything." Every now and again we got a tap on the head with the cricket bat. I wasn't any good at Latin.

We also had a number of student teachers and I feel very guilty now at the way we behaved towards them. We must have destroyed at least one fledgling career. I remember particularly an Indian with exquisite manners who tried to teach us mathematics. When he turned to write on the board we would hurl bits of chalk and other missiles at his back and he would plead: "Gentlemen, marvel at the board."

The headmaster, Mr Broome, was a wonderful Alistair Sim type of character. He asked me what I wanted to do for a living and I said: "Something to do with cameras, perhaps." He said: "You could learn Russian as well and become a spy. It would be a brief, but colourful career." He caught me once in the high street without my cap and greeted me with: "Fair cop I think we'll call that."

There was a geography master, Major somebody, who used to wrench people to the floor by their hair. He was in charge of the CCF of which I was a member. My father, who was a professional soldier, encouraged me in anything to do with uniform. His wanted me to become a fireman.

I liked school because I was gregarious. I was described as an "all-rounder" which meant I was a dilettante. English was my best subject and I was good at art and pretty good at languages – apart from Latin. I failed at maths completely. I was in the school drama group and in one end of term play played a BBC announcer in a dinner jacket. Everyone said I did it unnaturally well.

My father didn't believe in further education so I left school at 16 and became a teaboy at a publishing company before doing national service. I was 21 or 22 when I went for an audition at the BBC in Wales and the next week I was on the radio in *Children's Hour*.

GABBY LOGAN
TV sports presenter

I had three special teachers at my secondary school, Cardinal Heenan High School in Leeds, all of whom came to my wedding. I invited them because they were important influences in my life; all three were inspirational and encouraging.

Miss McMahon taught geography. It was a subject I loved anyway, but she had a very interesting, engaging way of teaching. She was an effervescent, glamorous woman with long blonde curly hair who took great pride in her appearance.

She also took great pride in her work and in everything that we did. She was good at giving pastoral care alongside her teaching at that important age between 13 and 16, which is all about goals and aspirations and when awkward things are happening to your body. She would surreptitiously drop in suggestions about what we were going to get out of life and how we were going to get it, without ever using clichés.

Until I was taught by Miss McMahon I'd thought of geography as being about learning about different countries, but I didn't realise that it includes things like the earth's resources and the preservation of the planet and crosses over into politics. Later, she went on to become head of another school and I think the qualities I admired in her would have made her a great head teacher.

Mr Flanagan, who taught me religious studies, was head of year in my fourth year and also a PE teacher, so I came into contact with him through the extra sport I did at school as well. Like Miss McMahon, he was probably in his late twenties. He was a great disciplinarian, he didn't suffer any nonsense in his classes, but unlike the other male teachers, he did it with a smile. He took religious studies way beyond learning the catechism and reciting prayers. He taught us about other cultures and places in the world, and how religion affected them. We were a hard-working class and he got a lot out of us. He opened up our minds, our horizons and our imaginations

Physically, he was sinewy, with red hair and a moustache. He used to run to and from home to school every day, which was about 10 miles, with a rucksack on his back. I found his self-discipline inspirational. I was already keen on gymnastics and aiming to compete internationally; but I ran because I was in training; he did it just to keep fit.

When my brother Daniel died in 1992, aged 15, Mr Flanagan, who had taught him too, read at the funeral and was very supportive to my family.

The other teacher who inspired me was Miss Woolliter, who taught PE. She, too, was really dedicated. This was a time when teachers were striking all over the country, but we never seemed to suffer like other people of my generation I've talked to since. Miss Woolliter continued to take us to netball matches and cross-country events in the mini bus and stayed behind with me at lunchtimes when I was doing extra training at high jump, in which I became city champion at 13. She was very supportive and always had a big smile on her face and made training fun. There was never any problem when I couldn't go to school sports practice or play in netball matches because I was doing gymnastics, probably because academically everything was fine.

I enjoyed my schooldays and although I was very involved in sport and drama, I was a high achiever. I still managed to do my homework and consistently got A grades. The more you do, the more you get done.

MALCOLM RIFKIND
politician

My secondary schooldays began at the local authority school, James Gillespie's, just round the corner from my home in Edinburgh. It was the male equivalent of the girls' school on which Muriel Spark's novel, *The Prime of Miss Jean Brodie*, was based.

Then two years later I changed to George Watson's College, an independent boys' school. It was the year of the Queen's coronation and I remember being thrilled to receive two commemorative souvenirs – one from each school.

There were a lot of good teachers at George Watson's but if I had to single out one it would be a chap called Robin Morgan, who taught history. He had tremendous enthusiasm for his subject and he was stimulating in the way he presented what we were studying. But what was most interesting was that he very often began lessons with a discussion on what was in the newspapers that morning. He was fascinated by what was happening in the world and stimulated my interest in current affairs. It was the end of the Macmillan era and the time of the Cold War and Kennedy. I was a bit of an extrovert and took an active part in class discussions.

I was already very involved with the school debating society, which had been formed by the English master, Michael Robson. He'd instructed me to "volunteer" to speak in the first debate, knowing I could perform in public having been in the odd school play. I'd been cast, most improbably, as Cardinal Wolsey in *A Man for All Seasons* and played the soothsayer in *Julius Caesar*.

That first debate was whether television was a good thing. I was speaking in favour, which you would think would be easy – but we lost. It was an inauspicious start, but I'd got the bug. Joining the debating society was the best thing that happened to me. We also had mock elections in which we not only had the traditional political parties, but we also used to invent parties one of which was called 3D – for doom, death and destruction. My support varied. I started off as a Tory but in my first year at university I flirted with the Liberals. Then I went back to the Tory club, which was much more fun.

At George Watson's all the masters wore gowns but Robin Morgan was a particularly imposing figure. He was tall and saturnine with dark-rimmed glasses and a marvellous loud, booming voice. He drove a sports car and had a rather grand background and lifestyle. He was fascinated by all things military. Some boys found him intimidating but I liked his style and he and I had an immediate rapport, though we had one unfortunate exchange. In my final year I was deputy editor of the school magazine, *The Phoenix*. We thought it amusing to take a well-known quotation and apply it to individual masters and in the case of Robin Morgan it was: "Get your facts right first, then you can distort them as much as you like." The day the magazine came out Mr Morgan asked me to stay behind after class and complained that we were making him out to be some sort of fascist who distorts the truth.

He left Watson's to become headmaster of a public school in Northern Ireland and then returned to Edinburgh as headmaster of Stewart's Melville. When I became a Member of Parliament he invited me once or twice to speak to the school.

I wasn't prominent at school at sport, or academically, and was never a prefect which I was rather narked about. By the age of 16 I was a bit stroppy and bored. I left at 17. Two of my friends were offered places at Edinburgh University, so I applied too. It was six months after the closing date and I had minimum qualifications because I was only in my fifth year. Nowadays I wouldn't even be interviewed, but I was offered a place to read law and the day I began at university I grew up.

Years later, when I was a government minister and was invited back to my old school to make the founder's day speech, the headmaster thanked me and in front of the whole school, said he wished to rectify an omission of many years. Suddenly he produced a small silver prefect's badge and presented it to me.

CLARISSA DICKSON WRIGHT
youngest woman to be called to the Bar, one of TVs 'Two Fat Ladies'

When I was 11 I was sent off with my trunk and my uniform from Harrods to board at the Sacred Heart Convent in Hove, East Sussex. I still remember the wonderful smell of beeswax polish, flowers and incense. The nuns wore full habit with a frilled wimple framing the face and appeared very gracious and dignified and had a considerable air of authority.

Mother April O'Leary was my favourite. She taught me English for A-level and was also my mistress of studies. She became one of the great influences in my life. She was in her early 40s then, a small woman with bright blue eyes. We later became great friends and now go away for holidays together. I cook and we talk and read and play backgammon – at which she is a fiend.

She was a wonderful teacher: exuberant, enthusiastic and full of life. She would read the comic bits of Shakespeare in a Warwickshire accent and directed us in school stage productions with gusto. Never shy or retiring, I was cast as Ernest in *The Importance of Being Ernest* and she taught me how to rub up tobacco and I learned to smoke a pipe. I was Arthur in a memorable production of *Le Morte d'Arthur* for which April constructed an amazing barge on wheels which was pulled across stage by the lacrosse team. Unfortunately, my baldric got looped round a wheel and it was very nearly the end of me. Everyone said it was most dramatic how my voice got fainter and fainter.

April O'Leary was very keen on Skeats' etymological dictionary (I have her copy) and we spent many happy hours researching the origin of words. My father was also a great teacher who had encouraged me to go and look things up and she took this one stage further and stretched my mind and taught me to look beyond the page immediately in front of me.

She was a very clever woman. If she hadn't been a nun I'm sure she would have been a brilliant Oxford don. We'd read Milton and Henry James, which I didn't like then, though I do now, and she would enthuse me. Her forte was Jane Austen. She wrote her PhD at Oxford on the role of the aunts in Jane Austen. We were all devoted to her, but my best friend, Christine, and I used to pester her to give us chores just so we could spend more time talking to her.

When my mother died I went to see April, who was then at the teacher training college in Roehampton, and she helped organise the funeral. We became friends and she became my spiritual counsellor. The Catholic Church can be quite rigid, but the great thing about April is that she has always worn her spirituality like a very comfortable garment. There have been times in my life when I have been separated from God and she accepted that and never nagged me.

She has always been very understanding. In my drinking days, when I was on retreat and supposedly giving up alcohol, she once took a swig out of my glass thinking it was water and found it was almost neat gin. She didn't say a word; she just looked at me quizzically. Later she told me she realised there was nothing she could do, so she prayed.

I was slightly apprehensive when I sent her a copy of my autobiography but she said she'd enjoyed it and when she got to the horrid bits she kept on reading because she knew the story had a happy ending.

TIM WATERSTONE
founder of Waterstones and Daisy and Tom stores

I was barely educated and barely fed at prep school. Then I went to Tonbridge which was a bog standard minor public school in those days, but it was where I encountered inspirational teaching of an extraordinary standard I'd never experienced before.

Mrs Austin was the wife of the school chaplain and wasn't actually a teacher, but gave extra English lessons on a one-to-one basis in the evenings. She opened up my imagination in a sensational way.

She was amazingly well read and talking to her was leagues above what I was getting from the nice English master who was teaching 23 of us in a class. I'd always had a natural affinity for writing and when I was 14 won the school short story competition – despite Freddie Forsyth being there at the same time. I wrote about one of the masters who was retiring and the prize was a book which I still have. I'd just got into Thomas Hardy and chose *Far From the Madding Crowd.*

Twice a week for two years I spent an hour with Mrs Austin in her little drawing room piled with books and usually with a pot filled with wild flowers. She'd give me a cup of tea and once on my birthday she baked me a cake. She was a lovely warm woman with a kind face

There was something of Doris Lessing about her in appearance and in her conversation. She was very left wing, which appealed to me enormously because my parents were right wing colonials. She dressed exactly like Iris Murdoch in those loose floppy sort of clothes. I've always liked that style of dress ever since. She was cultured, eclectic, imaginative, kindly, wise and intelligent. I really loved her.

Mrs Austin gave me *Odour of Chrysanthemums,* a short story by DH Lawrence, to read and asked me what it meant. That was an epiphany for me. I'd always read a lot and enjoyed the narrative but never realised that stories meant something. Then she moved on to Browning and got me to analyse every line. She encouraged me to get absorbed in the minor poets and to understand the significance of their work. She introduced me to authors I might not otherwise have read, such as John Steinbeck. It was blinding good teaching to a sympathetically inclined 15-year-old boy.

She taught me about music too, and sometimes played Nielson symphonies very quietly in the background. I'd volunteered for these extra lessons because even then I had Oxbridge at the back of my mind and I wanted to read English. I've always had goals – though sometimes they move – and tenacity.

As a schoolboy I was small, but fierce. I was terrified of boxing but taught myself and got into the school team. I became head of my house and a school prefect. There was absolutely no pressure on me from home, which was wonderful. My older brother and sister were very academic and my mother took one look at me and decided I was dim. She gave me lots of praise if I said anything in the least bit intelligent.

I wish teachers realised how much power they have to boost children's confidence. I thought I might become a teacher myself at one stage. I tried it for one term and absolutely loved it. Just before I went to Cambridge I had a call from a former teacher who'd become a headmaster. His English master had had a stroke two days before the beginning of term and they needed somebody quickly. But although I enjoyed teaching so much, I had other things I wanted to do.

QUENTIN BLAKE

artist, author and the first Children's Laureate

There were two teachers who were particularly important to me, though in completely different ways, and they both taught English at Chislehurst and Sidcup Grammar School.

I knew RQ Rahtz best as a friend. I was pleased to discover that his second name was the same as my first name and after I got to know him as a teacher I found out that he lived across the road from my home. He became almost a pseudo parent. I would pop across to see Mr Rahtz and his wife and three young children whenever I was at a loose end.

They introduced me to cultural activities such as the local film society and lectures about the arts at the local education centre and I became so much a member of their family that they even took me on holiday with them to the West Country. Unlike mine, their house was full of books and I pored over their pre-war editions of art books which had wonderful tweed covers.

However, our close friendship didn't influence our relationship in the classroom. I can remember being disappointed when I got an essay back from Mr Rahtz marked simply, *satis*. To me he was more interesting as a person than as a teacher. His classes were quite sober. You had to know him well before you discovered his sense of humour. But he encouraged me to get involved with the school magazine, which I edited and wrote in and drew in, and the dramatic society and school concerts.

My most influential English teacher was JH Walsh. He taught me right through to the sixth form and prepared me for the Cambridge exam. I got an exhibition to Downing College. He wrote for *The Use of English* magazine and publications of that kind and was very good at getting you to write about poetry and books as a critic rather than regurgitating facts.

Mr Walsh gave me an independence of thought and you can't have anything better than that. He wrote poetry himself, which was published. He died quite young but there are now plans to re-issue his work and I have been approached to do the illustrations.

Mr Walsh had a tremendous sense of humour. When we had to do punctuation exercises he would invent funny sentences which made it interesting rather than a chore. In those days you could get whacked for misdemeanours and he used a plimsoll to inflict punishment. He would offer the culprit a selection of numbers of whacks, which had no bearing whatsoever on how many you actually received, but it cheered up everybody else in the class.

Probably because of Mr Walsh's influence, I went on to read English at university, intending to teach because I didn't think I could make a living as an artist. I was at Downing when the literary critic FR Leavis was there so I sat at the feet of the master. I didn't think he was a very good teacher. Harold Mason, who was the supervisor, was really much better. You didn't get any give and take with Leavis until you got to his level and we were nearly all too frightened to say anything.

A nice woman called Mrs Jackson taught me Latin, not to much effect, and it was her husband, who was a painter and cartoonist, who introduced me to the idea of contributing to *Punch*. I had two drawings published when I was 16 and continued to work for the magazine for the next 40 years.

By the time I reached the sixth form most art masters didn't have much effect on me because they tended to adapt lessons to people who couldn't draw.

Then a teacher called Stanley Simmonds, who was a painter, came back from the War and he talked to me and gave me practical advice as one artist to another. I owe him a great deal. He showed me that lessons are not just about imparting information, they are also about creating a situation in which you get some kind of reaction from those you are teaching.

SOPHIE ELLIS-BEXTOR
singer and songwriter

Mr Trant was like someone's Dad: he had a thick moustache and glasses and wore a shirt and tie with a V-necked jumper over the top. We all liked him. He was my form teacher at St Stephen's Primary School in St. Margaret's, near Twickenham, Middlesex, when I was nine.

By the time Mr Trant joined the school we had already done one term of the school year so we only had him for two terms. He taught everything, but I particularly remember history lessons because he would walk round the classroom singing songs that were popular in the Second World War. He had a rich baritone voice and having a teacher sing to you made you feel special. He also told jokes. His lessons were great. He always had our attention and was a cut above all the other teachers.

Then one day somebody peeked at a letter on his desk that said which teachers would be teaching which forms the next year. When we discovered that he was going to another class a friend and I started a petition to keep him. We went round the playground in the lunch break collecting signatures but were discovered and sent to the headmaster, who told us that Mr Trant could have lost his job because of us. It was rather confusing at the time but I think we were in more trouble for reading the letter than because of the petition.

Back in the classroom Mr Trant didn't name us. He just said: "There are two girls here who nearly cost me my job today." I remember crying and great tears falling onto the book I was reading. I have a fear of authority and hated being told off.

I wasn't a naughty child at school but I was a chatterbox and mischievous. My reports were OK, but I wasn't studious. I loved taking part in school plays and enjoyed singing. I suppose I already had a bit of a predisposition towards showing off.

Mum [Janet Ellis] was on *Blue Peter* from when I was four until eight, which was a pretty big deal among my peers. I appeared on the programme twice. At first it seemed good currency to have a mother on television and everyone wanted to be my best friend, but then some kids turned against me and life at school was not so good. There was actually an Against Sophie Club at one stage.

Things got better when I moved on to senior school – Godolphin and Latymer at Hammersmith – where I had three brilliant English teachers.

Mrs Babuta, who was Welsh, married to an Asian, taught me when I first arrived. English in that first year was really cosy, mostly creative writing, which I enjoyed. I was into Roald Dahl and *Tales of the Unexpected* and wrote dark short stories about people dying and killing each other.

Mrs Stevens was quite different. She wasn't cosy; she was very articulate with a dry sense of humour and a passion for literature. She treated us like adults and would occasionally share an anecdote about something outside school, which made us feel incredibly grown up.

Miss Shadforth had an amazing way with words. She ran the school magazine, *The Dolphin,* which I wrote for and edited for a while. I had planned to read English at university and was quite interested in a career in journalism but I started performing and found that was what I enjoyed most.

I didn't keep in touch with any of my teachers. I wouldn't say that my schooldays were the best days of my life, but they set me up for the best days. My five closest friends are all girls I knew at school.

ROGER McGOUGH
poet

Most of my poetry friends are able to pinpoint one person who really changed their lives and I long for a teacher who had spotted something in me that was worthwhile, worth encouraging – but there wasn't one. There are several teachers I remember, though.

My first teachers, Miss O'Brien and Miss Crook, were delightful and kind to everybody, and I was good at things such as art and writing. Everything changed when I went to secondary school. Then, being good at art was not conceived as something worthwhile. You either took art or you took Latin and it seemed that the less able people took art.

At primary school we learned English by the look-say system from pictures around the classroom wall and I have retained a visual sense of words which I think stems from that. I see letters and words in colour. For instance, R is always red and H brown. We learned our tables by rote and recited poetry and I entered art competitions.

From there I went to St Mary's College, Crosby, where John Birt and Laurie

Taylor were my contemporaries. Laurie Taylor gave me my first kiss, when I was the Princess of Cleaves in the school play and he played the prince. It was an all boys' grammar school and we were taught by the Irish Christian brothers, most of whom were very fierce. The strap was a popular method of teaching. French and Latin verbs were literally beaten into me. But it wasn't a bad school; they took working class Catholic boys, gave them an education and got them to university.

My father worked on the docks and it was very important to my mother that my sister and I went to grammar school. She sent me to elocution lessons to try to lose my Liverpool accent. I didn't, but I garbled more clearly

There was one woman teacher among all the brothers – Miss Allen, who taught drama and elocution – and, encouraged by Miss Allen and my mother, I took part in competitions at Waterloo Music And Literary Festival.

Miss Allen was another kindly teacher. I had great respect for her and enjoyed appearing in school productions and reciting poetry, though I had no interest in reading poetry or writing it then. I failed English lit at O-level. I enjoyed English language and was good at that, but was too busy messing about to read books. I remember we had to read a chapter of *The Mayor of Casterbridge* every weekend and answer questions on it on Mondays. If you didn't get the answers right you had to write out the chapter and I pretty well copied out the whole book.

I went to Hull University at the age of 17, going on 15, to read French and geography. I chose Hull because a chap from the same church went there (Kevin McNamara, who became an MP) and also because I liked the scarf. I was put in the hall of residence where Philip Larkin was the sub-warden, though I never spoke to him.

When I was about 18 I started enjoying French literature and French poetry and began writing poetry myself. I sent Larkin some of my poems and he wrote back a very nice, encouraging letter suggesting I publish in the university magazine. I kept it fairly quiet, because poetry wasn't for blokes in those days. I realised that poetry was my vocation, but also that it wasn't an option as a career.

I took a PGCE and went back to Liverpool where my first job as a teacher was at St Kevin's Comprehensive School in Kirkby. The set text book was Palgrave's *Golden Treasury of Verse* which I'd had at school myself and not enjoyed, so I started telling the kids the poems I was then writing and they liked them because they were about grannies and football. I realised there was a market, that I was a poet. Now, of course, I wish I had talked to Philip Larkin – but I wouldn't have known what to say.

TONY HAWKS
comedian and writer

At first Mr Ackers seemed a perfectly conventional history teacher, just going through the motions. Then one day he turned up with a guitar and handed out photocopied lyrics of songs he'd written about the period we were studying. The tunes were catchy and the lyrics included all the dates and facts we needed to know. Suddenly we all started to look forward to history lessons. I can remember some of the songs, word for word, to this day. When we did our history O-level we sat in the exam room with eyes closed singing to ourselves. It was a very original and effective teaching technique. We all got pretty good results.

Mr Ackers was one of the younger teachers at Brighton, Hove and Sussex Grammar School, which is now a sixth form college. He'd been an Oxford blue at football and was quite a charismatic figure. He was a bit of a showman and appeared in school concerts. I remember him doing a funny version of the Rolling Stones' *Get Off Of My Cloud* in a very prim and proper Shakespearean way. From him I learned not only about history, but also about song-writing, not in any academic sense but subconsciously how you could take material and make a song out of it.

I already played piano and inspired by him, I took up guitar. It was thanks to Dave Ackers that I became a musician – which is the job I did first – and I think it was rather good to be inspired by a history teacher. The music teacher was no inspiration at all.

On Friday afternoons we had to take part in Army cadet training with the CCF. I didn't really want to get involved in the shooting and fighting, but I didn't want to be a conscientious objector and have to do charity work with old people, which was the alternative. I decided to join the drum corps and be part of the marching band and learned to play the side drums. The sergeant major of this platoon was Mr Ackers. Being able to play drums was useful years later when I was in a show called *Lennon* in which I played the part of Ringo.

Mr Ackers managed to lose us once. He took the whole band marching round the streets of Brighton and met somebody he knew, got talking, and we carried on marching. It was some time before we realised we had broken free. He was furious.

The other teacher I remember from those days is Mr Reeve, who was known as Killer Reeve. When I arrived at grammar school at 11 I was rather scared and Mr Reeve deliberately set out to frighten first year boys. He taught art, which you might expect to be taught in a free and easy atmosphere. I don't remember much painting. We did a bit of drawing, but my memories are mostly of being disciplined. He would insist that all the desks were precisely lined up on the nails in the floorboards, so the top left hand corner of your desk tallied with a particular nail. If it didn't, he would bellow at you and try to humiliate you. I think he was role-playing, just pretending to be unpleasant, because one day when he bellowed at me and I was feeling particularly confident, I said something cheeky back which he kind of liked me for.

It was the sort of school where the teachers wore gowns in class. When I first arrived I was diligent. I had it in my head that I had to work hard to keep up. Then I realised that by working very hard I'd come top or second, so I worked less hard and consequently dropped further down with each passing term. I became the class comedian, especially in lessons where the teacher wasn't good at keeping discipline.

I remember Miss Naish, who taught English, struggled to keep control. One day I was sitting in the front of her class balancing books on my head when the deputy headmaster walked by and hauled me out of the lesson and gave me a detention.

I took a year off after leaving school and went to Manchester University to study drama but only managed a term and a half before deciding student life wasn't for me.

JOHN BIRT
BBC former Director-General

I was educated at St Mary's College, Liverpool. It was run by the Irish Christian Brothers, who were dedicated to taking the sons of the Catholic working class and making them upwardly mobile. They developed a very tyrannical and rigorous approach to learning which was highly effective in that it got lots of boys through exams and into university, but it was rooted in rote learning with the sanction of corporal punishment hanging over you literally every moment of the day.

The hallmark of this punishment was what we termed "strapology." Brother Brickley, who taught Latin, was the most effective exponent of the art. He was a well-built, fierce-looking fellow with a menacing and sadistic sense of humour. He would drag a boy from behind his desk to the front of the class and lift his black leather strap – which he called Excalibur – high, drooping it over his shoulder and down his back, then whipping it down ferociously with all his considerable power onto the culprit's outstretched hand. Some boys were beaten for not being clever enough or for stuttering and stammering in class. Invariably, the punishment for failure to answer a question correctly was the strap. Even bright boys, like me, didn't escape because if someone was talking between lessons or being noisy in a corridor, the whole class would be beaten. It was education within a climate of fear.

Luckily, there were a few members of staff who avoided using corporal punishment. My favourite teacher, Mr BB Cooper (known as Norman), was one. He was a lovely man with a sweet nature and an absolute dedication to his subject, which was mathematics. He was round and cheerful, with a twinkle in his eye, and he had a squeaky voice and wore glasses and a three-piece suit. He taught us to love maths, explaining the most complex concepts with humour. He also broadened our horizons. He took *The Times* and every day would talk to us about current affairs. He read aloud from *War and Peace* and encouraged us to think for ourselves. It wasn't until I reached Mr Cooper's science sixth form that I began to be interested in ideas and knowledge, rather than just learning in order to pass exams.

Another influential person was Mr Kelly, a kindly, effervescent man with boundless energy, whose son was in my class. Mr Kelly taught at the prep school and didn't directly teach me, but he plucked me out of the crowd to be president when he started the school's charitable St Vincent de Paul Society.

We organised Christmas parties for pensioners and Mr Kelly would stand up on stage and to our amazement, tell dirty jokes. He was a natural comedian and had them all rolling in the aisles. Once I organised a seaside picnic for 100 children, aged between two and 14, from the local orphanage. I enjoyed being in charge and found planning and executing a complex task satisfying. I'd begun my schooldays as a quiet and reserved child but by the time I got to the sixth form I was 6ft 2in, confident and outspoken.

Another aspect of the Brothers' middle-class grooming was that we played rugby, rather than football, and were given elocution lessons to eradicate our accents, and classes in politeness.

Miss Bushell endeavoured to ensure that we spoke like gentlemen. She was as buxom lady with the posture of a thrush, with her bosom sticking forward and her bottom sticking out. I thought I'd lost my accent until I got to Oxford and found all Miss Bushell's hard work had been in vain. I only had to open my mouth for people to say: "Oh, you're from Liverpool."

Politeness lessons were the province of the headmaster, Brother Francis, a small, dour man with red hair. He taught us to doff our caps and to stand up for ladies on the bus. Brother Francis explained how we should eat soup, and the proper use of cutlery. "If in doubt," he advised "just start from the outside and work your way in." Whenever I see a table laid with lots of cutlery I always remember Brother Francis.

ANDREW MOTION
former Poet Laureate

My family was almost entirely unbookish. I grew up in the countryside on the borders of Essex and Suffolk. My father was a brewer as his father and his father's father had been but there was never any pressure on me to go into the family business. Because I liked birds and trees my parents thought I might go to work for the RSPB or the Forestry Commission. There was certainly no expectation that I would live a life that had anything to do with books.

I struggled in school. I was not very smart and I was frightened most of the time. At the age of seven I was sent away to a prep school I detested. There was a great deal of beating. We were beaten for minor misdemeanours, for work, for major misdemeanours. You name it; we got beaten for it.

There were two kinds of beating. There was beating at the end of the day in our dormitories where the head came round and slippered people and there was "the swish" (cane) administered in his study. This was in the early Sixties, but the regime was Dickensian.

Because school was so frightening, I found it incredibly difficult to think straight but somehow I scraped into Radley and once there I could hardly believe the difference. The man who changed my life was Peter Way, my housemaster.

He didn't teach me for the first two years, even though English was his subject, and I scrabbled through my O-levels. My brain was still deeply asleep and I got the bottom grade but one in all subjects except English. Then when it came to A-levels I had a genuine "Road to Damascus" moment. Thanks to Peter Way, suddenly school was a great place to be and I couldn't wait to get back after the holidays.

He was such a nice man: quiet, modest, withdrawn and shy. We immediately got on extraordinarily well. We still write to each other regularly and meet when we can. It's no exaggeration to say I love him. I liked his way of teaching and never felt threatened by him. I remember clearly my first lesson in his pink classroom, which he'd had specially decorated because, he told us, pink is the colour of concentration. We studied the poem by Thomas Hardy, *I look into my glass and view my wasting skin* in which Hardy looks into the mirror and regrets that he has a young man's desires, fears and yearnings in an old man's body. It was an odd poem to give to a group of testosterone-filled 15-year-olds but it went through me like a spear. It was quite extraordinary. I immediately thought not only that I wanted to read more of this, but also that I wanted to write something like it.

Peter Way loved poetry and taught it with tremendous spirit. He encouraged us to read permissively and I soon found I couldn't stop talking about poetry and had to rein myself in because the other boys would think I had gone mad.

I could have been Peter's favourite pupil – or his nightmare. He introduced me to the work of Wordsworth and Larkin and lent me his own copies of books. Then, in the middle of my A-levels, I was ill and had a year at home and our relationship was more or less a correspondence course.

Very soon after I returned to school my mother, to whom I was very close, had a bad riding accident and was unconscious for three years. When it looked as though she was not going to recover, Peter encouraged me to write about it, which was a catharsis. A lot of my best poems have been about my mum.

He guided my writing very, very gently and I won the school poetry prize three times. I went on to read English at Oxford, got a first and taught at Hull University where I got to know Philip Larkin.

As time goes by I realise more and more how much I owe to Peter Way. In class he would play us recordings of poets such as TS Eliot, Ted Hughes and Sylvia Plath reading their own work and this was the seed of the Poetry Archive which I set up in 2005.

EDWARD HEATH
former Prime Minister

I liked school. I was always a year ahead of my time at Chatham House Grammar School, Ramsgate, which made it a challenge. The staff were all of a very high quality when I was there from 1926 to 1935 and we were given every opportunity to develop outside interests. We had an enormous number of activities, both on and off the sports field, including music and drama in which I used to play a part.

The debating society, for which Mr. Wilsher, the geography master was responsible, was very active. I took part in debates continuously. We also had a mock election in which I took part (and won) representing the National government. It was in the school debating society that I first spoke against capital punishment, but the biggest debate of all was copying Oxford on "This house will not fight for king and country." I opposed the motion. The debate attracted an enormous audience in the school so we couldn't finish it in one evening and had to postpone it over the weekend and finish it off on the Monday when everybody hoped tempers might have cooled a bit. Amid a great deal of shouting the motion was defeated by 45 votes to 13.

The headmaster in my day was HC Norman. He used to take prayers every morning and was always there for sports, watching cricket and athletics and so on, and he showed great interest in the drama. He was not at all aloof, he knew us all by name. There were 450 pupils. I go to quite a number of schools today which are so large the headmasters find it difficult to know the names of their staff and to recognise them all, quite apart from the boys and girls.

Dr Alec Woolf, the second master and an inspiring teacher with a very good sense of humour, tried to urge sixth formers to learn Spanish, his favourite language. He considered it to be the language of the future, particularly in Latin America. I did not share his enthusiasm.

I regret now I didn't concentrate enough on modern languages. I did concentrate on Latin and I always attribute being able to make a speech without notes to a satisfactory Latin upbringing. It forces you to phrase your approach in the right way; it is of great value from the point of view of developing the mind. I always use Latin today when I give grace. I did that at Number 10.

Dr. Woolf was responsible for organising my first visit to Europe, which was to France when I was 14. He took a group of 12 of us. One night some of us looked in on the Folies Bergères – which I think I may have neglected to mention when I recounted the events of the trip to my parents.

My housemaster was Mr Derome who taught mathematics. He was meticulous, wouldn't let anything pass. And "Tufty" Goodram, the senior English master, conducted the school orchestra. I had been taught the piano when I was seven and was in the parish church choir when I was nine. Then, when my voice broke at 14, I took up the organ. Mr Goodram allowed me to conduct the school orchestra when I was 15. It was a very good orchestra, properly balanced with all the right instruments, and everybody agreed it always put on a good performance.

Another housemaster, Mr Pearson, was a great cricketing man and we had a very good team. Kent County used to come for a one-day match every summer and the school team held its own. For a couple of years I was scorer; I didn't play. I was a cross-country runner.

After I left (I got the organ scholarship at Balliol) I corresponded with the headmaster for several years, and told him what was going on at Oxford. I have been back to the school many times. I have attended three speech days and we have old boys' reunions. I look back very fondly on my days at Chatham House.

SARAH BEENY
property expert

I think I was probably quite difficult to educate. I wasn't very good at being told what to do and could be quite obnoxious. I didn't really see the point in half the stuff I was being taught at school. Now I do, but at the time I couldn't see how geography or history was relevant to my life and I remember tormenting the science teachers in particular.

But Mrs Evans was great and I found her inspiring. Rather than tell me what to do, she suggested what might be a good idea and they were always positive suggestions. She encouraged me in directions in which I was interested, which I think is the sign of a clever teacher.

She taught English at my secondary school, Luckley-Oakfield in Wokingham, where I was a weekly boarder. I didn't get particularly good grades, but I enjoyed English lessons and Mrs Evans planted a seed of interest. I was always a bit lazy and a bit slapdash and when writing an essay I would begin with gusto and get really carried away and then give up and the essay would peter out. Instead of saying, "This is too short, you haven't put in any effort," Mrs

Evans would say, "The start is really good, if you continue like this all the way through you'll have a great essay."

She encouraged me in drama too. At the time we didn't put on any school plays but we had a stage that was full of old chairs. With one or two friends I decided to clear out the stage and put on a production. Mrs Evans was very encouraging and the school started putting on plays again. I had a leading role in Brecht's *Caucasian Chalk Circle* and quite liked the idea of becoming a professional actress. My classmates were all heading for university, but it was clear I wasn't going to get the necessary grades. Mrs Evans inspired me to believe I could do something different from the careers that were traditionally expected. With her encouragement I went on to Queen Mary's Sixth Form College in Basingstoke where they had a fantastic drama course and a theatre.

I planned to go on to drama school but I didn't get in, so ended up travelling round the world for a while and then did lots of jobs including window cleaning, sandwich making and door-to-door vacuum cleaner selling. I assumed I'd be self-employed. At weekends I used to go looking at property that was for sale, despite having no money to buy anything. That gave me a very good idea of the market. It took me a few years to get it off the ground, but I set up my own property business.

After I left school I had no further contact with Mrs Evans and I often wonder what happened to her. When she was teaching me she was probably only about 30 or 35. She was glamorous and sexy with long blonde hair. She wore high heels and nice dresses. She had a vivacious charm and was slightly scatty in an energetic way. I think it was her energy that I found so inspiring. I had a bit of a crush on her and wanted to be like her.

Apart from Mrs Evans' lessons, I hated school pretty much right through. It began badly. I remember at four being pulled out of the house screaming and kicking and being forced into the car to go to school. None of the children or the teachers liked me – apart form one kind woman called Mrs Prince. It probably didn't help that my parents were a bit alternative, leading a self-sufficient "good life" and would come to this city school wearing overalls.

My school reports were increasingly poor. I found one recently that said: "Sarah has very little knowledge of the world around her and clearly has no intention of finding out any more."

JOHN MORTIMER
QC, novelist and playwright

My father didn't have a very high opinion of schoolteachers. When I was nine and sent to board at the Dragon School in Oxford he told me that for the next four or five years I'd be rubbing up against second rate minds. "At a pinch," he said, "you can take their word for equilateral triangles and the Latin for parsley, but life is a closed book to schoolteachers."

I think that was a bit harsh. Perhaps teachers in general don't know much about life – but the Dragon was a terribly good school and I remember the masters there with gratitude because they taught me to work hard.

The school produced great academic results but was quite liberal in many ways. We were allowed to bicycle round the town and every year put on a Shakespeare play and a Gilbert and Sullivan opera. And we had girls there – including Antonia Fraser, who became captain of rugby football.

The teacher I remember best is Francis Wylie, who taught English. He was a handsome man who was very pleased to listen to himself reciting poetry and as I was also terribly pleased to hear myself reciting poetry, we got on well. I needed no encouragement. I was a shy child, but not shy about acting. I used to act the whole of Shakespeare to my dad, taking all the parts because I didn't have any brothers or sisters.

Mr Wylie would recite in a John Gielgud voice and was, I think, a frustrated actor. He realised that I was allergic to any form of sport or games so he used to send me with a bar of chocolate to the Oxford Repertory Theatre, which was then near the Dragon school. Instead of playing sport, I sat in the matinées eating chocolate and enjoying the plays of Bernard Shaw. I think everyone was very pleased I missed games. I once played cricket and every time they said, "Over" I moved further and further away. I sat in the long grass reading Henrik Ibsen.

I was completely stage struck and my one ambition when I was in my final year at the Dragon was to play the leading role in the school production of *Richard II*. It was a very democratic school and the pupils voted for who got what part. There was one boy who was very handsome, and I think came from an acting family, so he was a dead cert for Richard II. But when we went back after the summer holidays, the voting had swung, and I was to play the lead. I left in a blaze of glory and a notice in the school magazine which said, "He threw away his life with that careless elegance which becomes a king." One of the girl pupils played the queen and was the first girl I got to cuddle.

These productions were put on by another English master whose real name I can't now remember, but whom we called Cheese. Most of the masters – with the exception of Francis Wylie – were known by a nickname. There was Tubby (Mr Haigh) whose speciality was hurling books. He had shrapnel lodged in him from fighting in the First World War, which made him slightly dodgy. He hurled books at random and if he hit you he would be very sorry afterwards and give you money. I made a fair bit of pocket money.

The headmaster, Mr Hum, a sweet man with long white hair, used to summon us to supper by ringing bells. He so enjoyed ringing those bells that he went on doing it long after supper had finished. Mr Hum was always changing his mind. For example, one week he told us all we should wear boots, not shoes, and the next week (after we'd sent home for boots) he said the reason we had weak ankles was because we were wearing boots and we should all wear shoes.

I didn't like Harrow, where I went next, but I enjoyed my time at the Dragon. English was my best subject. I was also good at history, but I had a problem with maths. I never understood why people had to learn geometry and trigonometry and never got to grips with equilateral triangles.

ANNA FORD
former BBC news reader

Bill Thompson had thick grey hair, wore a gown that looked as though it might disintegrate at any moment, and smelt of Gauloise cigarettes. He looked like a Frenchman, had that Gallic charm and would have been perfectly cast as Simenon's Maigret – yet he came from Carlisle.

He walked around the classroom with his hands in his pockets, relaxed and smiling, talking to us as though we were a group of friends in his house. He taught A-level French and gave me a fantastic love of French and France which I still have. He stands out in my memory because as well as being a brilliant teacher, he provided a sense of calm in my fragmented and chaotic school career. My family was constantly moving house because of my father's job (he was an actor who became a clergyman). I was always arriving somewhere at a different stage in the curriculum, just before exams. Though I made superficial friendships, throughout my schooldays I felt an outsider and my teenage years were lonely and desperately unhappy, but my feelings were kept hidden because good behaviour was the order of the day.

There is a peculiar pressure being brought up in a vicarage. You are economically working-class, but socially middle-class because you live in a big house and your father is a social figure. I was not quite accepted and it was unfortunate that almost as soon as I arrived in the sixth form at the White House Grammar School in Brampton, Cumbria, I was made head girl which probably didn't go down very well with the others.

The White House was a small co-ed school in what had been a country house. Classes were small – there were only 14 in the sixth form and four of us in the A- level French group – so it was like having private tuition. We had a number of set books but Mr Thompson read much more widely. He read us a lot of French poetry in a lyrical voice and introduced us to the work of Maupassant and Vigny and books like Balzac's *Le Père Goriot*, which isn't easy. He always explained the background to what we were studying which gave us an introduction to the French way of thinking, French society and life. He played us records of singers such as Edith Piaf, talked about current affairs and told anecdotes about what he had been doing and where he had been.

He treated us as equals and expected us to behave as equals.

I was terribly serious for my age and, probably because I was a clergyman's daughter, used to speak out against injustice. I was grown up long before I should have been. I was the only girl in a family of four boys. By the time I was six I had three small brothers and because my mother was often ill, I had to look after them.

However, I did once get involved in the tail end of a silly end of term prank. A group of sixth-formers dug a trench across the school car park to prevent access and painted "condemned" on the pavement. Because we had damaged school property, Mr Thompson took me and the head boy, Roger, down to the police station. Mr Thompson was terribly relaxed, as if what we had done was of no consequence. The policeman took down our names with a wink.

A special assembly was called and it was decided that I should be the one to make a public apology. I had to stand up in front of the whole school and apologise to the caretaker and staff. All throughout this Mr Thompson was completely non-condemning and like an adult friend, smiled and said it wasn't the worst thing that ever happened in the world.

Sadly, I didn't keep in touch with him after I left school. I went to Manchester University and read social anthropology. I would have preferred to do art, but my parents discouraged me. I drifted into teaching and then into journalism. When I was a teacher myself I took into the classroom with me Mr Thompson's informal technique and, as he did, made a point of listening to what my pupils had to say.

MATTHEW PARRIS
parliamentary sketch writer and former MP

Mrs McLeod taught me in Standard 2A at Borrowdale Primary School in Salisbury, Rhodesia. She was a Scot, had an educated Scottish accent, was kindly though stern and had an absolutely fixed view of the world and of right and wrong. She entertained no doubt about any of her values, nor suffered any of her pupils entertaining any doubts.

She was my class teacher for just one year. She taught everything except mathematics, but English was her great love and she was very keen that it should be pronounced properly. She didn't like Rhodesian accents, which luckily I didn't have. She particularly hated the way Rhodesians pronounced the word "school" – *skule*. Her discipline was effortless and total. I imagine she had been at the school for many years, she seemed such a fixture.

She looked like a rather trim, grey koala bear: chunky but not fat. She was always very well-dressed and carefully made up and her hair was always perfect. All the teachers were smart, but she was particularly well-groomed. She was a little like Margaret Thatcher – in whose office I worked for two years – in that respect.

Mrs McLeod seemed to me then to be of enormous age, but she was probably only about 45. She had a husband called Jim and one daughter, Fiona. Part of the aura that surrounded Mrs Mc Leod was that we didn't know her first name.

She was very keen on drama and reading aloud and recitation, all of which had to be done with exaggerated articulation. I was good at these things and got better at them under her tutelage. I wasn't teacher's pet, though. Mrs McLeod didn't have favourites, but she and I got on well.

She taught me English spelling and grammar and to enjoy reading aloud. She wasn't a visionary, she wasn't inspirational; she simply provided an anchor. She knew the rules and you knew the rules and life was ordered and had a structure to it, and for a little boy whose family was constantly moving round the world, that was important.

My father was an electrical engineer and was posted from country to country. I was born in Johannesburg, but we left when I was about a year old and went to Yorkshire and then to Cyprus before Rhodesia. When I left my school in Cyprus we were just about to learn decimals, and when I reached Borrowdale they had just done them, so I never really learned decimals. I have been trying to get the hang of them ever since.

Mr Moffatt, who taught mathematics, was another Scot, as was the other teacher I remember from Borrowdale, Mr Milne, my form teacher after Mrs McLeod. Mr Moffatt was quite a martinet. Mr Milne I also looked up to and admired. If anyone complained in his lessons he would say:" My heart pumps custard for you," which we thought very funny.

Mrs Mc Leod was a very ordered and disciplined person, with complete moral certainty about everything – manners, right and wrong, the way words should be pronounced and spelt – and it was all very important that you did everything right. But she also had a great sense of fun.

As a child I had absolutely no interest in games, and a lot of the teachers were keen on sport and you pleased those teachers by being good at games. I liked Mrs McLeod because she was a believer in things of the mind. I remember her telling me that moral courage was just as important as physical courage. That struck me forcibly at the time, probably because it was something I wanted to hear.

I am the eldest of six and was a very sensible child. I was a bit of a goody-goody. Perhaps Mrs McLeod helped to inculcate the qualities of the goody-goody in me.

In personality she was very different from Mrs Thatcher, who had an abrasiveness and stridency that Mrs McLeod didn't have, but I certainly learned from Mrs McLeod how to handle strong women.

HELEN BOADEN

head of BBC news

When I was five I found school so overwhelming, I used to sit under the table. I was an anxious, nervous, shy child and Mrs Cheadle persuaded me to come out. I think she twigged that I was being slightly bullied because she used to let me hold her hand in the playground, and very slowly I came out of my shell. It also helped when it was discovered that I was so short-sighted I could hardly see what was going on around me.

I came from one of those families where there was quite a lot of shouting and plates whizzing through the air. I found school a great relief from home life because it was calm and ordered. After Rushmere Infants, I went to Rushmere Junior School in Ipswich and then, when I passed my 11-plus, to Northgate Grammar School for Girls where there were some fantastic teachers.

I particularly remember Miss Stone. She was rather round with iron-grey hair which she wore in a bun. Like all good teachers, she managed to make every child feel special. She had terrific ambition for her girls. and decided, despite the fact that I was dreadful at maths, that I'd make a good doctor. And I bet if I'd stayed at the school I would have ended up a doctor, but I left after two years because my dad got a job in London.

My father was a FE lecturer in geography and then worked for a teaching union. I was rubbish at geography. English, history and drama were always the subjects I was good at. I don't know why Miss Stone thought I'd make a good doctor. I wasn't especially good at science, but I was rather good at Latin and I think it was just decided I had the sort of brain that could be trained.

Next I went to the Cedars Grammar School in Leighton Buzzard where I really flourished. I had a great teacher in Miss Metcalfe who taught maths and understood how frightened I was of the subject. She de-mystified numbers for me, which was a great achievement. She was rather an elegant woman who wore quite short skirts and had long brunette hair.

Once I moved into O-levels and GCSEs, Mr Lloyd taught English and introduced us to the pleasures of culture. He took us to the theatre and we saw Peter Brooks' production of *A Midsummer Night's Dream* which is now considered a classic. And one half term holiday about six of us went into school every day and listened to Wagner's entire *Ring Cycle* with him.

But Mary O'Keefe, who also taught English, is top of my list because she was such a great role model. She married another teacher at the school, but kept her maiden name, which was remarkable then. He was younger than she was, too, and their relationship seemed so passionate and romantic. We all clubbed together to buy them a wedding present.

I thought she was so glamorous. She wore nail polish and quite a lot of makeup and lovely slightly floppy crepe dresses. In those days no women teachers were allowed to wear trousers, but one day she and all the other women teachers came in wearing trousers and won the battle.

I remember doing Hardy's *Tess of the d'Ubervilles* with her and Milton. She had spiky writing and would go through my essays writing very intelligent comments that actually added to the learning process, rather than making you think you'd got it wrong. Sometimes she would invite a group of us to her house to catch up on work, particularly coming up to A-levels, and I played the lead in her production of *The White Devil*.

I went on to read English at Sussex. Then it was all a tutorial system, you didn't have to go to lectures, which Miss O'Keefe and Mr Lloyd knew would suit me. I kept in contact with Mary O'Keefe for a while, but we drifted apart and I'm really sad about that because she was a big influence on me.

ALAN TITCHMARSH
broadcaster and celebrity gardener

Harry Rhodes was my form teacher at All Saints Junior School in Ilkley, and also my Sunday school teacher. He grew cacti, which I bought from him for sixpence a time at church and school bazaars and coffee mornings and that's how I started gardening.

Mr Rhodes was the kindest man. He had a Roman nose and rimless spectacles and to me then at the age of eight he seemed as old as God, but I guess he was probably in his thirties. Although you didn't mess with him, and he was no pushover, he personified the word "avuncular". He was the only male teacher who called the boys, as well as the girls, by their first names.

He had a wonderful way of teaching, which was bouncy and enthusiastic and engaging. He was the sort of teacher you found yourself listening to with your mouth open. He taught everything and he was also in charge of the music for morning assembly. The partition between two classrooms would be slid back to make one big room and as the headmistress, Miss E. Hickinson, left her office to join us, Mr Rhodes would herald her arrival by lifting the needle of the gramophone onto a record of something like *Greensleeves* – or if he was feeling mischievous, *The Arrival of the Queen of Sheba*.

Miss Hickinson was a statuesque, rather austere lady with glasses, grey hair, an aloof expression and a mouth which turned down at the corners. I discovered when I tripped over and broke my leg in the school playground that she was actually very kind. She sent me a large envelope full of schoolwork – but also included some crayons and a letter, which said: "Try not to do too much and enjoy the colouring."

By the age of ten I'd decided that I wanted to be a professional gardener. I toyed with the idea of acting, which I enjoyed as an amateur, but that would have been too much for my father, who was a classic Northener. My dad was a plumber. He hated gardening, but his father and grandfather were keen gardeners and so was Mum.

Having started with the cacti I bought from Mr Rhodes, which I kept on the windowsill in the loo at home, I graduated to growing more exciting things like spider plants and then geraniums. I bought packets of Mr Cuthbert's seeds from Woolworths with the money I earned from my paper round. I was quite good with nasturtiums and mesembryanthemums which I planted in the back garden between Mum's hydrangeas (I never had a plot of my own). I soon found taking cuttings more thrilling than growing from seed and I remember giving Mr Rhodes cuttings from time to time.

School palled somewhat after I failed the 11-plus and went to Ilkley County Secondary School. In the first year I had one term of what was called rural studies. It included gardening, taught by a burly man with the unforgettable name Ernest Wilberforce Heath. He was broad with a bristly moustache, glasses and a head shaped like a bullet. He had a piece of willow bound at both ends with sticky tape and he used to whack it down so hard on the desk if you were talking you would spring back thinking he was going to hit you – but he never did.

Unfortunately, because I was in the A stream I only had one term of rural studies which I regret. I think it's desperately important for children to be taught gardening and to learn to value the countryside and nature.

I didn't enjoy school much after the age of 11 because I seemed to be funnelling more and more towards subjects I wasn't keen on or good at. My reports said things like: "Alan tries, what a shame he doesn't always achieve his full potential." Art was my strong subject and I took my art O-level a year early, passed and then left at 15 to do an apprenticeship at a local nursery. On my first day I knew I'd made the right choice. I couldn't believe I was getting paid for doing something I loved so much.

SAM TORRANCE
professional golfer and commentator

My dad was a golf professional and I started playing the game when I was five. By the time I was nine and was at Largs high school I was playing every day. I remember Mrs Drynam, one of my teachers, telling me I had to work harder in class because I'd never make a living at golf.

She was a lovely woman with wavy hair and I liked her a lot. We were an unruly bunch and she was very patient with us. Many years later, when I'd made it as a professional golfer, we met up and she remembered what she had said and we had a good laugh about it.

Another teacher I remember is Mr Murphy, who I think, taught geography. When he was new to the school, a friend of mine, Douglas Wraith, and I decided to go round to Mr Murphy's home and ring his doorbell and run away – just for a laugh.

The following day Mr Murphy came into school and I have never seen a man looking so angry. He threatened to punish the whole class, so we owned up and he told us to see him after school. We were absolutely terrified because he looked so menacing. But he took us to his home, gave us a cup of tea and some cakes and explained that his wife was new to the area and having someone ring the bell and run away really scared her.

He taught us so much about consideration for other people in the half-hour we were there. After that Mr Murphy and I became friends and we played golf together and Dougie and I never rang his bell again.

Football was the main sport at Largs High and we had gym several times a week. Although I had a good eye for a ball, I wasn't particularly good at games. I remember the gym teacher, Mr Murray, smacking Dougie with a table tennis bat so hard the bat broke. I got the strap once, but I can't remember why. We played golf matches against the teachers and sometimes we won. The headmaster, Hugh McGhee, was the best golfer on the staff.

Mr Black taught us metalwork and I made pokers and ashtrays. I think my mum still has one. And I remember Mr Rose taught science. I was useless at that. I never pushed myself at school. My whole life centred on golf; I couldn't wait to get out of school to go and play. But I never bunked off; my parents wouldn't have allowed it. I left when I was 13. The school leaving age was 14 then and my birthday was on August 24th so after the summer holidays I just didn't go back.

It was a 20-minute walk from our home overlooking the bay at Routenburn golf course, where my father was the professional and greenkeeper, to Largs High and the next step would have been for me to go on to the Adrossan Academy in Irvine which involved a 10 to 15 minute train journey. However, my father saw the potential in my golf and I'd turned professional by the time I was 17.

I'd started whacking balls around the course when we lived at Rossendale in Lancashire and by time we moved back to Scotland, golf had begun to take over my life. Within a year of leaving school I was playing off scratch. Dad taught me to hit the ball as hard and as far as I could, with a big shoulder turn and the emphasis on distance rather than accuracy. "We'll straighten it up sooner or later," he said. I swung how Dad told me to swing. I worship my father – but he can be very tough and our sessions on the practice range generated a lot of electricity because we are both very strong willed.

My father is the hardest-working man I know and one of the greatest coaches in the world. Even now, in his seventies, he stands for hour after hour on the practice range coaching some of Europe's finest golfers – including my son, Daniel.

JOHN INVERDALE

TV presenter

There were two teachers at Clifton College in Bristol who had an influence on me and I have stayed in touch with both of them.

Terry Whatley was the tennis and racquets coach and he was more than a good teacher, he was a mentor as well. I was a big sports fan, played in the first team at most games and was captain of both the racquets and tennis teams. Terry tried to instil in us the right sort of values in various sporting arenas and he and I had a good rapport.

He was fit, athletic, witty, charming, tall, dark and good-looking and almost like an elder brother – though he could also crack the whip on occasions if you pushed things a little bit too far. I think we called him Mr Whatley for the first year, then, like most of the sports staff, he was addressed by his first name. All the other masters were called "Sir".

Terry Whatley was also the first person to get me drunk. We had played an away match and stopped off at two or three pubs on the way home. I got to know him well and to meet his wife and kids. When we played away matches we invariably went back to his house for a bite to eat.

But although I was sports mad, I also loved English. My English master at Clifton was a guy called Brian Worthington who loathed sport and I think had sports people down as Ds and Es, not As an Bs – although I got an A at A-level.

He had been a pupil of FR Leavis, the doyen of English criticism. I think he thought sport was intellectually demeaning – though he seemed to have a secret grudging admiration for people who were good at it. He was very erudite and educated, a great scholar and intellect. If anybody ever got slightly above their station he had the most wonderful selection of put downs which left you in no doubt at all that he was your mental superior. He wasn't cruel, but he could occasionally be acerbic, sarcastic or mocking. I'm sure some people didn't like his manner, but it used to make me smile and I always felt that he was on my side.

Occasionally I found the set books boring because we were always analysing things, and I just wanted to enjoy reading them. I remember *The Portrait of a Lady* seemed to drag on forever and one day I was caught reading *The Sporting Life* in class. Brian Worthington came out with a wonderfully erudite put down, which made me look a complete buffoon, and everybody laughed at me. I folded up the paper neatly and went back to page 802, or whatever it was.

He had a very successful formula for getting good results. He encouraged free debate and free thinking in class. He was immensely proud of getting people to express themselves well. If you made a point in class which wasn't very coherent, as often it wasn't, he would say: "Now, hang on a minute, how much better would it be if you had put it like this?" People who were in his A-level English class got a lot of benefit from that sort of encouragement.

I went to his 60th birthday and retirement party and he looked exactly the same to me as he had on the first day I walked into his class. He looked old before his time then and now looks much younger than he is. He organised careers talks and I've been back to speak to the school on several occasions. I'm sure he was pleased that someone who spent so much time on a muddy sports field also has the ability to string two words together. He must take a lot of the credit for that.

I also see Terry Whatley occasionally. He left Clifton to become the commercial director of Chepstow racecourse and then the commercial director of Clifton Rugby Club.

KIRSTY WARK
TV presenter

My mum believed very strongly in the value of nursery education so when I was three-and-a-half I was sent to St Ola's, a small private nursery just round the corner from my home in Kilmarnock. It was run by Mrs Tulloch and I looked forward to going each day enormously.

I can remember sitting at very small tables on very small chairs. And I remember clearly the little tin I took with me that had my play piece in [play piece is the Scottish word for the snack children have in their mid-morning break]. I always had the same little tin with a snow scene on the front of it, which must have been an old sweetie tin. In it I would have two digestive biscuits with butter in the middle of them and once a week, I got a Kit Kat.

Then when I was four-and-a-half I went to the state primary, Kilmarnock Grammar School, which sadly is now no more. Miss Smith was the infant mistress in Primary One there and Mrs Kelly was my teacher in Primary Two. They were both enormously encouraging and seemed very happy to allow expression. I remember big, bright classrooms and walls covered with artwork. It was a very stimulating environment for learning.

They were quite opposite in looks. Miss Smith was very tall and thin and wore specs and Mrs Kelly was roly poly with dark hair. Their classrooms were next door to each other.

Miss Smith was a very kindly person and I can remember on Friday afternoons we sang songs like *Yankee Doodle* and were allowed to career around the classroom.

The exciting thing about Primary Two was that Mrs Kelly was particularly keen on artwork. She was a very warm woman and I cannot remember her ever shouting. In her classroom the walls were covered with collages. We made wonderful things, like Easter bonnets, from tissue paper. I wasn't particularly artistic, but I got a great deal of fun out of making things and everybody had something up on the wall.

I was enormously happy at the school, despite the fact that later up the school I used to get belted – probably for being cheeky. We only lived round the corner, so I walked to school every day. I can remember everything about every single room, it is so imprinted on my memory. My mother still lives nearby which gives me a great sense of place. I think both teachers are probably dead now; they were getting on a bit by the time they taught me.

At the age of 11 I took the bus to Wellington School for Young Ladies, which was a misnomer if ever there was one. It was like McTrinian's, the girls were pretty wild. It was a private school and I think my parents sent me there rather than to Kilmarnock Academy because they thought I would have more opportunities because the classes were smaller.

Miss Logan, who taught English, was very Scottish, very dour – absolutely like Miss Jean Brodie. She was a rigorous teacher. I was quite good at English and wrote for the school magazine which was run like a co-operative. I remember on my final report card Miss Logan advised me not to bother with university, just go straight into journalism. I think she thought because I was nosey it would be a good career for me. I was a bit of a flibbertigibbet, interested in drama and lots of other things and didn't stick into my work enough.

There were two very good French teachers there, too, whom I admired – Miss McKechnie and Miss McCallum.

Despite Miss Logan's advice I did go to university. First I went to Stirling for a year and read English, history of art and sociology. Then I went to Edinburgh to do honours in Scottish studies. And then I went into journalism. The timing was great. I was at Wellington in 1966 just when people started talking about women's liberation and there was a great sense of "can do."

MICHAEL EAVIS
founder of Glastonbury Festival

My schooldays began when I was just a few months old. Mum was a supply headmistress, and when she was working I went to school with her on the back of her bike. My earliest memories are of dinner ladies cooing over me as I played with beads in a playpen in a corner of the classroom.

Mum was a good teacher. I was the eldest of five and there was a lot of pressure to succeed and we've all done pretty well, really. My brother, Patrick, was the clever one of the family and became a headmaster in Northumberland; Peter runs a hotel in Yorkshire; Philip has a chain of shops; and Susan has a hotel in Bath.

When I was five I went to the village primary school, but the presumption was that I wasn't going to pass the 11-plus so I was sent to Wells Cathedral School at the age of nine, first as a day boy and then as a boarder. Both my brother, Peter, and I took the choral test, but we both failed despite the fact that we had really good voices. I was a boy soprano and loved singing. I had a bit of a stutter and singing was part of the therapy for my speech impediment.

One teacher I really liked at Wells was a Welshman called Mr Howell-Jones.

He was my form master and English teacher, and the great thing about him was that he saw the talent in kids who were nervous, as I was. He made me think I had something to offer. Although he looked a bit scary with his black curly hair and horn-rimmed glasses, he really cared about everybody. He was a real star; he knew his stuff and taught with a passion.

Mr Howell-Jones gave me top marks for the first time in my life, for an essay I wrote about my holidays. We didn't go away on holiday as a family; my school holidays were spent working on the farm so I wrote about haymaking and life on the farm. That was the big breakthrough in my education. Once I realised somebody was interested in me and what I could do, my attitude changed.

Between lessons we used to have fights with rubber bands and paper pellets and one day Mr Howell-Jones walked in early and got caught in the crossfire. He was generally pretty tolerant, but he was really cross about having pellets in his hair. We all thought we'd be given 1,000 lines, but he didn't say much, he just made us clear up the mess. The next day, however, he came in with packets and packets of elastic bands and piles of paper pellets already made up and we spent the whole lesson firing them. It was quite a novel way of dealing with us. Shooting each other with pellets wasn't wicked any more. We all got fed up and didn't do it again.

Another favourite teacher at Wells was Nikki – I forget her surname – who gave piano lessons and was married to one of the masters. She was gorgeous. She was Scandinavian, about twenty with long blonde hair and marvellous bosoms. She would lean over me to demonstrate how to play and I was so jittery I couldn't concentrate. I never got anywhere with the piano, but I loved the lessons.

I have always loved music and was crazy on Elvis Presley and Pee Wee Hunt when I was a kid. When I became a boarder, I listened to the Top Twenty on Radio Luxembourg on a little transistor set hidden under my pillow. The housemaster, Alan Tarbat, caught me listening after lights out one night and gave me ten whacks with a hairbrush. He obviously didn't bear a grudge because he later made me head boy of Cedars house.

That was a big deal, I was so chuffed. Suddenly I lost my shyness. I started a bird watching society at school and in the holidays organised a camp down on the farm for about a dozen kids from the village. It was like a miniature festival. We generated our own electricity with upside down bicycles and played team games. I found then that I really enjoyed being with lots of people and trying to bring them on board and persuade them to make things happen.

JILLY COOPER
novelist

I went to a rather austere girls' boarding school, Godolphin in Salisbury, where I was desperately homesick. I missed my pony dreadfully. I missed my family, but I missed the pony much more. However, I had a wonderful housemistress, a sweet woman called Miss Pointon, who arranged for me to ride racehorses on Salisbury Plain in the evenings after school. I was absolutely terrified because I was only 11 and these horses were 17 hands, but it was thrilling and I think the experience probably inspired my novel, *Riders*.

My star teacher, though, was Miss Aphra Lloyd who taught English. I dedicated a book to her, an anthology of poetry and prose entitled *The British in Love*, which pleased her, though she didn't like it when I later started writing novels. She wrote to a friend: "Isn't it tragic that Jilly now writes nothing but pornography."

Miss Lloyd was Irish: tall, dark and elegant and looked like a glamorous bird of prey. She must have been about 32, but she seemed to me then, like all teachers, to be terribly old. She made English literature hugely exciting. She had us reading *The Mayor of Casterbridge* and Sir Roger de Coverley at the age of 11 and brought these great literary characters to life. We acted everything out. She also made us learn verse by rote so even now poetry constantly drifts into my head because I remember it from school. Nobody ever cheeked Miss Lloyd; she kept order well. If she noticed you gazing out of the window daydreaming she would sidle up to you and suddenly ask you to recite something you were supposed to have learnt for homework.

Her classes were a joy. She would transfix us when she talked. She knew just how to pick out the lovely bits so your hair stood on end with excitement. She set us essays with interesting titles. I remember "A Day in an Italian Square" and "A Day in the Life of a Penny". I wrote about Italian men for the first and about being stuck in the loo (which cost a penny in those days) for the second. I had quite a good imagination, despite Miss Lloyd's comments years later that she never thought I would go on to be a writer because I had no imagination. I think she was joking. She could be quite sarcastic.

I was never top, but I must have been quite good at English because I was expected to get to Oxford. I was all programmed to take the exam at school in the autumn, but was completely boy mad and bullied my parents into sending me to a crammers where I went out with men every night for two terms and ploughed the exam. I had an interview at St. Hilda's College, but they took one look at me and said "no". That was as near as I got to further education. Instead I became a cub reporter on the *Middlesex Independent* where, thanks to Miss Lloyd's influence, I never went anywhere without clutching some volume of poetry, which doubled as a notebook.

I was terribly badly behaved at school. I was known in the staff room as the "unholy terror." I think I was the worst pupil they ever had. I always giggling and awfully rebellious. I refused to kneel down in church and things like that. I was also very untidy and if you left two or three things out you got sent to the headmistress, Miss Gerrard. I lived outside her door. I admired Miss Gerrard too; she was very fierce, but very beautiful.

Another teacher I remember is Miss Williams who taught science. She never had any eyebrows because she was always blowing them off in experiments. A cry would go up from this black smoke: "Oh, it worked for the other group!"

My three mates and I were terrible. It makes me blush to remember now that we de-bagged Miss Harris our absolutely sweet junior housemistress, poor darling. She was pretty, but rather wet and we took off her cardigan, her shirt, her tweed skirt and her shoes and there she was wriggling like a fly in her petticoat when the housemistress caught us. I think our punishment was to be denied cake for a week.

BEAR GRYLLS

action man, TV presenter and survival expert

Mike Town taught geography. I was only in his class for one year because he taught the top group and I soon slipped down to the bottom set, but we became great friends through a shared passion for climbing. Mike was a mad keen mountaineer and I'd been climbing with my father since I was about five around the sea cliffs on the Isle of Wight where we lived.

I found Eton quite scary at first, but the school's great strength was to encourage pupils to have a real interest in something. It didn't matter if it was stamp collecting or bird watching or whatever, as long as there was something that sparked your fire. With Mike's encouragement I ran the school mountaineering club and, inspired by Mike who was also keen on martial arts, started a karate club and became one of the youngest second dan black belts in the country.

My identity at school came from being the boy who could climb the highest building and put a pair of underpants on the highest flagpole. There was one particularly high spire which hadn't been climbed since Ranulph Fiennes was at Eton and since then masses of barbed wire had been put all round so there was no way you could get up onto the ledge to even start the climb.

Night after night I tried to find a way up and eventually discovered a lightening conductor running up the side of the spire. Ranulph Fiennes had had to steal clamps from the woodwork department to make a ladder up the buttresses, but I found I could get under the barbed wire and shin up the lightening conductor. When I eventually got to the top there was a lead flashing with the initials "RF" ground into it. I added "BG" and scuttled down.

I never got caught on my escapades, but I had a near miss once when I tried to show a friend the way up a tower. To reach it we had to cross the housemaster's garden. It was midnight and as we crouched behind a bush the master (who'd been a marathon runner) came out with his dog for a late night cigarette. The dog smelt us and as we sprinted towards a 10ft wall my friend, who was half a second behind me, was grabbed.

Academically I did OK at Eton and went on to do a degree. But having really worked hard to get there I got rather distracted by my extra-curricular activities and occasionally my name would be read out at the end of term as a "GFT" – which stood for general total failure. Deep down I think that gave me more determination to excel at climbing and karate, things I enjoyed and was good at. They "flicked my switch" much more than team games like cricket and football.

Mike Town had a cottage in the Lake District and in the school holidays I would go and stay with him with friends and his Burmese mountain dogs, which always came with us as we climbed the peaks. After I left and was with the SAS, he lent a group of us his cottage so we could go there to train. He was brilliant. He's a bachelor and his former pupils became like his family. I thought of him as an uncle.

Another brilliant teacher at Eton was a guy called David Cooper, the school chaplain, who'd been a colonel in the SAS. He also encouraged me in mountaineering and he ran the CCF which I was very involved in too.

Mike and David both inspired me to follow the path less trodden and to do whatever it was I really loved. Both became great friends. When I got married David conducted the service and Mike played the organ.

BERYL BAINBRIDGE
former actress who became a novelist and playwright

Miss Peck was excessively thin, completely flat-chested, and had a very distinctive hairstyle, parted in the middle with plaits wound in coils around the ears. She looked a bit like a creature from outer space. It was impossible to tell her age. To me she seemed very old, but I suppose she was about 40. Like all the other women teachers at Merchant Taylors' in Liverpool, she was unmarried.

She taught English and I liked her because I enjoyed what she taught and later, because she was the only one who stood up for me when I was expelled.

My first real memory of feeling she was different was when she sent us off to read *Sons and Lovers* by DH Lawrence at home. I'd read most of Lawrence by the time I was 12, thanks to Miss Peck. She also put me on to Rudyard Kipling, not just the poetry, but also *Stalky and Co.* I never read children's books.

Our set books at school, included *The Mill on the Floss* and we did Shakespeare, of course. I didn't understand a word of it, though Miss Peck did try to explain.

I suppose I liked school. The building was lovely. It was originally built for boys in 1500 and it had Elizabethan oak panelling and high ceilings and was set in a park in

Blundell Sands on the outskirts of Liverpool. It was a public school. Right from the beginning I had a nickname. I was called Basher because I used to fight. I got told off for being unladylike.

We all wrote rude limericks and when I took one home to illustrate it, unfortunately I left it in my gymslip pocket and my Mum found it. Sex was never mentioned in our house and my mother just couldn't cope and took the offending rhyme straight to the headmistress. I was sent to Coventry at home, my brother wasn't allowed to speak to me, and I was made to sleep in the bathroom. At school my punishment was to walk around with a little book about the birds and the bees at all times and the maths teacher wouldn't have me in the classroom. I was allowed to stay on till the end of term, but then I had to go.

I didn't know until long afterwards that Miss Peck pleaded for me to be given another chance but Miss Williamson, the maths teacher, said no, I was obviously a rotten apple and that was it. Miss Williamson was a horror, a real cross patch, always snappy and a fiend not just to me, but to everybody. She was a St Trinian's kind of teacher with an Eton crop who wore a costume and tie.

Miss Peck was much more gentle. I was good at writing essays and she encouraged me. She talked a lot about style. I remember writing about a church outing and saying that the vicar had a reputation as grubby as his dog collar. She was very taken with that. I don't think she ever suspected I'd become a writer. A lot of us wrote all the time then. We didn't go out to play, because you might meet somebody not nice, and there was no telly, so we all wrote little stories. I wrote a full-length novel called *Filthy Lucre* when I was 12 or 13, which was published years later.

My parents' ambition for me had been to go to university. My father wanted me to be a doctor. I was sent to private elocution lessons and I remember Jean Alexander, who played Hilda Ogden in *Coronation Street* and Auntie Wainwright in *Last of the Summer Wine,* went to the same teacher.

But I had no more schooling after about 13½. I went off to a boarding ballet school after Merchant Taylors' but didn't like it and left after a year and my father got me into the Liverpool Playhouse and I became an actress.

From time to time my name was in the papers and when I moved to Salisbury Rep I got a letter from Miss Peck, who had retired and then lived in Salisbury, asking me to look her up. I did. I went to see her in the house where she lived with her sister and had tea. It was all terribly polite and ladylike. She didn't seem to have changed at all. She never knew I became a writer because she died before I got down to serious writing.

JOHN NETTLES
actor

I went to St Austell Grammar School in Cornwall, known to its pupils as Borstal-on-Sea. When I first arrived it seemed a rather oppressive place, and I don't think the quality of the teaching was very good. All that was to change, however, after I'd been there four years with the arrival of the exotically named Frederick Farnham-Flower and Fred Waring.

They set about reforming the school and giving it style, direction and purpose. We learned from them that there was more to life than football and young ladies, smoking and gymnastics; that there was life beyond Plymouth and that it wasn't effeminate to pursue a career in the arts and to enjoy reading Wordsworth.

Until they arrived, I had no inclination towards the arts. I wanted to become a pop singer or a professional footballer, although I had no ability in either field.

Mr Farnham-Flower taught English and Mr Waring, French. Farnham-Flower was the man who really changed things. He introduced us rather insular Cornish boys to a world of literature and drama. There was no theatre in Cornwall, no opera, no singing, no dance – just the clay mines and the boats. There was no question in those days (the 1950s) of outings to Stratford-upon-Avon or London, because of the distance and the cost involved. Farnham-Flower took us to see a couple of touring groups, but I didn't see a professional theatrical production until I was 21.

Farnham-Flower was a striking man – tall and good-looking with an aquiline nose and swept-back hair. He wore a natty, three-piece suit and sometimes a bow tie, which we boys thought was a bit flash. He had a classy, cultured accent we'd never heard in Cornwall before. His approach was very personal. He took a proper pedagogic interest in his pupils, whom he saw as his disciples. He even changed the school uniform, designing the blazer, badge and the logo on it.

Suddenly, through him, the gates were opened on the intellectual world. He provided the key – it was as simple as that. I'd read hardly anything apart from *Hotspur* before he arrived. His teaching, particularly in the sixth form, was adventurous. He used the set texts but also encouraged us to read other things. He introduced the school play and swept boys and staff along with him with his canny mix of enthusiasm and authority.

I remember a newly-appointed physics master providing the pyrotechnics for an interesting version of *The Critic* by Sheridan we put on. He allowed me, bravely I thought, to play Macbeth when I was 15.

Waring and Farnham-Flower were friends and had taught at the same public school that had closed down. They bought houses next to each other. One had gone to Cambridge and one to Oxford. Farnham-Flower's house was painted dark blue and Waring's, light blue.

Waring was a little older than Farnham-Flower. He was an avuncular fellow who always looked rather sad. He was good-looking in a craggy way and smoked a pipe. He was just as I imagined Maigret would look – indeed he introduced us to the Simenon books. In much the same way as Farham-Flower introduced us to the joys of English literature, Waring introduced us to the joys of French literature. As well as the set texts he pointed us towards contemporary French writers and European philosophy. I got very interested in existentialism and the European idealists.

Both men encouraged me academically in English and French and then I applied myself in the same way with my other subjects. My parents suggested a career in the Hong Kong police force, but Farnham-Flower persuaded them that I should stay on and go to university. I read philosophy and history at Southampton.

Over the years I have kept in touch with my former teachers. Farnham-Flower made an annual pilgrimage with his wife to Stratford-on-Avon when I was performing with the Royal Shakespeare Company and offered acting hints.

JENNIE BOND
former BBC royal correspondent

I spent all my school life at St Francis' College, Letchworth, where I was a day girl. I remember my schooldays as happy, but my daughter was recently reading my old diaries and tells me I had written how much I hated school. I remember that the workload was great and being conscientious, working fantastically hard. I didn't like being told off so was hideously well behaved. It is a matter of embarrassment to me that I never got a detention or a conduct mark.

Most of the teachers were nuns so it was very refreshing when I got to O-levels to have a lay English teacher who dressed rather sexily. Mrs Cherry had hennaed hair and a gravelly smoky voice and we could see her legs under her black gown. She was of the school of thought that I came across later at university: that books are fine, but are a means of making you think. However, the most illuminating thing I remember her saying was that we'd know when we were really in love with a man because we wouldn't mind sharing his toothbrush.

Another teacher I remember well is Sister Christophane who taught biology. She was completely batty. She would spend most of the lesson feeding her stick insects saying to them in a shrill voice:"This is for you…and this is for you…" She made us cut up frogs and things, which I loathed, and took us on nature walks and would wax lyrical about cow parsley. I liked her scatty approach to life. Sadly, she fell off a bus and died shortly after I left the school.

Sister Agatha, who was Irish, taught Latin, and was a bit of a rebel. She always had little strands of red hair peeping out from under her veil. I found Latin rather boring, but she managed to make me interested in the readings of Cicero and helped me to understand the logic of the language. However, one day when I turned up for my Latin A-level lesson she wasn't there. She had last been sighted running down the road outside the convent with her red hair flying and wearing white stilettos, never to be heard of again.

Then there was Miss Wilson, the maths mistress, a tiny lady who shouted a lot. She was very strong on discipline and terrified me. I never enjoyed maths lessons. I found the subject hard and I don't think her method of teaching was helpful.

But Mrs English, who taught French, was delightful. She was gentle and interested in us and in our lives and had a relaxed way of teaching. She inspired me and made me enjoy speaking the language. I liked working on pronunciation and enunciation. I thought at that time I would probably become a French teacher myself. English and French were always my best subjects.

I went to Warwick University to read French and European literature, planning to teach, and as part of the course was sent to France to work as an *assistante* for a year. By a stroke of good luck my placement was at a lycée in Juan-les-Pins in the South of France where I taught senior children conversational English. I only had to work eight or nine hours a week, but I was hopeless and soon learnt I could never be a teacher.

My big mistake was to walk in and say,"Call me Jennie, not Mademoiselle Bond." From then on I had no authority whatsoever and the students played me up terribly. They used to take cigarettes out of my handbag in the middle of the lesson and one of the boys would ride round the classroom on his bicycle. One day someone lit a fire under his chair. I was hauled up in front of the headmaster for talking to the students about Jimmy Hendrix and the drug scene in England. I wasn't actually fired, but it was close.

When a couple of my friends went into journalism, I thought it seemed like fun, and got a job as a cub reporter on the *Richmond Herald*. I had no idea I would end up as the BBC's royal correspondent. I wasn't particularly interested in the royal family as a girl. My family had a normal middle class respect for the monarchy, but life didn't stop for the Queen's Christmas message.

BRENDAN BARBER
TUC general secretary

I was a pupil at St Mary's Grammar School, Crosby, Merseyside, in the days when corporal punishment reigned. My elder brother, John, was at the school before me so he tipped me off about the teachers it was best to keep on the right side of. A lot of them used the strap big time, but those I remember fondly had a rather different style of keeping order.

Mr Rigby was a lovely man who never needed to use physical punishment. His subject was maths and he managed to convert me from being a disastrous student with zero confidence and poor exam results into someone who really enjoyed the subject and sailed through to get a top grade at O-level.

Somehow he made maths fun and we all looked forward to his lessons. He used his Scouse humour to great effect. There would be lots of jokes, and yet he cracked people along so they were learning all the time. He set us problems that related to our lives and he had a nickname for every lad in the class. He was a very experienced teacher, I guess he was in his fifties, and a tall, thin, angular man.

My other special teacher was Mr Slade, who taught music. St Mary's placed immense store on its speech day, which was always held in the impressive surroundings of the Liverpool Philharmonic Hall. As well as prize giving, there was a performance from the school orchestra and choral and speech choirs. Mr Slade took great pride in organising this occasion and pieces were chosen and auditions and rehearsals for the next year began as soon as the last speech day was over.

I sang in the choir. At first I was an alto then later a tenor and I distinguished myself by having a voice that was so loud that I could be distinctly heard above everyone else (something which was to prove useful in later life when I became a trade union official). I wasn't in the school orchestra – I'd tried to learn the trumpet without success – but I was in the speech choir. One year half the choir got lost backstage and I ended up having to do most of the solo lines.

Mr Slade constantly reminded us of the importance of appearing and doing well on the concert platform. He was stricter than Mr Rigby but he, too, communicated his enthusiasm and passion and commanded respect.

When I reached the sixth form I became a prefect and ran the cultural and social society and organised dances and folk concerts and political debates. I was in the school team that entered the *Observer* Mace competition and we got through to the finals, encouraged by Miss Keenan, who taught elocution. I was in a couple of drama productions we put on with the girls' school across the road and played Professor Plonk in the pantomime, *Old King Cole*.

Then I became a teacher myself. I taught English, Latin, history and geography at a Catholic missionary school in Ghana through VSO. The pupils ranged in age from 12 to 29 and I was just 18. I coped by emulating Mr Rigby and using humour in the classroom.

While I was in Ghana I got a letter from my father to say that there wasn't time to consult me about university applications so the school had put me down for a mixture of subjects in a variety of institutions. I went to City, in London, where I read social sciences.

A few months into my first job I became a trade union official. At school I had developed an interest in social and racial justice as well as learning organisational skills and how to speak in public. St Mary's also taught me to get along with many different types of people because the boys came from such a wide mix of backgrounds.

MICHAEL BOND
creator of Paddington Bear

The day I left school was one of the happiest of my life. I was 14 and got away as early as I could. The teacher I remember best was Brother Ambrose, known as Hambone. He had a terrible temper. I can still hear the rustle of his gown when I fell foul of him one day. He leapt on me from the platform on which he taught, boxed my ears and knocked me to the ground because he thought, wrongly, I had thrown an ink bomb. I remember lying on the floor thinking: "I hope I get a mastoid, then he'll go to prison."

The Irish Jesuits who ran Presentation College in Reading, Berkshire, were strict disciplinarians. They kept rubber straps, about 10 inches long and an inch wide, under their black gowns and whacked us at the slightest provocation. Ear-tweaking was another punishment. Caning was the headmaster's prerogative. Bullying was rife. When it was my turn to be picked on, I'd wait outside until the bell went for lessons. Being a day boy at a boarding school, as well as a non-Catholic, I was a bit of an outsider.

Paddington would probably have coped with Brother Ambrose and Co by giving them his hard stare, although it's a technique I have never used. Paddington's stare deflates people. He is also good at the quick answer – which I have never been. It takes me several days to think of a smart retort. I gave Paddington many of the attributes I would like to have.

I was one of the founder pupils at Presentation College. There were only 20 to 25 of us when I first went there and in the early days we were often taught together. At the age of seven I would find myself sitting next to someone of 14. By the time I left there were more than 200 pupils.

On my way to school I would try to fall off my bike and hurt myself so I could get out of school. Another ploy was to swallow pellets of soap coated with sugar to make myself sick.

We had a science lab, but it was rarely used. It only seemed to be open when parents came with prospective pupils. I don't think the Brothers believed in science; they believed in religion. We had half an hour of religious teaching at the start of every day. There was a school library, but that was kept locked as well.

Brother Ambrose taught English, and any flight of fancy in essays was stamped on. I remember my friend John writing a composition about gardens in which he wrote that his parents grew rhubarb and put manure on it. "I prefer custard on mine," he joked. Brother Ambrose read this out and we all roared with laughter, including Brother Ambrose. Then he gave John a whack with his strap.

My school reports mostly said things like "needs to try harder." One complaint was that I "suffered from a sense of humour".

The school failed to inspire me. Now I have a home in France, I wish I had realised how useful French would have been. Miss Camion, who taught us, was a bit of a dragon but at the end of the first term she underwent a transformation, turning up in a flowery dress and hat, with her fiancé in tow. That was the last we saw of her. From then on the Brothers took over.

It wasn't until I was in the RAF that I came across a teacher who inspired me. I cannot remember his name, but he had been a master at Eton and made mathematics interesting and fun.

After the War, I returned to the BBC where I met someone who wrote short stories. I thought: "If he can do that, I'm sure I can." I sold one in 12. About 12 years later, by which time I was a cameraman, Paddington came along.

The main thing I learned from my schooldays was how to survive. English schools in my day prepared you for the worst. It was like serving a prison sentence before you committed the crime, and gave me a valuable insight into the fact that life is unfair.

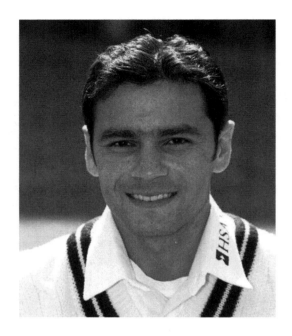

MARK RAMPRAKASH
cricketer and past 'Strictly Come Dancing' champion

Mr Kerswell was the deputy head at Grimsdyke Junior School in Hatch End, Harrow, and I'll always remember him because of the calm and fair way he dealt with a difficult situation on my first day at the school.

I was nine, my family had just moved house and I'd left all my friends behind in my old school in Wealdstone. I was a bit apprehensive about going somewhere I didn't know anyone and the other kids had already formed friendships. Being a new child at school you stand out and are an easy target for being picked on, and that's what happened to me. In the playground on that first day one boy in particular (joined by two or three of his mates) started name-calling and bullying me.

I was not only the new kid on the block, I also had a bit of a suntan and they didn't take to me. News of the scuffle got back to the teacher on duty and we were all marched in to see Mr Kerswell. He spoke to us all together and explained that fighting wasn't acceptable and wouldn't be tolerated.

What struck me was the way he handled the situation. He didn't shout;

he didn't frighten the boys. He simply explained in a very calm and objective manner, on a very basic level to small boys who didn't know much about the world, that they should try to help anyone new to integrate. He also warned them that if the bullying continued, stronger measures would be taken and parents informed.

The next day Mr Kerswell met my parents and listened patiently to their concerns. My father is Indian, from Guyana, and my mother is English and he reassured them that the school was totally against bullying and racism would not be tolerated. He promised to keep an eye on me. I felt his interest was very genuine and my parents were impressed by his determination to nip any trouble in the bud.

I soon settled down and fitted happily into school life. I was never actually taught by Mr Kerswell but we shared a common interest in sports and saw a lot of each other. Football was my big passion then, cricket came later and we certainly didn't do any dancing at school.

Everyone respected Mr Kerswell. He dressed smartly, always in a tie and shirt. He was about 5ft 8ins with dark hair and probably in his late thirties. He was particularly good at projecting his voice when necessary and he spoke with authority. But it was his demeanour that was so impressive. He could be your friend and joke and smile with you, but he also knew when he had to be firm.

We could tell what was required by the tone of his voice. I think when you're dealing with children of that age you need a special balance between making them feel at ease and helping them learn, but also knowing when to harden up to get respect, make sure they are standing in line and not talking and that sort of thing. He was very good at that.

The ringleader of the bullies and I never became friends – there was always a bit of tension between us – but I was never taunted again. The way Mr Kerswell handled with such calm and fairness what could have been a very difficult situation was a very good lesson to learn early in life.

PETER SNOW
broadcaster and author

I was sent away to school when I was seven, which was much too young. I had no idea what I was in for and was terrified, so I took my teddy bear, Patrick, with me. I soon discovered that the other boys hadn't brought teddy bears so I wrapped Patrick up in a parcel after two days and sent him home.

I quickly settled into school life. I was pretty resilient and learned to throw myself into study and games and all that sort of boyish stuff that is no doubt character-building and made me hugely independent and fairly tough.

I had two key teachers, one at Wellington and one at Oxford. George MacMillan who taught Latin and Greek at Wellington, was the head of the MacMillan clan. What was so amazing about George was that he was virtually blind and yet wholly able. He had a curious magnifying glass and at huge personal effort, could just manage to read a short piece of prose, but he couldn't read my essays or my Latin and Greek translations, so I had to read my work to him and we would discuss it. That is common at university, but something which you don't often experience at school.

He was a brilliant man and he obviously did a lot of preparation for his classes. He was so interesting and human and fascinating to listen to. No-one ever took advantage of his disability because he was such a sweetheart. He would have been about 30 then. He's the nicest man I know and we are still in touch occasionally. I don't think I ever called him George at school. It would be "Sir" in those days but he didn't call me Snow, always Peter. He was absolutely devoid of any pomposity with students.

To me Latin and Greek are the most wonderful languages and when I went to Balliol College, Oxford, I read Greats. My tutor in ancient history was Russell Meiggs who was also prefectus of Hollywell Manor where I lived in my first year. Being at Hollywell was wonderful because Russell loved drama and so did I and we used to produce these extraordinary plays in the magnificent gardens and Russell was always in the audience laughing.

The most notable thing about him was his long grey hair, which reached down to his shoulders. He was a wonderful character with piercing eyes and bushy eyebrows. At first he appeared frightening, but when he started talking you realised what a gentle, kind and understanding man he was. He was a good listener, too. His lectures were wonderful because they were so amusing. He talked with enormous enthusiasm and at a rate of knots so you had to listen very hard to follow him. Quite possibly his delivery has rubbed off on me.

I have always had boundless enthusiasm and have never been shy. As well as being involved with theatrical productions at Wellington, I hugely enjoyed taking part in Latin and Greek reading competitions. I did a lot of acting and directing at Oxford and went to ITN intending to be a director, but within a week I ended up a journalist. Since then have never thought of doing anything else – apart from one occasion, when I might have become James Bond. I was working for ITN when I was invited to go round to an address in Mayfair to meet the James Bond film people. But when I knocked on the door faces dropped when they saw that I am 6ft 5in. I was told I was too tall to be James Bond.

After National Service I taught at a prep school called Arnold House in St John's Wood in London for three months. I found it hugely satisfying to teach those who wanted to be taught, but frustrating with those who didn't.

I suppose there's an element of teaching in what I do now, though in history television it's more a question of getting people interested and imparting knowledge, passing on your enthusiasm for something you greatly enjoyed learning about and making it come alive to others.

JOE ROYLE
football manager

All the kids at Ranworth Square Junior School in Liverpool thought the world of Dave Bessell. He was a gentle man with blond curly hair; always smiling, always encouraging and he never shouted at us. He taught religious studies, but his passion was football and he was the first person to introduce me to any kind of soccer training.

We had a good school team and Dave got us to stay behind after lessons for shooting practice. I spent hours kicking a ball against the old bomb shelters in the school yard. In the summer months I played football morning, noon and night, kicking out the toes in my shoes so hard I needed a new pair every week or 10 days. My Mum had a cupboard full of brand new left shoes and worn out right ones until Dave Bessell taught me to kick with both feet.

At eight years old I was an all-round sportsman, good at anything to do with synchronisation and timing. I was the city high jump champion and swam for Liverpool and played cricket to a good standard. But football was my big love and in my first season in the school team we won the league and got to the cup final. Every young kid in Liverpool wants to be a footballer and Dave offered us organisation and structured training and coaching.

The headmaster, Dave Mackay, was also a big influence on my future career because he was the person who encouraged me to go to Quarry Bank High School when I passed the 11-plus. John Lennon had left just as I joined the school but his reputation was well established. The Beatles phenomenon was starting to take off and a lot of school textbooks with Lennon's name in them suddenly went missing.

Mr Mackay thought it was the best school for me because of its reputation for being good at sport as well as getting top academic results. He was a man of few words and a lot of smiles. He smoked a pipe and was tall and dignified. We all lived in fear of him for no great reason, because he certainly wasn't a tyrant. Mr Mackay was the secretary of Liverpool boys' football team and he tipped off the team's manager, Tom Saunders, to watch me play with the result that I became the first high school boy to represent Liverpool boys.

At 14 I was training twice a week with Liverpool boys, playing twice a week with them and for the school and swimming for the city. I was also opening bowler and batsman for the Quarry Bank cricket team. I was exhausted. Eventually I had to make a choice between football and swimming – and soccer won hands down.

One day I arrived home to find a Manchester United scout waiting for me in one room and an Everton scout in another. Scouts from Aston Villa and Chelsea had also, unknown to me, been watching me play. I was a big lad for my age who could kick with both feet, head the ball and had a good leap. I played for Lancashire boys and was selected to captain the North v South in the England boys' trial, but the school refused to let me go and insisted I play for them instead that day.

That was what prompted me to make the decision to leave school early and join Everton full time. I was middle stream academically. I wasn't going to get straight As or go to Oxford or anything like that, and my parents supported my decision. The teachers at Quarry Bank tried to talk me into staying on – especially Arthur Emmett, the head of sport, who hoped I'd play cricket for England. But football was my number one priority and I left school with no qualifications at all. I took a couple of O-levels at night school, but by then my head was turned and very little studying was done.

My ambition had always been to be a professional footballer. Even my essays were often about football. I had a terrific education and enjoyed school. It was a big risk to walk away, but once I knew that professional clubs wanted me my mind was set on kicking a ball for a living.

WENDY HOLDEN
journalist turned novelist

Mrs Symons joined Whitcliffe Mount School as deputy head and head of English when I was in the lower sixth, just starting A-levels. I was determined to go to university and intended to read history, which up to then had been my favourite subject. I was vaguely hoping to work for the National Trust and if it hadn't been for Vanda (Mrs Symons) I would probably have ended up dusting off manuscripts in a basement.

Everything changed when she came and I realised that English was really the subject I wanted to do, entirely because of the way she taught it. She did what no teacher had ever done before; she managed to relate the subject to every aspect of life. She made me realise that English literature isn't just the flower arranging of academia, it's the whole of life. Everything you could ever experience, every place you could go, everything you could think, is somewhere in a book.

Because it was an A-level course, we were studying Shakespeare and the Romantic poets. Keats was her burning passion and she was able to make his work absolutely comprehensible to a motley collection of Northern sixth formers, some of whom weren't terribly interested. She did it by relating Keats to our lives. For instance, I vividly remember her reading in her broad Yorkshire accent:

"Love in a hut, with water and a crust,

Is – Love forgive us! – cinders, ashes, dust."

She explained you might think you're in love with someone when you are 16 but if you get pregnant and have no money it could turn out to be "cinders, ashes, dust." She encouraged us all to aspire to things we possibly hadn't thought of doing. When I decided to try to get into Cambridge University, which was a bit of a long shot, it was Vanda who encouraged me to have a go.

She talked to us as if we were grown-ups. She was only 36, but she was always moaning about her age. She would say how much she loved chocolate and how she worried about becoming fat. She communicated effortlessly with us like a friend and she was the first teacher I'd come across who did that. And she combined this with an absolute passion for her subject. We all did well in our exams because we were taught so well.

Vanda Symonds even looked different from any teacher I'd ever had. She was glamorous, always well dressed. I see her in a crisp white blouse, smart black skirt and high heels with her brown hair wound up in a chignon. She always smelt lovely too. Because she was deputy head, she had her own office and it was full of flowers and all over the walls she had enormous photocopies of lines from Shakespeare or her favourite poems.

I worshipped her, but she was popular with everybody. When we were sitting exams she would put little bars of chocolate on every desk. She took us to the theatre, to an amateur production of *The Merchant of Venice*, and to Stratford to see *Macbeth* where we also went to the Black Swan pub where all the actors drink. She took us to the cinema and arranged a special showing of the Alan Bates/Julie Christie film of Hardy's *Far from the Madding Crowd*.

Her husband, Paddy, was also an English teacher, though at a different school. They were an exotic couple – the Burton and Taylor of English teaching. We've kept in touch. Vanda read some Yeats at my daughter's christening service.

I still feel bad about switching allegiance from history to English because my history teacher, Mr Perrin, was such a lovely man. He had a jolly red face and floppy white hair and brought humour to his subject. Somehow he managed to make Corn Laws, free trade and tariff reform interesting and fun.

I have always wanted to write a novel but it wasn't until I had a job ghost writing Tara Palmer-Tomkinson that I found a subject. Vanda thought that was great.

DENIS HEALEY
politician

In the sixth form at Bradford Grammar School I was taught English by a young man just down from Cambridge called Leslie Shepherd, known to us all as Giggling Gus because of his infectious laugh. In my time masters didn't giggle and Gus excited our interest because he made jokes and also because he really knew his stuff. It was through him I got to know some of my favourite writers like Virginia Woolf, DH Lawrence, Wyndham Lewis and TS Elliot. He was a brilliant teacher and also a very nice man. He had studied under Frank Leavis and knew him and his wife, Queenie, well and he introduced us to a lot of the Leavis' favourites as well as his own.

I was a voracious reader right from childhood. I used to buy little sixpenny copies of the classics with cardboard covers from Woolworths – I still have one or two of them. Basically I was a classicist, but I loved English and always came top. I won the National Book Council junior essay prize the same year as Alan Bullock, who later became vice-chancellor of Oxford University, won the senior prize.

Bradford Grammar School was proud of its reputation as one of the best schools in the country and the cleverest pupils had to learn Latin and Greek to enable them to sit scholarships to go to Oxford or Cambridge. The man who first gave me my love for the classics was "Tock" Lewis who was a great friend of Gilbert Murray, Regis Professor of Greek at Oxford University. Tock Lewis was bald with a white beard and a good deal older than Giggling Gus. He had a house at Mawgan Porth in Cornwall and I often used to spend a week of the summer holidays with him there. After a day on the beach or walking along the cliffs we would listen to recordings of classical music together.

I found Greek hard, but I enjoyed it enormously and was passionately keen on the Greek lyric poets like Sappho and Alcaeus and the dramatists, Sophocles and Aeschylus. I preferred Greek to Latin but I also liked some of the lyric poets in Latin, such as Catullus, very much. It's a pity so few schools teach Greek now. I still consider Thucydides to be the best writer about politics ever.

I was also very keen on drawing and painting and still doodle compulsively, though I paint very little now. We had a good art master called Frank Maddox. I learned water colour painting from him and went to lessons out of school at his home. He got me to copy paintings by De Wint and Ethelbert White. Later I learned classical painting from Alex Keighley. I used to buy picture postcards of all the great Impressionists from the church bookshop with my pocket money. If circumstances had been different I think I might have become an artist. Some years after my time, David Hockney was a pupil at Bradford Grammar School.

I have always had a lot of interests. At school I was keen on acting and took part in school productions. I played Polly Perkins in *The Grand Cham's Diamond*. I was also involved with the literary and debating societies. I was an enthusiastic cyclist. I went to the Hallé Orchestra's subscription concerts at St George's Hall and heard all the great musicians conducted by Sir John Barbirolli and Hamilton Harty, which were wonderful.

My studies came easily to me and I enjoyed them, but I wasn't good at everything. I'm a bodger when it comes to technical things. I played a bit of cricket and football, very badly. I dropped out of the Officer Training Corps, which seemed to me an absolute waste of time. I became a pacifist, much influenced by an English master in the junior school, Mr Benn, who had been wounded in the First World War.

I can only remember once getting into serious trouble at school. That was when my great friend, Arthur Spencer, and I bunked off for a day to go to see Donald Bradman play cricket at Headingley in Leeds. The headmaster, Mr Edwards was very nasty about it and we had to write a lot of lines.

CHRIS BONINGTON
mountaineer

Bunny Lake, the headmaster of University College Junior School, London, was a wonderfully theatrical character who taught Latin. He would walk into the classroom carrying a spear, and if he was in a good mood the base of the spear would be directed towards us, that was *pax,* and if he was in a bad mood, the spear head would be pointed at us, meaning *bellum.*

My parents split up when I was small and I'd had a fragmented education, my spelling was awful and my handwriting has always been terrible, so there was no way I would have passed an entrance examination. Fortunately I got into the school on interview. I stood up to Mr Lake and wasn't cowed by him, apparently.

When I moved on to the senior school the teacher who had the most influence on me there was Mr Darlaston, who was master of the history sixth form. He was a very good teacher with a great sense of humour who made lessons interesting and held your attention. He was preaching to the converted, because history was my favourite subject. I wanted to read history at university and got a place at London conditional on passing three A-levels, all at the same time, one of which had to be advanced Latin. My plan was to become a librarian.

I passed Latin and did well in history – I'd won the history prize the previous year – but I got nought per cent for one of my English papers. I was pretty good at English and it was surmised that the reason for the disastrous mark was my illegible handwriting. My confidence was completely destroyed. I went off to the RAF to do my national service with the thought of going into mountain rescue and then doing a physical training instructor course. But I found I had no aptitude for flying an aeroplane so I transferred to the Army, went to Sandhurst and after a spell in the Royal Tank Regiment, became an instructor at the Army's outward bound school and began climbing in the Alps.

I'd started rock climbing when I was at school. I was 16 when I persuaded a school friend to hitchhike with me to Wales where we stayed in a youth hostel and set off the next morning to climb Snowdon, completely ill-equipped. I had a pair of hobnailed boots and my friend, Anton, had his CCF boots and we both had on our school gabardine macs. I'd cut my down to make it look more like an anorak. I tried to persuade the sports master, Mr Lewis, who also enjoyed rock climbing, to help me form a school climbing club, but he wisely said "no way".

It was after I made the first British ascent of the north wall of the Eiger that Lydia Gollanz asked me to write my first book, *I Chose to Climb*. Lydia was the daughter of the publisher Victor Gollanz who had persuaded her to give up being a French horn player to go into the family business. I had a deadline of one year to complete the project – and I took three. Lydia was immensely patient and taught me everything about how to structure and write a book and never gave up on me.

My other mentor as an adult was Lord John Hunt. He was chairman of my expedition management committee in 1970 [Annapurna, south face] and 1975 [Everest, south-west face] and gave me tremendous support. I got to know him well and he wrote to me frequently. In a way my career has followed his. John's Everest expedition in 1953 really provided the blueprint for future expeditions. He didn't actually give me advice; I learned from seeing the way he did things. Running an expedition is like a military operation and my experience as a troop commander in the Army was helpful. You have to plan and get the logistics right, but you also have to be flexible. Once you get to a mountain you can't drive people, the only way to lead is by commanding their respect.

DEBORAH MEADEN
entrepreneur and 'Dragons' Den' panellist

Miss Jefferies was a bit of an ogre. To me, aged seven, she seemed 10ft tall. She wasn't particularly attractive, nor was she soft. She certainly wasn't a cuddly mother figure. But she was extremely confident and extremely fair and she helped me to settle at boarding school (the Hall, Wincanton, Somerset). I was terribly unhappy about being sent away from home so early. At the time I thought my parents didn't love me; now as a grown up I see it was a good option since they were both working.

Miss Jefferies taught maths and history. I've never been brilliant at anything academic because it didn't engage me, but I was comfortable with maths. I had a little stall selling flowers from the garden at the age of seven and in the school holidays helped my parents count money from the tills in their leisure business for as long as I can remember, so I was good at adding up.

We all behaved ourselves when Miss Jefferies was around. We weren't scared of her, but we were very respectful. When you did a good job she'd say, "Well done" and when you did something badly, she'd say, "You need to go away and do better" and explain how you could improve. I liked that. Fairness has always been really, really important to me.

Lessons with Miss Jefferies were also fun. I remember her spreading out a pack of cards and we had to pick two. The numbers we had chosen were the times table we had to recite. Her history lessons were also interactive. We worked towards an end of term play, which brought the subject alive. One year we re-enacted the Roundheads and the Cavaliers and I can remember being disappointed at not being chosen to be a Cavalier because I wanted to have long curly hair. I enjoyed performing. I was never a shy, retiring child. I always had plenty of confidence and was pretty outgoing and gregarious – and noisy. If lessons didn't interest me I could be disruptive.

My other favourite teacher was Miss Chisholm, who taught English literature and English language at Godolphin School in Salisbury. She was also a very fair woman. She walked with a limp – legend had it that was because she had very bad verrucas. She wasn't physically attractive, but she had a very engaging personality.

Although I loved the subject, I didn't get great marks. Recently my father looked out my old school reports and plonked them on my desk. Miss Chisholm had written:"Deborah answers intelligently in class, plans her work carefully and her work has been excellent." By contrast, the woman who taught divinity – which I couldn't get the point of at all – remarked:"Deborah works with enthusiasm, but needs to be calmer and more methodical." People who watch *Dragons' Den* may be surprised to learn that my housemistress described me as:"Friendly with a happy personality."

I was never made a prefect – probably because I was a bit naughty. If a teacher was not strong enough to control me I could be a nightmare. I played up the Latin mistress, who was a gentle soul, and was sent to the headmistress, Miss Frazer, who told me not to mistake kindness for weakness. I've never forgotten that advice.

Reading those old school reports I see myself as a schoolgirl very much as a young version of the person I am now. And the teachers who inspired me were strong, robust women who said what they meant.

NIGEL HAVERS
· actor

When I was six I was sent off to board at Nowton Court Prep School near Bury St Edmunds, a wonderfully romantic mock Gothic building in glorious parkland. "Don't cry and never sneak on your mates" my father [Attorney General and Lord Chancellor, Michael Havers] wisely advised.

The school was run by an eccentric whisky-quaffing trio, two brothers and a sister – Charles, Neville and Betty Blackburn – who encouraged pupils to call them by their first names. Charles was the eldest and in charge of the Shakespeare productions put on in the school grounds every summer. He picked me out to appear as Mamillius in *The Winter's Tale* and so was entirely instrumental in my choice of career. From that moment I knew absolutely that I wanted to be an actor.

Looking back, Charles was very modern in his approach to education. He had an open and friendly manner and yet he was strict concerning manners and discipline. We felt we were treated as adults. We were given responsibilities. We were left alone a lot, both to learn and to go off and do things. There were about 40 acres to knock around in and we didn't have to be in bed until 9pm. We went fishing in the grounds, rode bicycles, climbed trees – did almost anything we wanted to do.

Neville Blackburn didn't teach but he organised all the costumes for the school plays and painted the scenery and was in charge of school administration. Betty taught divinity and some sport.

Charles brought us up on Shakespeare right from the beginning and we all loved it and understood it. I'll thank him for that for the rest of my life. A lot of people have been put off Shakespeare because they were badly taught. It was of no relevance to them, but to me it was really relevant and fun and interesting.

Charles was tough, yet kind. He was a big man with a moustache and receding hair. He wore glasses and dressed in tweeds and sometimes smoked in class. He was well-educated and had been to Oxford. He loved the theatre and was very knowledgeable about it. The Blackburns had a number of pretty high profile friends in the artistic community. George Baker, the actor, was a friend and also Angus Wilson, the writer. Angus was one of the guys who, having seen me perform, told Charles he had to convince me to go for acting as a profession.

I was an average student. I just chugged along. I didn't do any more or less than was needed, except when it came to doing the plays and then I put in long hours. As a child I think you only excel at things you enjoy. I liked cricket and football and was in the school teams.

I became head boy in my final year but I was pretty bad at it. My elder brother, Phil, had been a particularly good head boy and I suppose the Blackburns were hoping leadership ran in the family. But I didn't want to discipline people; I wanted school to be a free for all. It didn't work, but it was fun while it lasted. I let the boys get away with murder and even introduced cigar smoking onto the curriculum.

At 13 I went off to the Arts Educational School. My brother had gone to Eton but I realised pretty quickly it wasn't the place for me.

Soon after I went to the AES, the school's resident theatrical agent called me in and I got my first professional job – playing the part of Billy, Mrs Dale's grandson in the radio programme, *Mrs Dale's Diary*, mainly because I had the right speaking voice.

I kept in touch with Charles Blackburn right up until he died and he followed my career closely. I owe him a lot.

MAEVE BINCHY
novelist

ister St Dominic was absolutely wonderful and an incredible guiding light. Sadly, she's dead now, but she's not forgotten. The faces of a whole generation of women who were taught by her light up just at the mention of her name. She worked mainly in England, but we had her for ten starry years in Ireland.

When I was nine I thought she was 100, but she was 92 when she died a few years ago so she can only have been in her thirties when she taught me at the Convent of the Holy Child in Killiney. She was tall and thin and of course in those days nuns wore black habits and a white wimple. She had round metal-framed glasses, which shone like a torch from constant cleaning, and a jolly laugh. She was one of those people who once they start laughing, can't stop.

Her main subject was geography, which I wasn't a bit good at, but she was the prefect (mistress of the school) so I would have her every day for other things, including religion. She made religion absolutely splendid. None of us had the slightest problem with it because she made the whole thing completely reasonable and acceptable, even when some of us had become "collapsed Catholics." I was easily bored, but I was never bored in Sister St Dominic's lively lessons and would ask all kinds of leading questions such as "Is Judas in hell?"

She was a natural psychologist. She seemed to know what would appeal to children to encourage them. She really loved children and would have been, I'm sure, a marvellous mother. She saw the dignity of children and when I became a teacher myself I based everything I did on Sister St Dominic.

When I was doing my teaching diploma I contacted her at St. Leonard's on Sea where she was then working and told her I needed somewhere quiet to study and also asked if I might practise on some of her children. She was delighted and sat at the back of the room while I taught. Afterwards she'd say: "You were a little too hard on that girl, she was trying" or "That talkative one…you should shut her up a bit because the others get bored," or "Try to discover something that little mousey one is interested in and able to do." She understood every child in the class and showed me that teaching was all about caring about children and bringing them forward, not just pushing facts into them.

Her enthusiasm was infectious. I remember her lessons as if they took place yesterday. Her eyes shone as she talked about St Paul's visit to Ephesus as if she'd been there herself.

I was a good little girl and very devout. I wanted to become a saint, not just a nun – I was going to be the first Saint Maeve – because Sister St Dominic had such respect for saints and people who were good.

When I was in the fifth form I was made a Child of Mary, which was a bit like being given a religious Duke of Edinburgh Award, and had a big blue ribbon to wear. Unfortunately, it was taken away when I was discovered to be posting letters for the boarders to their boyfriends. Sister St Dominic caught me red-handed when some letters fell from under my tunic.

English was always my best subject and I liked history too, which I read at university. My essays were long and rambling and I'd be told: "Stick to the facts Maeve, stick to the facts," because I embroidered and exaggerated. My reports said I was lazy and didn't try hard enough, but Sister St Dominic would wrap her comments up nicely and say something like: "For a bright girl with an imagination it is a pity that Maeve doesn't apply herself more."

Sister St Dominic's approval was very important to me and I sent her copies of all my books. About five years before she died she wrote me a marvellous letter saying she thought she had the beginnings of Alzheimer's and wanted to say goodbye while she was able to. We kept in touch right to the end.

MARTIN BELL
former war reporter and politician

GK Morris had been a colonial administrator in the Gold Coast before embarking on a career as a schoolmaster. He taught Latin in the days when Latin was big in the school curriculum and he taught it with such enthusiasm that I diligently slaved away at the reams of exercises and translations he set us and got to be quite good at it, though I've forgotten it all now. Learning Latin taught me the meaning and the roots of words and I think it helped me later to develop a sparse style of writing.

When I was eight I was shipped off to a small prep school near Norwich called Tavernham Hall to be a boarder, which seemed normal in those days. The classes were small, about eight or ten, so we were under strict personal supervision. It was a deferential age and I was a deferential pupil. The bloody-minded elements of my character and a resentment of authority didn't manifest themselves until I was in the Army doing national service.

GK Morris – I didn't know the first names of the other boys, never mind the masters – was a big, hairy man. He had hair bristling out of his ears, his nose, everywhere. He wore glasses and the traditional schoolmaster's tweed jacket with leather patches under his academic gown. Some masters would throw chalk to get attention, but he never needed to. Lessons were conducted in silence.

I was a swot because my parents never had any money and I felt I had to repay them for all the sacrifices they made to send me and my twin sister and my bossy older sister to quite expensive public schools. Looking back, I certainly worked too hard when I was at Cambridge. I got a first, but now I wish I'd had more fun.

Between the ages of eight and 22 I was in all male institutions – two schools, the Army and a college. I moved from Tavernham Hall to the Leys School, Cambridge, which had been the school of the original Mr Chips. I enjoyed sport enormously and was in the second teams. I was shy, but that was overcome when I became a journalist. My grandfather was the news editor of the *Observer* in its heyday and my father had a weekly column in the *Eastern Daily Press*. His great claim to fame, though, was being the founder of *The Times* crossword. I intended becoming a journalist myself from the age of 12 but I kept that quiet at school. When I went back to the Leys for some old boys' function at the time when I was rushing around war zones on television I was accused by one of the masters of having wasted my talents.

One of my tutors at Cambridge was the eminent literary critic, George Steiner. He had just arrived in Cambridge and was a rather controversial figure because he was outside the normal mindset of literary criticism. I was in awe of him. He made me feel inferior, but he was very kind with it. I used to submit weekly or bi-weekly essays, which he would criticise as I sat in an easy chair in his study. He was totally fluent in French and German as well as English and from him I learned that English literature was not the be-all and end-all of literature.

I was reading English, specialising in moralists, and he was well versed in all kinds of things, and had such a wide reading and grounding in so many areas of life and literature, he set me thinking in directions I wouldn't otherwise have gone. He had been a refugee from the Nazis and he talked a lot about the Holocaust. We would explore topics such as the nature of evil.

Even as a child I was interested in the rights and wrongs of human behaviour. I had a quiet, rural upbringing and learned my moral values at home, but George Steiner was probably much more influential than I realised at the time. He'd been close to evil. Even though I am no longer an MP, I still bang on about trust in public life and the inequities of what goes on in Parliament.

PETER HILLARY,
mountaineer and explorer

High up in the Himalayas or on a long journey of exploration in the Antarctic, especially in a situation of sensory deprivation, memories are your companions and I have often found myself thinking back to my schooldays and two guys in particular: Mr Carter and Mr Jefferies. Mr Carter was my form master at King's Prep in Auckland and Mr Jefferies taught me physics when I moved on to the senior school, King's College.

I really owe Mr Carter because he saw I had an interest in natural history, especially ornithology, and he encouraged me to pursue it. Who would have thought that this interest would eventually lead to me taking a trip on behalf of the New Zealand Department of Conservation to photograph one of the rarest birds on the planet, the flightless parrot? There are only 62 of them in the world and they are huge, weighing about 4 kilos, and they creep around in the forest on Stewart Island.

My maternal grandfather sparked my early interest in nature. He was on the board of Tongariro, one of the first national parks, and used to take me as a small child to the bottom of our suburban garden and show me where the cicadas left their cases on the bark of a tree, where to find the giant weta, a big insect that is extinct everywhere except in New Zealand, and how to tell when a fig was ripe.

At school natural history was probably my best subject and Mr Carter's encouragement was important to me. He was an elderly man, probably in his early sixties. He was soft-spoken, quite formal in his grey suit and tie, and very likeable. Everyone in the class liked and respected him. He was one of those teachers who stood out. As well as teaching natural history, he encouraged our art, getting us to draw birds and animals in their natural habitat, which I loved.

At King's College I was in one of the top forms but I wasn't an outstanding scholar. I was a member of the bird club and the photographic club, not mainstream activities. I wasn't in the first XV, which was something that got you high points at that school. In winter there were two choices: rugby or rugby, and in summer: cricket or cricket. Rugby didn't appeal to me at all. I thought the whole idea of people hurling themselves against one another was rather undignified. I wanted to put my energies into skiing or climbing. I'd started climbing when I was about ten. Dad [Sir Edmund Hillary] took me into the mountains in the Southern Alps of New Zealand with his Sherpa but I didn't start climbing in a serious way until I was 15 or 16.

Mr Jefferies, who taught physics, was British. Like Mr Carter, he was an extremely good teacher who had total control of the class. He had a capacity to talk about physics in a way that made it wonderfully interesting. Physics is extraordinary stuff because it underscores everything – how a plane flies, how radio works and the internet and everything we use. Mr Jefferies was an intense fellow, quite a skinny man, balding and with glasses. And, like Mr Carter, he was very encouraging. The two men became role models; their encouragement was really important to me.

After I climbed Mount Everest with my father in 1990 I was invited back to the college and was given an honours tie for all my climbing expeditions and also for some of the work I have done with the schools and hospitals we have in Nepal. Mr Jefferies was still there, but about to retire.

Over the years in remote places around the world I've thought about these two teachers often and found myself skiing along with a smile on my face. They were good men. One of the great things about expeditions is that you step away from the frantic pace of modern life for a while. These periods of contemplation can be some of the most memorable and best parts of an expedition.

MICHAEL ROSEN
author and broadcaster

I fell in love with my first teacher. She was tall, dark, pretty and kind and I was about two and a half. She was called Miss Hornby then, but she's Mrs Forcer now and I had a letter from her recently to say she'd enjoyed an article I'd written. "Just think," she said, "It all started at Tyneholme Nursery School."

I moved on to Pinner Wood Primary where I was very fond of Mrs Hurst, an older teacher who was also very kind. My friend, James Gray, and I discovered where she lived and one day decided to go and knock on her door. She asked us in and gave us tea and I remember sitting in her little cottage drinking orange juice and eating cakes.

At seven and a half I was transferred to a brand new school called West Lodge. Being a founder pupil gave me a feeling of great importance and there was something magical about being taught in a new building. My favourite teacher there was Mr Bagg, who took us for football. I wasn't much good at football but, probably because of my enthusiasm, I was in the school team. Mr Bagg was tall and grey-haired and very approachable. He thought jokes were important and told us stories about his time growing up in Wales. The school seemed obsessed with the 11-plus exam and there was a lot of pressure. Because Mr Bagg had a more relaxed approach I gravitated towards him. I wrote a poem about him, which was published in one of my books.

I passed the 11-plus and went to Weald County Grammar School (now Weald College) where Barry Brown was my favourite teacher. He was a new graduate, came from Manchester and wore suede shoes. He sat with his feet on the desk. He often broke off from whatever we were supposed to be doing to tell stories and we soon recognised, too, that he had a glad eye for the women teachers. He was active in the local am dram society and asked me to join. My first performance was in *The Merchant of Venice* playing a little boy assistant fanning one of the potentates. I was immediately hooked and was given the part of an ant in a play called *Under the Sycamore Tree* he was directing at school. I bumped into Barry Brown on a station a short while ago. I hadn't seen him for 40 years but we recognised each other. He's become a theatrical agent.

When my parents moved house I went to Watford Grammar where in the sixth form I had a fantastic Shakespeare teacher in Mike Benton who is now I believe professor of education at Southampton University and a writer. He was just out of college then and I was 17 or 18 so found it easy to relate to him. I was already keen on Shakespeare, having been taken to a number of productions by my parents. My father taught English and then went into teacher training, ending up at the Institute of Education where he became a professor and my mother was a primary school teacher and later went into teacher training. The special thing about Mike was that somehow in reading a play he was able to bring it to life and at the same time show the seriousness of it.

The other teacher I remember from Watford is Dickie James, a short, plump man who smoked a pipe. He was diabetic, which meant that occasionally he would doze off and if this happened we had to quickly give him something to eat. We'd have to revive him about once a term. He kept a lump of sugar or a bit of chocolate in his jacket pocket for such emergencies. His subject was chemistry but he also directed the school plays and he cast me as Sir Toby Belch in *Twelfth Night*. Two days before the opening I got knocked down and ended up in hospital and Mr James had to take over my part.

I left school intending to become a doctor. I had this fantasy that studying science would make me a total human being like Jonathan Miller, but I soon switched back to the arts.

159

ANGELA HUTH
novelist and broadcaster

Miss Winifred Barrows, the headmistress at Lawnside, Great Malvern, was a legend in her own time. She had beautiful arched eyebrows and a lovely smile and charged around the school in navy blue dresses and shoes with Louis heels and little straps.

She was rather eccentric and wonderfully old-fashioned in both her outlook and her demeanour. She seemed to have been friends with most of the interesting people of the 1930s. George Bernard Shaw and Elgar used to play duets on the school piano I learned on, and Laura Knight did sculptures in the assembly hall. We were taught singing by Elgar's best friend, Sir Ivor Atkins, and tennis by Dan Maskell, the Wimbledon champion. Lionel Tertis and Leon Goossens came to give us private concerts.

Like all prospective pupils, I was taken for lunch by Miss Barrows with my mother to the smartest hotel in Malvern. Miss Barrows paid for the lunch out of her own pocket. She also organised and paid for parties for the entire school every term. She had huge vitality and was interested in everything to do with the arts, which suited me very well. If you were keen on maths or science, it was the wrong school. We didn't have a geography teacher for a year. But we all learned how to get up on stage and talk on any subject for five minutes. Miss Barrows was keen on public speaking because she said we would all be asked to open fêtes when we grew up.

Miss Barrows' best friend was Gwendoline Parke, another spinster, who taught piano. For a while I had a vague dream of becoming a concert pianist and practised for four hours a day. Miss Parke was terrifying. She a red face and her anger always seemed about to burst if you hit a wrong note. In the middle of music lessons the butler would come in with a glass of sherry on a silver tray to calm her down.

One of the lovely things about Lawnside was that if you weren't good at something you were allowed to change to another subject. I was chucked out of the maths class because I couldn't keep up and was allowed to take extra French, which I enjoyed. Instead of hockey, I did art and extra tennis.

About a year after I arrived Rosemarie Dillon Weston joined the staff to teach English. She'd been to Oxford and I think would have been a don if she hadn't had to look after a sick sister. She was one of those teachers who had a profound influence on hundreds of girls' lives, even those who weren't remotely interested in English.

Miss Dillon Weston had a Rossetti face, good bone structure, huge wide-apart brown eyes and a delicate little nose. Her hair was worn in a long plait wound round her head and almost every day of her life she was dressed in a brown tweed suit. She never wore tights or stockings, just ankle socks pulled up high, and walking shoes.

When she came into the classroom there was absolute silence. We wanted every minute of her time; lessons seemed too short. She taught us composition and literature and took us to the theatre. Reading Shakespeare with Miss Dillon Weston was one of the most exciting things in the world. She taught us to be curious and to observe and to write in a way that grabs the reader in the first sentence – things that have been incredibly useful in my career.

I kept in touch with her for 40 years. When I began in journalism I sent her everything I wrote and she listened to everything I did on radio and gave me her comments.

When I went back to Lawnside to give away prizes I was so nervous I stopped off in a cornfield to practise my speech. At the ceremony Miss Dillon Weston was standing at the back of the hall in her summer version of the tweed suit and ankle socks and when I publicly thanked her for all she had done, the entire hall stood up and cheered.

ANN WIDDECOMBE
former MP and Shadow Home Secretary

Right from the first lesson Latin was my favourite subject and Sister Mary Evangelista was a superb teacher. I was a boarder at La Sainte Union Convent in Bath and Sister Evangelista supervised the senior dormitory and as well as Latin, taught me religion for the O-level syllabus. She had a tremendous influence on me and even made a huge impact on girls at the school she never taught. A few years ago I organised a reunion at the House of Commons and almost the first thing everyone asked was: "Is Sister Evangelista here?"

I have kept in touch with her in the intervening years and so did my late brother, who was a vicar in Bristol. She was intensely interested when I started making a name on the political scene, but whether she shares my politics I don't know. I never asked and she never told me.

Although I enjoyed the subject anyway, her teaching contributed very much to my decision to read Latin at Birmingham University. She was pleased but there was no question of any pressure. I also like history, ancient history and English and might have studied any of those subjects, but I decided on Latin. In other circumstances I might have been a Latin mistress myself. Indeed, I considered it. Law was another option. I think I was probably the first girl from the school to go into politics. Having decided on a political career, I went on to read politics and economics at Oxford.

Sister Evangelista kept order by the force of her personality. She was also patient and if you didn't understand something she would go back to basics and start all over again. She invented funny little rhymes to help you remember things such as when to use the dative case. And if you were struggling through a translation, she would stop you every so often and invite you to picture the scene, rather than just concentrate on the words.

She was a nice person. I remember one occasion when, still hungry after supper, a group of us went and picked apples from the garden of one of the school houses. Sister Evangelista caught us munching them outside on the steps. We thought we were going to get into trouble, but when she found out why we had taken the apples, more were brought to us.

She took us on school trips to Rome. We went all round the ruins and had the traditional mass audience with the Pope. The first time we stayed in a sister convent, which was perfectly ghastly. There were large open dormitories so we had no privacy and the food was awful. We didn't stay there again.

I was a hard worker and very competitive but, like all girls, occasionally got up to mischief. There was tradition that on St. Cecilia's night (St Cecilia is the patron saint of music) a ghost walked, so a few of us dressed up in sheets and went wandering through the convent in the dead of night and played the piano. Unfortunately we got caught. There were three or four of us in the beginning but only two of us saw the whole thing through and actually walked through those dark corridors.

The next day in class we were going through the second book of Virgil's *Aeneid* where Creusa's ghost appears and Sister Evangelista remarked: "There will be a few unhappy ghosts on Saturday when you won't be allowed out."

The school was strict in many ways. For instance, we all had coverlets on the beds which had to be folded in a particular way so you had two very sharp creases down the centre and a series of very sharp creases going across. This was produced by folding this flimsy material very tightly in a special way, putting it between two pieces of cardboard and pressing it under the bed overnight. Everybody else's coverlet came out with the creases in the right places but mine came out like a rag, every day, and I used to get into trouble. Eventually I did a swap with another girl. I did Lucille's Latin homework and she folded my coverlet. We continued this arrangement for my entire school career.

RONNIE O'SULLIVAN
snooker champion

Snooker has ruled my life since I was eight. I hated school, which I saw as something that interrupted what I really wanted to be doing. I started playing on a little 6ft × 3ft table when I was seven, and by the time I was eight Dad was taking me along with him to play in his club in the West End. I won my first tournament when I was nine and when I was ten I made my first 100 break.

I went to Wanstead High School. I wasn't very clever. I was all right at maths. I was good at adding up because of snooker and I was good at woodwork and at sport, but hopeless at everything else. I just sat there going through the motions. I used to watch the clock waiting for 3.15pm when I could go home. I had just nine minutes in which to run to the bus stop and catch the 148. I'd rush into the house, throw down my schoolbag, grab my cue, ring for a cab and be in the snooker club by 3.50pm.

Because I spent so much time mixing with adults I got on better with some of the teachers than I did with the kids at school. The headmaster, Mr Challon, was a snooker fan. He was elderly and walked around with a walking stick. He had that look that meant you didn't mess with him, but he was as good as gold with me. He couldn't believe it when I started winning cheques for £1,000 at the age of 12 or 13, and asked me to bring my trophies into school to show him. He would have me pulled out of class to go and have a cup of tea and a chat with him in his office. He was like an uncle.

Mrs Abbot, the deputy head, was one of my favourite teachers. She had a soft spot for me and I loved her. When she saw me on the telly playing snooker when I was 14 she wrote to my mum and dad saying how proud they must be of me.

I've always been pretty quiet and shy, but I was disruptive at school and in the third and fourth years ended up in a class with all the naughty kids. At lunchtimes three or four of us would go down to the snooker club where I'd play for money to buy us all fish and chips and a Coke. We were often 15 or 20 minutes late getting back for lessons. I got a very bright kid called Fasel Nadir to do my homework for me for a fiver a time. I told him not to make it too good or the teachers would know it wasn't mine, but I didn't bother to copy it out in my own handwriting because he was in the top group and it was marked by different people. Nobody ever found out.

One lesson I did enjoy was woodwork, which was taught by Mr Townsend. I made a beautiful case for my snooker cue, but unfortunately I got my centimetres and my inches mixed up and it came out much too big. It took me a year to make and was a work of art, but it wasn't much use. I liked sport, too, but the master, Mr Gleeson, used to get frustrated with me because I wouldn't run. I was more of a skills player. I could probably have made the grade to be a professional footballer if I'd put in the same dedication as I did to snooker. I was a bit overweight – but so was Gazza, who was my hero.

Mrs McPhee, who taught cooking, was tough if you got on the wrong side of her, but she and I got along great. She taught me to make macaroni cheese and basic stuff like that. I love cooking. Another cookery teacher, Mrs Hayes, was also one of my favourites. She was beautiful and had the patience of a saint.

There were a number of teachers I liked, but the person who really taught me more than anyone else was my dad. When I was a kid I wanted to be famous. I dreamed about being on the telly playing snooker. Dad saw how much I loved the sport and helped me to fulfil my ambitions. He has been my rock and I love him. When he went to jail [serving a life sentence for murder] it was time to do something for him. The whole family fought to get his sentence reduced. It was terrible that someone got killed in a fight, but we always thought of it as an act of self-defence on Dad's part.

JOANNA TROLLOPE
novelist

Miss Woods was the sister of Peter Woods, the BBC newsreader who had a rather long, lugubrious face. She didn't have a lugubrious face, she had a rather sweet round one, and she taught me A-level English with such passion that I blossomed.

Until I reached the sixth form I had been deeply average, so much so that Miss Williams, the very nice headmistress at Reigate County School For Girls, called my parents in and said: "I do hope you're not hoping for university for Joanna because if you are, your hopes will be most surely dashed."

Miss Woods inspired in me such extraordinary enthusiasm that I wrote a long over-excited essay about Wordsworth's *Prelude* for S- level which made Oxford and Cambridge look at me in a way they would never have contemplated before. Lower down the school I'd been quite good at English, but not outstanding, and I remember being told not to let my imagination run away with me. Miss Woods, however, encouraged me to use my imagination. She encouraged me to speak out and to argue and implied that it is all right to dare, to be bold and brave and express enthusiasms and opinions.

She had this extraordinary ability of getting you inside what you were studying. For instance, with *King Lear* she would make us visualise why Lear was behaving as he did and the jealousy the elder daughters would have felt for his adoration of Cordelia. She made us read Shakespeare aloud and took us on theatre trips. We saw Paul Robeson and Mary Ure in *Othello* at Stratford and a very young Judi Dench as Juliet at the Old Vic.

I can remember getting very excited about English classes. Miss Woods was probably in her fifties then, a spinster with a precise old-fashioned delivery. I visualise her as being plump and buttoned into unremarkable grey flannel suits – but there was an inner fire. She made me, and everyone in the class, feel special.

I started writing huge adolescent novels when I was 14. I wrote furtively and endlessly in notebooks and nobody was allowed to see them, and they remain under lock and key. It wasn't until I was pregnant with my first daughter that I wrote my first adult novel. I think Miss Woods' attitude that there is no such thing as an ordinary life or a dull person was seminal in my growth as a novelist.

Another influential teacher was Miss Walters, who taught Latin. I was terribly bad at it, but she was very persevering. I longed to be good at Latin. I think if I'd got her going on Catullus or Virgil it would have released her passion. I think, like Miss Woods, there was a banked fire within. I think too that if the curriculum had permitted her to teach me Greek we would have done much better together.

I had enormous respect for both women's intelligence. There was a kind of dignity in the classroom then; teachers weren't trying to be your mates. They were there because of the distinction of their minds and their commitment to imparting what was in their minds with a degree of stoicism and unselfishness which is rare now.

When I got to Oxford my moral and English tutor was Rachel Trickett, who rose to be principal of St Hugh's. She was absolutely the most charismatic teacher you could possibly imagine. There was also an extraordinary very sophisticated Polish woman called Mrs Bedronovska who taught Chaucer and gave my tutorial partner and me glasses of sherry.

It is an enormous regret that I never expressed my incredible gratitude to my teachers. It is only years afterwards that you realise how much you owe to someone as generous and inspirational as they were.

HOWARD JACOBSON
novelist

When I was nine one of my teachers at Bowker Vale Primary School in Blackley, near Manchester, sent a letter to my mother which she put in a frame and treasures to this day. It was from a lady called Aster Herman who was so impressed by one of my essays that she wrote:" Howard has great potentialities in English." I grew up with this letter standing on the mantelpiece in my bedroom.

I was a bit of a swot when I was at primary school, and introverted. I am the eldest of three: I have a brother, Stephen, four years younger and a sister, Marilyn, six years younger. I felt their arrivals very strongly, especially that of my brother. Until then I'd held sway in a house full of women. My father was away because of the War and I had the rapt attention of my mother, my mother's mother and my mother's sister. I danced for them and sang for them and told them amazingly clever jokes. When somebody else arrived on the scene it was a big shock.

The essay which had so impressed Miss Herman was about the importance of newspapers and Miss Herman, who was a student teacher then, said she was going to take it back to college as a showpiece. My family have never been readers of newspapers, but that didn't stop me from having an opinion about them. I have opinions now on books I've never read. Opinions, I'm not short of.

I passed the 11-plus to go to Stand Grammar School in Prestwich, which was a cause of much celebration at home, and I regained my position as number one son. At secondary school there were several memorable teachers all of whom, except one, taught English.

My first English teacher, whose name I cannot remember was, I thought, dashing and clever and wonderfully louche. He, too, was impressed by my essays and asked if I would like to contribute to the school magazine. When, because I was intensely shy, I replied:" I don't know, sir," he was very angry and accused me of having no ambition.

Then there was Mr Ogden, the father of John Ogden the pianist. He was a very interesting man, very serious, and I enjoyed being taught by him. We discovered he had suffered from schizophrenia and had written a book about it. We found a copy. It was very well-written and upsettingly frank about the condition including stuff about sexual dreams. We were unbelievably giggly about all that.

One of the things Mr Ogden taught us that stays in my mind was Charlotte Bronte's punctuation system which is, if I remember rightly, a colon followed by three semi-colons. He described it as the classic form of the English sentence.

Mr Ogden helped me through O-levels and then Mr Clayborough came along. He was terrific. He wore the sort of tweed suits Alan Bennett wears. He was a big man, and funny. He made a big impression and a lot of us modelled ourselves on him.

Somewhere between O and A-levels I was taught by Alexander Baird who was mad on William Golding and Graham Greene. He was small, dark and Scottish. I think he went on to write a novel.

My final English teacher at Stand was Mr Parkin whose long white fingers I can still see on my desk as he leaned over me. He introduced me to F R Leavis and he was the reason I ended up going to Downing College at Cambridge. He was a Downing man himself and Downing men are a very special breed. Many of them are austere and introverted and I think in me he spotted a fellow spirit.

But the teacher I probably admired more than any and liked most was a history master called John Hunter. History was the other subject I was good at. Mr Hunter encouraged me and made me feel I could write.

All the teachers I remember were people who set an example. You aspired to be them, they didn't aspire to be you like modern teachers do or try to ingratiate themselves by talking to kids about football.

BETTY BOOTHROYD
first woman Speaker of the House of Commons

I thought Miss Smith was wonderful. She was my form mistress when I was about ten. She travelled a lot and after the summer holidays she would get out the atlas and the globe and tell us where she had been and what she had done. She'd even been to Australia, which was very unusual in those days. It was an absolute eye opener to me that anybody from my small town of Dewsbury had such an expansive mind and was adventurous enough to do all these things.

Miss Smith took us out and about. She explained how magistrates' courts worked and how the local authority was elected. We went to council meetings and to the Dewsbury Empire, right up in the gods in the threepenny seats to see Gilbert and Sullivan. She had very wide interests and she broadened my mind in every way and gave me a thirst for travel.

The War had just begun and one day when she was talking about politics she asked those of us who were Labour supporters to put up our hands. My hand shot up and she went on to talk about the War and the fascist movement in Germany and how they were persecuting the Jews and the gypsies and left-wing people. Because I had dark curly hair and a sallow skin she warned that if the Nazis came to England I'd be a target because I looked like a gypsy. I wasn't frightened by what she said, but I was determined the Nazis wouldn't get me or my friends and immediately made plans.

My friends and I found out where the nearest police station was and where the air raid shelters were. We decided we'd hide in the caves in Caulms Wood and take sandwiches and apples with us. We had it all worked out.

Miss Smith wasn't very glamorous, but she had a most attractive personality. She was plump and jolly and loved life. Miss Ganter, the headmistress, was a tough cookie however, and a great one for punctuality and from her I learned never to be late for anything. She sat at a desk on a raised platform so she could see through the glass partitions that divided the classrooms and spot any latecomers.

At primary school I was taught by Miss Fox, who was also a Brown Owl. Since I was a Brownie we got on well. Miss Fox had short, cropped hair held in place with a slide. I remember her teaching me to read and to count with huge playing cards with sums written on them all round the wall.

I wasn't a particularly good scholar. I failed the 11-plus, but I got a scholarship to the technical college and there I had two good teachers. Miss Gregory, who taught typing, and Miss Harvey, who taught shorthand, shared a house. They both wore thick lisle stockings and Miss Gregory had patches on hers. There was another teacher who taught French whose name I can't remember, but I do remember her making me sit in front of my school dinner until I finished it. It was congealed fatty mutton, which wouldn't have tasted nearly as bad at 12 o'clock as it did when I finally got it down just before school finished at half past four.

I never won any school prizes, but I won prizes at Sunday school. I was quite good at sport and got a medal for life saving. At technical college I was captain of the Spartan house and wore a badge and organised things and jollied people along. My father's ambition for me was a job in the town hall – preferably in the rates department where it was warm and dry and I'd be sure of a pension. I wanted to be a window dresser.

I never got to the rates office. My first job was as a cashier and typist at a posh shop called Bickers for £1 a week and a few years later I joined the Labour Party's HQ. But the job people are never going to let me forget is being a Tiller Girl. Quite frankly, it was 1947 and a lot of young women who were much better dancers than me were in the Forces. I was only a Tiller Girl for about two months. Father didn't approve, but mother wisely thought I should get it out of my system.

BRIAN BLESSED
actor

I wasn't interested in school, I was interested in dinosaurs and nature and adventure and I paid for it by being put into form 1C which was considered the dud's class at Bolton-on-Dearne Secondary Modern.

At first we were under the watchful eye of Mr Dalton, a teacher with a stocky frame, thinning hair and tired eyes that looked at us with a kind of weary fatalism. Then the headmaster, Mr Brown, decided a change was needed. Mr Dalton went and his place was taken by a teacher described to us as "a giant".

On the day the new teacher was due, we waited with bated breath in the classroom. The door opened and Mr Brown, with a twinkle in his eye, introduced us to this "giant" of a teacher – Mrs. Brown, his wife. Mrs Brown was about 4ft 11in tall. She looked like a little pixie with spectacles on the end of her nose and woollen cardigans festooning her upper body. She wore thick woollen socks and slippers. There was a long silence as the woollen pixie surveyed us. Then she did two pirouettes on the spot, drew a deep breath and turned round to wipe the blackboard.

One of the bolder members of the class imitated the pirouette, provoking much laughter. It is doubtful in the history of warfare that a missile has ever been propelled with such force as the wooden board rubber that then hit him on the side of the head. In less than a second the pixie whipped out a small thin cane from the folds of her cardigan and lashed out on the fists of the gigglers who had not had time to hide their smirks or their hands. With amazing energy and speed, the boy who had caused the trouble was propelled through the classroom door to the headmaster's study. There was not a vestige of ill-will or temper in Mrs Brown's behaviour, just an awe-inspiring demonstration of discipline that made a lasting impression on me. She never needed to hurl the board rubber again.

Mrs Brown taught us about Einstein and read to us from Shakespeare, Shaw, Masefield, Keats and Wordsworth. Tears ran down her cheeks as she told of the wanderings of Odysseus. She was brilliant. She promised us that in six months' time we would have a knowledge that would astound the rest of the school. We were popularly known as the Wooden Tops. "Is that how you wish to remain?" she demanded, adding: "I will do all in my power to drag you into the light so you can hold your heads up and be proud of yourselves."

I became teacher's pet; she loved my deep voice. We all worked hard for Mrs Brown, trying our utmost to please her and to meet her high standards and she gave us apples, oranges, comics, magazines and books. Once when I won three essay prizes in a row she took me to see *Henry V* at the local cinema with the headmaster himself. I sat between the pair of them. It was a great honour, but an unnerving experience.

Every day I went home for lunch and for several Wednesdays listened to Conan Doyle's *The Lost World* on the radio which made me late for afternoon school. Every Friday afternoon I appeared on the podium to be caned, and on the eighth occasion the headmaster asked me why I was repeatedly late. When I told him he dropped the cane, stared long and hard at me and motioned to me to join the rest of the assembly. Later he came into the classroom and publicly apologised. "I was in the wrong," he said "I am giving you permission, Blessed, to listen to the last two episodes of *The Lost World* without fear of further punishment." He also asked the English master, Mr Jones to read the book to the entire class.

I kept in touch with Mrs Brown after I left school. She frequently wrote me scathing notes. She thought I was in *Z Cars* too long. She didn't approve of what I was doing until I played Augustus Caesar in *I Claudius*. She she was pretty harsh about my television work but she adored the *Flash Gordon* film.

BENEDICT ALLEN
explorer

Murray Argyle had extraordinary presence. He was a large, elderly man with thick white hair, fearsome blue eyes and bushy eyebrows. He was my biology teacher at Bradfield College, Berkshire, from the age of 13 to 18 and I found him inspirational. He was charismatic in a quiet way, a rather mysterious character who had served in the Navy before becoming a teacher and there were rumours about him having been torpedoed in the War. There seemed to be some magic about him.

I always wanted to be an explorer. My dad was a test pilot and he brought home all sorts of exciting things from Africa like a weaverbird's nest and a stuffed crocodile, which fired my imagination. Most of the teachers, especially the art master, dismissed me as a dreamer, but Mr. Argyle understood. Looking back now I think he had a soft spot for me, though I didn't realise it then. I got the feeling that he put in a good word for me with other members of staff from time to time.

Mr. Argyle could control a room full of boys with a look. When he walked in

– always very slowly – there was total silence. He didn't suffer fools gladly, but he was never nasty to anyone. I always looked forward to his lessons and yet I was always slightly scared.

He brought lessons alive with his enthusiasm for his subject rather than by telling funny stories. When we were busy dissecting rats and worms he would say that your best tools are your hands. He even managed to make equations for photosynthesis and respiration seem interesting.

He had extraordinary confidence, which is one of the keys of charisma, and I think what I looked up to in him. He was someone I wanted to be. He was a teacher of the old school who knew the name of every one of the 500 or so pupils. You would find him in some remote playing field inspecting the pitch, jabbing at the turf with a walking stick, or stalking round the school late at night on his own picking up litter, which he loathed.

He was solitary, but also gregarious, a little bit aloof from people and yet at the centre of everything. I think all the other masters as well as the pupils were in awe of him.

Always conventionally dressed in a tie and tweed jacket with elbow patches, he appeared a smart, but slightly untidy, bachelor. After I'd been at the school a couple of years I'd talk to him when I bumped into him in the corridors, often about my collection of insectivorous plants. He was instrumental in my development from a total dreamer to someone who by 18 was starting to get his act together and won a number of prizes for biology projects.

I told Mr Argyle about wanting to be an explorer and he helped me to realise my dream. I think I was the sort of pupil he liked to encourage, someone who wasn't top of the class, wasn't academically brilliant nor a sportsman, but different and needed to be told or needed to feel that he could make a difference in the world.

The last time I met him was when I went back to the school to give a lecture. He was quite doddery and I was flattered he had made a special trip to be there. I wanted to give him a copy of one of my books, but he made a great point of opening up his wallet and taking out a crisp £20 note and insisting on paying for it.

Sometimes when I am feeling very alone on one of my expeditions I think of Murray Argyle. I remember at the end of one very exhausting day, having walked 30 miles across the desert, bending down to clear up the rubbish round my campsite and having a little chuckle as I recalled his hatred of litter. I felt his presence, like a sort of guiding spirit.

JOAN SIMS
actress

Miss Wilson, my elocution teacher at Brentwood County High School, was responsible for me going on the stage. I adored her because she was so glamorous. She was very smartly dressed, wore bright red nail varnish and a lovely diamond and emerald ring. She reminded me of the stars I'd see on the silver screen every Saturday morning at my local cinema.

She made lessons fun and she was terribly encouraging and enthusiastic as she tried to get rid of my flat Essex vowels. Elocution was the one subject at which I didn't feel a failure.

I was rather slow and not very clever at my studies (I failed school certificate twice). My school reports usually included the comment: "Joan could be very good at this subject if only she would concentrate." I think I have always been slightly dyslexic because I have never found reading a pleasure and have to learn my lines by putting them on to a tape recorder.

Encouraged by Miss Wilson, I joined the local amateur dramatic and operatic societies. I was playing Madame Arcati in Noel Coward's *Blithe Spirit* by the time I was

15. I began my lessons with her when I was about nine. She taught me in a building which was detached from the main school and all its rules and regulations. The lessons were one to one, of course, and to me that was magic.

Miss Wilson and Mr Hill, the warden at the youth club where I belonged to the drama group, persuaded the Essex Education Committee to finance my theatrical training. I was an only child with no theatre connections. My father was a stationmaster and my mother was a housewife. They were a bit horrified at the suggestion that I should go on stage and insisted I had a proper training, though they couldn't afford to pay for it. It was mainly thanks to Miss Wilson that I got the funding to go to RADA.

At school I took great delight in entertaining my fellow pupils by impersonating the teachers, and later I modelled some of the characters I portrayed on the mistresses at Brentwood.

Miss Goodwin, for example, who taught PT, was the inspiration for Miss Allcock in the *Carry On* films. I copied the way she ran with her chest pushed forward. She was a well-endowed lady, and she had a whistle which used to bounce on her bosoms as she ran about.

Then there was Miss Hodge, the English teacher. She was very slim, always wore a neat suit and her silver white hair curled up into a bun. She was absolutely lovely, but we played her up mercilessly. She rode a bicycle to school and years after I left I heard that she had been knocked off her bicycle and killed.

Miss Vasher-Bacon, who taught maths, was divine. We called her Rasher Bacon, of course. She had a rather mannish gait and I remember she wore flat lace-up shoes and Bermuda shorts. I was dreadful at maths.

I enjoyed my schooldays and liked all my teachers – apart from Mr Higby, the headmaster at my primary school, St John's in Billericay. He was a vicious and deeply unpleasant man who used to pinch you sharply on the top of the arm when he was talking to you. At St John's I fell in love for the first time, with a boy called Colin Blanks who gave me my first kiss. We were caught and sent to the head. I got a ticking off, but Mr Higby gave Colin six of the best.

I won a prize at my first school, though I can't remember now what for, and inscribed inside was a very sound piece of advice:

Life is an echo, all comes back
The good, the false and the true;
So give of the best that you can give,
And the best will come back to you

STEVEN BERKOFF,
actor, director and writer

Mr Shivas taught English with such persuasive charm, as something it would be delightful to learn, that it soon became the subject I was most interested in. For the first time I began to understand grammar and the structure of sentences. He encouraged me to be creative, writing essays and later, verse. These essays were along the usual lines of "What I did in the holidays" or "A day in the life of a penny", but writing made me aware even at the age of 11 that I wanted to earn my living doing something that would enhance my creative output. Mr Shivas encouraged that ambition.

At the end of my first year at Raines Foundation Grammar School in Stepney I came top of the class in English with 90 per cent. It was a phenomenal start and the first time I'd been top in anything. I remember Mr Shivas writing on my report that it was "A great beginning."

I had a passion to learn and was in the A stream then. (I didn't do so well when two years later my family moved house and I had to change schools). I was very excited to be going to grammar school and I remember taking a case with me on my first day, just as I'd seen boys do in the movies, to carry all my books.

Mr Shivas made the English language seductive and quite fascinating. He was an extraordinarily refined, handsome man. He had silver grey hair, blueish eyes and dressed well. He always had a smile playing upon his face, appeared to love children, and was receptive to our responses. Everybody liked him, but I liked him most of all.

There was a bit of the actor about him. He had a very precise manner and carried a handkerchief in his sleeve, which he took out from time to time with a flourish. When he read to us in class I was enchanted. Probably because I didn't have a very good relationship with my father, I bonded swiftly with older men who showed me any affection and I had a big crush on Mr Shivas. After school I'd run after him to chat on the way to the bus stop. He encouraged me to write and to believe I had a flair; and that confidence never left me.

Two years later we moved house and I went to the Grocers' School in Hackney which is now Hackney Downs Grammar school. I had another good English teacher in Mr Brierley who would proudly tell me how well Harold Pinter, who had just left, was doing as an actor. But I was put in the C stream at Grocers' School where we were not encouraged to be creative or even allowed to be in the school plays. I became deeply frustrated, rebellious and anti-social. I left as fast as I could, before I was 15.

I didn't keep in touch with Mr Shivas but curiously many years later I met his son, Mark Shivas, who became a very influential film and television producer. I had a play on at the Donmar called *West* and Mark Shivas televised it. It was a strange and wonderful coincidence that my teacher's son then took over where his father left off and guided me. And finally I was able to pass on my thanks to his father for giving me the key that enabled me to open the door to a creative career.

JOANNE HARRIS
author

I really wish I'd had one special teacher, someone who would have been a mentor. I think it would have helped me enormously to have had a teacher who encouraged creative writing. Most of my English teachers were much more occupied with teaching the syllabus. There was a great deal of comprehension and received wisdom in literature whereby we read texts and were then told what to think of them.

I went to an all girls' school, Wakefield High, on a bursary. I had a number of good teachers, but a lot of the things I learnt were learned outside the classroom. For instance, we all had to go outside at break, whatever the weather, so I volunteered to tidy the old book room which was full of texts which had been abandoned because they were unsuitable or old-fashioned or in some cases, downright pornographic. I managed to spin out the tidying for the whole winter and spent my time reading.

There was a history teacher called Miss Hardcastle who was dynamic and creative and when she wasn't teaching history, she would talk to us about her own interests: mythology, sociology, culture and civilisation. Miss Hardcastle was tall and slim and looked a bit like Sigourney Weaver. She was a brisk, no nonsense woman and extremely good at depressing pretension. In those days it was common for teachers simply to dictate notes for the entire lesson, but she never did that. She was good at making dull topics interesting.

I had a sweet Latin teacher called Miss Smith. She had a problem with her throat and couldn't speak in a normal voice, but was able to control 38 kids just by peering at them and whispering in a threatening manner. One day I fixed a bright green fluffy frog I'd won on a shooting range to the blackboard with a system of pulleys, so when I pulled the string the frog would appear above the board and wave. Poor Miss Smith, with her back to the board, didn't understand why everyone was laughing. Eventually, of course, she caught me and made me conjugate "Yonder frog is very amusing" in a number of tenses.

I was a daydreamer and spent a lot of time in lessons writing stories and poems and plays. I detested French because having a French mother and speaking and reading French at home, I already knew the language. I was very unruly in lessons because I desperately wanted to be thrown out. Mrs Wigglesworth, who taught me for several years, had no sense of humour. But in retrospect I feel sorry for her because I was a deeply troublesome pupil.

There was a certain ethos at the school that encouraged you not to show too much individuality. I got into trouble for doing silly things which were quite harmless, but didn't fit in with the school's idea of how a high school girl should behave. I was reported for eating ice cream with mathematical instruments on the bus and drinking Coca-Cola from a can.

There was a rigid uniform, which even dictated what colour your knickers were (navy in winter, sky blue in summer). I only wore uniform knickers for games, when I put them on top of my normal ones. I was constantly losing them and on lost property day this pair of school knickers with my name on them would keep turning up and deeply embarrassed, I would have to step forward and claim them.

When I moved to sixth-form college, it was a teacher who didn't actually teach me, but ran creative writing sessions, who was most helpful. On a one to one basis Mr Northern would read my work and discuss it and managed to encourage me without making me complacent. He taught me structure and started me writing short stories.

I've kept in touch with Mr Northern and sent him copies of my books. I also send copies to my primary school teacher, Mr Middleton, who was a big influence when I was eight or nine years old. I wrote a story called *Flesh Eating Warriors of the Forbidden Mountain* for which he gave me a star. I persuaded my best friend to copy it several times and we sold the copies and bought sweets with the proceeds.

ANTONY WORRALL THOMPSON
TV chef and restaurateur

I was a troublemaker at school. I was a bit like a Jack Russell, little and always snapping at teachers' heels. School was great fun. I enjoyed being naughty and the centre of attention.

My parents split up when I was young and I boarded from the age of three at a nursery school and then at Milner Court prep school, attached to King's, Canterbury. The headmaster, Rev John Edmunds, was a complete bastard. He ruled by the whip and the cane. I was always being beaten. His aim with a blackboard duster was extremely accurate, too.

Rev Edmunds was the scripture man and a teacher of doom. He was quite small but very chunky and he had close-cropped hair like an American GI. He would have made a good commando in a war zone.

My mother was warned that if my behaviour didn't improve she would have to find another school for me. I was always having bright ideas like unfurling fire escape chutes and abseiling from top windows. Once I pushed a teacher's car into the swimming pool. I was very aggressive. I used to kick the head boy. The headmaster was called in and dared me to kick him. I did. As a result, I was belted on the head and sent flying across the corridor. But nothing deterred me.

One of the teachers at the school was sexually abusing boys. I had no idea what was going on and was rather jealous that I wasn't invited to join the group who went to the master's room at night. I thought they were watching television.

Then, one day one of the boys told me what was happening and said he couldn't take it any longer. I ran to tell Mr Edmunds and set myself up as the fall guy. The predator was gone the same night. It was my finest hour and that year I was awarded the prize for the most improved student.

Another teacher I remember from junior school had the same name, but spelt differently. Mr Edmonds taught maths and I was pretty good at that. He was tall with an enormous Roman nose and stood up for me in staff meetings.

I was one of those boys who didn't concentrate in lessons, but always managed to pass exams. That annoyed staff. I was told I wouldn't get into the senior school, but passed with flying colours.

When I arrived at King's senior school, I was greeted with: "We are given to understand that you are a troublemaker and we are going to knock it out of you." I was beaten several times for various misdemeanours, but some of the staff had a soft spot for me because I was so small. I was only seven stone as a teenager.

I continued to be a rebel, letting off stink bombs and doing all sorts of wicked things. I saw no reason to be serious. Fagging was still in operation and I got three times the going rate because I could cook. It dawned on me then that there was money to be made from providing good food. I'd learnt to cook when I was six or seven. We had au pairs who were such bad cooks that the only way to get a decent meal was to make it myself.

At senior school I was moved from class to class because I caused trouble. It wasn't until I was 15 or 16 I started taking an interest and got involved in school activities. The headmaster, Canon Newell was tolerant and seemed to understand me.

My school reports went to my grandmother who paid my school fees. She wanted me to go to Eton as my uncle had done, or Wellington, where my grandfather had been. My mother insisted on King's. Grandmother was a powerful army wife, married to a general. She had lost her son in the War and I became a substitute.

I wanted to train to be a chef, but Grandmother insisted I did a hotel management course. I studied at Westminster College Hotel School where Graham Leedon was a big influence. He was chief lecturer and inspirational, though he did write on my report: "This boy should stick to accountancy, not cookery."

OLIVER SACKS
neurologist and psychologist

The day that Francesco Ticciati, a passionate, excitable Italian came to the house to give piano lessons is one of my earliest memories. He was a brilliant teacher, a Bach lover and a Bach maven [expert]. He drilled the preludes and fugues into me and my three older brothers and probably determined that my own first and most constant musical love would be for Bach.

Ticciati would shout and bang his fist on the piano in frustration when things went wrong. He was choleric, but without any malice or sadism – unlike the hideous abusive headmaster who darkened my life between the years of six and ten when I was evacuated to Vernon House in the little village of Brafield near Northampton. He was a monster: vicious and sadistic, and he regularly beat us with relish. There were some pleasant things though: a lusty young woman taught horse-riding, I had occasional piano lessons and cups of tea with Mrs Clayton in her cottage and I learned to love the countryside.

When I came back to London my music lessons continued with Mrs Silver, a red-haired woman who died in childbirth, and then with Ticciati's son, a mild man who gave me a mug of Lapsang suchong tea which I had never had before and I thought tasted of kippers.

Formal school was of little use or interest to me as a child. All my enjoyment was extra-curricular. My real educators were the public library, the museums and my uncle's electric light bulb factory.

Uncle Dave (whom we called Uncle Tungsten) inducted me into the joys of chemistry and I shared his passion and delight in chemical transformations. I watched him at work in a wing collar, his shirtsleeves rolled up, as the heavy, dark tungsten powder was pressed, hammered, sintered at red heat then drawn into finer and finer wire for the filaments.

At that time I was doing classics at school. I got a scholarship to St Paul's and also to Oxford so I suppose there was some part of me absorbing on automatic. I probably simulated attention but I didn't enjoy school. I wasn't sporty (apart from swimming, which is still a passion) and didn't like team games. I am rather a solitary person.

From about ten to 14 I wanted to be a chemist, then I moved towards biology and marine biology – medicine was a relative late-comer – and met the teacher who had the greatest influence on me and many others. Sidney Pask was splendid. He was also narrow-minded, bigoted and had a hideous stutter, but like Ticciati, he was marvellously passionate and he demanded that we were as dedicated and single-minded as he was.

Three of us – Jonathan Miller and Eric Korn (who is now an antiquarian bookseller) and me – formed an inseparable trio and would go with Sid on fresh water expeditions and to the marine biology station in Scotland. There were weekend plant collecting trips, sometimes in freezing winter. He instilled in all of us a lasting passion for biology. I had a particular love of cephalopods (squids and cuttlefish).

Some of Pask's pupils were repelled by his intensity and found him an impossibly demanding and exacting taskmaster, but to those who responded to his challenge he was the most influential teacher of all. There is now a group of about 70 of us who call ourselves the Pasquidae who still keep in touch and we are planning to endow a laboratory or a prize in his honour.

ALICE THOMAS ELLIS
novelist

My education at Bangor County Grammar School for Girls in north Wales came to an abrupt halt when I was 16. I was expelled – but it was an amicable arrangement. My poor mother was always plodding up to the school to see the headmistress and finally she was told that I'd got as much out of school as it could possibly give me, so I'd better leave. Miss Hughes, the headmistress, wasn't spiteful. She let me go back to take Higher School Certificate a year later.

I never knew Miss Hughes' first name. She was far too august a character to be asked. She looked a bit like Queen Victoria. She was well-upholstered, wore her hair in a bun and dressed in rather formal frocks, lisle stockings and strapped shoes and always wore a brooch.

Miss Hughes taught English literature. I was good at it, but I can't say I had a rapport with her. You didn't have a rapport with Miss Hughes – she was far too regal. She was a Greek scholar, a thoroughly well-educated woman. All the teachers at the school had degrees and I was very well taught. I must have learned by osmosis, though, because I spent an awful lot of my time in class gazing out of the window across the fields to the Snowdon mountains.

I had a tendency to be over elaborate in my writing and to embroider. Miss Hughes taught me to be more concise. Once, when I used the word "hometown" in a composition she said it was a dreadful Americanism and I must never use it again. She had a huge influence on me.

English and art became my favourite subjects, though I much preferred being at home, where I led a wonderfully wild life roaming the hills, to being at school. I always did the absolute minimum homework.

Until I was 13 I did well at school. I came top of the county in the scholarship examination. I remember my mum sending a telegram to my father, who was serving in the War in the Middle East, to tell him.

At first the grammar school seemed a bit daunting. It was a huge building with shiny parquet floors and it smelt of polish and dinner – and sick. My little primary school in Penmaenmawr was near the sea and smelled of chalk and milk and biscuits and hot coals. During my first year at Bangor I was one of the good girls and was made a form captain and had a little red badge to prove it.

Then puberty hit me and things went downhill and I started getting into trouble. I wasn't a joiner; I had not one ounce of team spirit. I would get sent to Miss Hughes for running in the corridor, talking in class and minor breaches of school regulations. Even wearing more than two grips in your hair was against the rules. To be caught eating in the street while wearing school uniform was a terrible crime.

My other special teacher was Miss Daisy Smart, who taught art. She was a quiet woman, short with big eyes and a big smile who dressed in light, flowery, feminine clothes. She took an interest in me and encouraged me and nurtured my talent.

Miss Smart's lessons were fun. I remember the first thing she got us to paint was a clown's face. She put me in for all the eisteddfodau. I once won a prize for a painting at the National Eisteddfod. After I left Bangor, Miss Smart encouraged me to go to Liverpool Art School.

Many years later, I was sitting at home remembering how significant she had been in my life and I decided to write to her. She invited me to tea. She looked exactly as I remembered her. She said she'd kept my school paintings for years but had recently thrown them away. I was upset, because I have none of my work from my schooldays.

I only stayed at the art school for about a year. I don't think I am schoolable. As a girl, there seemed to me something unnatural about going to school when I had so many other much more interesting things to do.

NORMAN BAKER
politician

Aubrey Pope wore John Lennon glasses, a tweed cap and cycled to school on one of those bikes with very small wheels. He rode a bike for environmental reasons, not because he didn't have a car. He was very "green" long before it became fashionable.

He was quite unlike any other teacher I ever had. He taught me German and Russian at Royal Liberty School in Essex, and I still clearly remember his first lesson. He taught us a complete sentence in German, which would translate: *"After the two children had left the house, they go into the park to play football."* It was an extraordinary thing to learn on your first day, but a very good sentence because it contained many of the rules of the German language.

In French, we began with numbers and verbs and even six weeks on had learned virtually nothing, yet with him we were straight into sub clauses. He taught us the rules of grammar too, but he did it in a very dramatic and idiosyncratic and effective way. And he marked our work in the German style. Instead of eight out of ten or whatever, it would be one (excellent), two (good) three to four (average) and five (useless). He would also give credit for length on essays.

You knew the route map with other teachers, but you never did with Aubrey Pope. His approach was always unexpected. He knew I was keen on the Beatles, for instance, and came in one day with a half-hour tape of a radio programme discussing the lyrics of one of their songs – I think it was *Sexy Sadie* – in German. I don't think he was into pop music himself, but he knew it would interest me and of course I listened to it and learned from it. He was very creative in that way.

He was also ahead of his time in the way he used language labs before they became fashionable. He would take us to see Brecht plays performed in German and was good at explaining why the author wrote as he did and what he was trying to say, which I found very interesting.

He didn't indoctrinate or push you into doing things; he just made things available and encouraged you to think, as a good teacher should. In Russian lessons he would have *Soviet Weekly* lying about because he thought if you were going to learn a language, you had to learn the culture as well. Once, off my own bat, I entered a competition in the paper and he said: "You shouldn't have done that, you'll be on the security service's data base now." I think he was joking, but having subsequently become home affairs spokesman, I'm not sure he wasn't right.

I have probably used my German twice in about 25 years and I haven't used my Russian at all since I left school. However, the good thing about learning foreign languages is that it broadens your mind. You learn about different lifestyles and different ways of thinking and pick up concepts that have no English equivalent, like the German word *bildungslücke* (a sort of cultural gap).

Having Aubrey Pope as a teacher made me more open-minded and taught me to question things. I grew up thinking that the Soviet Union was a big bad place and the West was good, and he explained that there was good and bad in all countries and gave me a more mature outlook. It wasn't until I reached the sixth form that I discovered he was political. He was very left wing/green and often wrote to the local papers about environmental issues.

I shouldn't think he knows I became an MP. If he does, I think he would be surprised. I remember him saying to me once in class when I was being particularly obnoxious: "I've never hit a pupil, but I've come nearer it with you than anybody else."

CONNIE FISHER
singer and actress

I first met Marilyn Lewis in a power cut. I was sitting on a sack on stage reciting an extract from *Good Night Mr Tom* in a Young Farmers' competition, when half way through my piece the lights failed. I carried on in the dark and won the competition. Marilyn was in the audience and afterwards came up and congratulated me on my "The show must go on" attitude and said if ever I wanted to have singing lessons she'd be happy to teach me. She said she could tell I had a melodic voice from the way I spoke.

A few weeks later I started having lessons at Marilyn's home after school. She was a colourful character, very warm and welcoming with rosy cheeks and dressed in bright, floaty outfits. She lived on a farm in the Preseli Hills in Pembrokeshire and was well known locally for her children's choir, Cor iau newyddion da (The Good News Choir).

I trudged through the farmyard, leaving my muddy boots by the door. I had confidence through reciting in public, but I was in awe of her at first. I came away from the first few lessons crying my eyes out because I thought I was good and she said I needed to work, work, work. She broke me down before building me up again. She was tough, but encouraging. She said I had a pure sweet voice which would be good for folk singing and if I did well I could join the choir, which I soon did. She helped me to learn Welsh and we won lots of competitions at eisteddfodau. I was the only English girl in the choir and was soon singing solos. We spent every Saturday rehearsing and on Sundays we toured all over Wales performing.

Marilyn was brilliant. I owe everything to her. She had a way of teaching children to sing in beautiful unison. She was never pushy, just very strong and a fountain of knowledge. She made each member of the choir feel individual and special but also a team player, something which was very useful to me when I played Maria in *The Sound of Music*.

I was 11 or 12 when Marilyn first taught me and I didn't know anything about technique. She showed me how to breathe low and how to avoid tension. She would never let us go on stage unless we were at our peak.

She became like a second mother and took us to the eisteddfodau in her caravan. She was full of useful tips like gargling with warm salt water and drinking honey and lemon to kill phlegm. Occasionally she'd put a little nip of whisky in it to steady the nerves.

By the time I was 15 or 16 Marilyn suggested that the way ahead for me was the musical theatre, but felt she couldn't teach me any more because that wasn't her area of expertise. I auditioned for the National Youth Music Theatre and she helped me prepare. She was so proud when I got in. It was the springboard to my career. Marilyn has followed my career every step of the way, constantly saying: "I know you're going to make it. I'll see you in the West End one day." Her attitude to rejection was "Move on to the next project."

Even though she was in New Zealand visiting family when I was appearing in the television show *How do you solve a Problem like Maria?* she kept calling me, giving me tips. The night I won she was so thrilled she sobbed down my voicemail. She came to see the show with three coach loads from Wales. Boy, was I nervous that night.

MICHAEL WINNER
film producer, director and columnist

Miss KM Hobbs ran a tutorial establishment in Buckingham Gate, near Buckingham Palace, to which I persuaded my parents to send me when I was about 17. I'd been to St Christopher's, a free and easy co-educational Quaker boarding school in Letchworth, Hertfordshire, for 11 years and learned nothing. It was a dreadful place in those days. The standard of tuition was poor, and the teachers, to put it kindly, were eccentric. It scarred me for life.

I resented being at a school that should have educated me but didn't, and took myself off to Miss Hobbs' crammer. My parents were insistent that I went to university and I said to them: "Look, I'm not getting any education. If you want me to get to university, this is where I'll have to go."

Miss Hobbs said I was illiterate. Of course, she was exaggerating, but she was not far off the truth. She was one of those wonderful Margaret Rutherford characters – portly, upper-crust, very businesslike, certainly of the old school and a very nice person. She ran two crammers, one in Guildford and one in London, and she placed me in the Buckingham Gate establishment, where there were only about eight of us.

One of the teachers there, a red-haired lady, was outstanding. It's a tragedy I cannot remember her name because there is no question it was thanks to her that within a year I got into Cambridge University. I dearly wish I was able to write to her and say: "I would like to give you a major present, my dear, whatever you want, because you were the only person in the world who educated me."

She was about 35, a neat, thin, nice-looking woman and well-spoken. Her lessons were like a breath of fresh air after St Christopher's. She explained things so clearly it was like a curtain was drawn back and light had flooded into a dark room. Suddenly I understood. She put into focus all the things that were swimming about. The size of the classes also helped: you knew there was no escape, you couldn't play around and you couldn't think of anything else.

They were all nice people at Miss Hobbs' — pupils and teachers. At St Christopher's they were peculiar. I'm sure a lot of the students ended up as biscuit salesmen. The staff were inept and the sexual leanings of some were a bit odd; the geography teacher had in his room photos that he had taken of naked boys on rocks.

Miss Hobbs' establishment was brilliantly run and all the teachers knew what they were talking about. Most of the teachers at St Christopher's did not and, if they did, they were incapable of expressing themselves coherently. The school's academic record was poor. It claimed to be run by the students through the school council, but it wasn't. It also prided itself on being immensely tolerant.

I left St. Christopher's with six or seven O-levels. I failed Latin, which I needed for university, and went to tutors in Redcliffe Gardens and then Holland Park. At Miss Hobbs' crammer I studied history, geography and economics at A-level. I'd been offered a place at Downing College, Cambridge, subject, of course, to getting the A-levels. Then I discovered that the college had its own entrance exams four or five weeks before the A-levels and you got the results of these within two days. If you passed the college exams, you didn't have to do the A-levels. It was a no-lose situation. I went to Downing to take the entrance exams.

Never short of confidence, I remember looking round the room at the other potential students and thinking, if these people can pass the exam, I can. And I did.

My mother kept every one of my school reports and when she died they came to me. They make interesting reading. The nicest comment was: "Michael Winner always takes up the cause of any child he thinks is unfairly treated." Some of the others were rather iffy: they said I used bad language, that I sought to draw attention to myself. The ongoing theme was: "He spends far too much time going to the cinema" — as if it was an evil influence.

LYNNE TRUSS
writer and broadcaster

It is only quite recently I became a stickler for correct punctuation. At school I regularly came a cropper with its and it's. Time again my homework would be returned with the floating apostrophe struck out and I didn't know why. Miss Fitzsimons, who took me for English, couldn't believe that my classmates and I had got as far as the fifth form without having being taught grammar. We'd been taught French and Latin grammar, but English grammar was something it was expected we'd infer from our reading. Spelling and grammar were corrected in our homework and we were supposed to learn as we went along.

I went to Tiffin Girls' Grammar in Kingston-upon-Thames, which was a pretty academic school. I liked it there because the headmistress, Miss Weedon, wasn't all that bothered about sport and I was not a great athlete. My school career began well, but then started to slip by the third or fourth years. Fortunately, I did much better when it came to A-levels.

Miss Fitzsimons was a great teacher because she taught English as a subject that you used every day, not just to pass exams. She was short with strawberry blonde hair and glasses and a bit tweedy. Occasionally she would talk about things outside the curriculum, which was unusual in those days. I remember when we were studying Shakespeare she told us about going to see Alec Guinness in *Troilus and Cressida*.

She gave us little glimpses into her world, which made me realise that what we were doing in the classroom could link into life outside school. She edited the school magazine and encouraged me to write for it. When we all went to see the film version of *Hamlet* she asked me to review the film for the magazine. It was my first commission.

Like any good teacher, when we were studying a text she would mention how other authors had written about the same topic, so if you were interested you could run off and compare them for yourself. Although she was a stickler, she had a sense of humour and I respected her and enjoyed her lessons.

There was another wonderful teacher called Mrs Cuthbertson who taught Latin. She was Czechoslovakian by birth and had a strong accent. She was married to an actor who had appeared in an edition of *Fawlty Towers* and we were all very excited when we saw him on TV.

Mrs Cuthbertson was also my form mistress one year. She was very keen on yoga and fresh air and I remember her suggesting I should do deep breathing exercises before I went to sleep. She must have thought I was a bit tense. I was quite a fearful schoolgirl and took things seriously. Once when the maths mistress wrote, "come now" on the bottom of my work I misunderstood the comment and rushed to the staff room to find her.   Looking back on my schooldays I realise that like most people then, I was conscientious and law-abiding. We were all well behaved; I don't remember anybody being rebellious. The most daring thing we did was roll up our skirts to make them shorter and I carried an airline bag instead of a satchel. Now and again if there was a lesson I really disliked – usually sport – I would stay at home and get my mother to write me an excuse note.

I was a form captain a couple of times but I was never made a prefect. Once when I was voted form captain one of the teachers asked the class to reconsider. I was probably thought to be too apathetic to be given responsibility.

It was only after I became a columnist I learned to take a stand and speak out about things like punctuation and manners as I have on radio and in my books. There was no public speaking or debating at school, but at the end of our last term my friend, Laura, and I wrote and performed a show, which Miss Fitzsimons praised.

STEVE JONES
geneticist

Ebeneezer Titus Ebenorufon Fury taught Latin at Wirral Grammar School and was, I believe, the first African teacher in a British grammar school. He was a magnetically powerful man who believed in the African method of teaching, which was basically to beat it into us. He kept discipline with the aid of a slipper and was very formal, very magnificent. We were all terrified of him.

His classes were formal; he always wore a gown. Education was chalk and talk in those days. I got beaten a number of times, but my misdemeanours were minor. I can remember Mr Fury angrily saying to me: "Jones, you were dragged up through the gutter," but I can't remember why.

I have to say I never learned much Latin because I always resented having to study it. It was compulsory because in those days the Oxford and Cambridge admission system demanded it. I found the subject boring and spent my time in class slumped reading a book. Mr Fury's nickname for me was Senex (old man). We weren't friends, but I respected him. He was frightening, but likeable and popular in his own way.

I never got my Latin O-level and my first set of A-levels were rather feeble so I re-took them while working as a fitter's mate at a power station and then managed to get into Edinburgh University to do a zoology degree. It was in Edinburgh I realised there was a big world out there about which I knew nothing.

Ebeneezer Fury was studying law while he was teaching us part-time to finance his own studies and in 1962 or 1963 he went back to Sierra Leone, just after independence, and became the Attorney General there. Then, of course, things began to go wrong rather quickly and he was fired from the government.

I had an opportunity to visit Sierra Leone in the mid-Seventies, some years after I had left school and been to university. One of the reasons I went was in the hope of coming across Mr Fury. I asked around and people were rather coy about talking about him because under the dictatorship he was not then very popular, but finally I tracked him down.

It was tragic because he had changed from being this magnificent 10ft-tall figure breathing fire I remembered to being a grey-haired and bent old man living in a slum in a small hut made of corrugated iron. Of course, he didn't recognise me, but we talked and he remembered the school well.

There is a wonderful story about Dylan Thomas: somebody goes back to his old school and asks the schoolmaster, "Do you remember young Thomas?" "Remember him?" replies the teacher, "I remember him by thousands." It's the same with my students. I have taught thousands of them and I certainly don't remember them all individually.

Some years after my visit, the story of Ebeneezer Fury ended in a very African way. I live in Camden Town in London and a man from the council came round to see me about some boring thing to do with planning. He was an African and his name was Johnson, which is a very common Sierra Leonean name. I asked if he came from Sierra Leone and if he knew Mr Fury. He looked startled and said that he did and, yes, Mr Fury was well known. He asked if I had heard what became of him. Then he explained that Mr Fury had fallen into a deep depression and ended up in a mental home where he had been murdered a few weeks before.

That this tremendously hopeful, enthusiastic young teacher in the Fifties ended up being murdered in a lunatic asylum really summarises the tragedy of Sierra Leone. If he'd stayed a teacher he might well still be around.

BETTY JACKSON
fashion designer

Having been a Brownie I knew how to thread a needle, but I couldn't sew when I was at school and I had no idea I would one day become a fashion designer. Bacup and Rawtenstall Grammar was a very academic school and art was a subject that was considered a bit of an also-ran. I took art as one of my A-levels, but not with a view to a career. I was planning to read English and history at university.

However, Jim Cawthorne, the art teacher, was a big influence. He was a flamboyant character and inspirational. He looked like a tall version of Toulouse-Lautrec in his black gown with a little beard and half spectacles. The A-level curriculum at that time involved learning about perspective and drawing things like a pot or your own hand – but he made it all exciting. He knew a lot about the theatre and music and would talk to us about the arts in general. Sometimes he did odd things. For instance, we'd be sitting in the art studio with our HB pencils poised and suddenly he'd say, "Nobody's doing anything that's remotely interesting, let's go out and run round the block. When you come back you'll all feel better." He made us look closely at things. I remember being sent off to find a bright green leaf and then being told to mix up exactly the same colour paint.

When I said I wanted to go to art school instead of university, all hell broke loose at home, but Mr Cawthorne was thrilled. I still had no idea what I wanted to do for a living, but I was a bit of a rebel and I fancied going to Hornsey College of Art where they were having a sit-in at the time. My father insisted I went to Rochdale to do a foundation course, and the most amazing thing was that when I got there I knew it was the right decision. I felt I was absolutely in the right place with the right people.

Rochdale College of Art had a fantastic still life department, fine art department, printing department and textile and embroidery section. Art was no longer just drawing and painting; a whole new world opened up. Mrs Booth was a frightening lady, but she ran an amazing department and knew everything about embroidery and the history of textiles. She taught us about machine embroidery, tapestry, collage and appliqué and I got a portfolio together which enabled me to go on to Birmingham College of Art to take a degree in fashion and textiles.

That was where I met Zandra Rhodes, who was one of the tutors. She was amazing. She used to walk through Birmingham with her bright orange-red hair and chiffon frocks causing quite a stir. Zandra was the most colourful person any of us had ever met. She wore bright green and black in layers and sometimes yellow with red or with pink, and everything was printed. We'd never seen anything quite like it. At that time (1970) everybody was into Biba and Bus Stop and muted colours.

Zandra would come in and see what we were doing, give advice and then wander off and sit down and fall asleep because she'd been up all night printing – or doing something more exciting. We used to make pilgrimages to her shop at the weekends. I bought a long white chiffon scarf with a running stitch print, which I still have.

In my final year I won the RSA student design award for women's fashion and I finally knew what I wanted to do. I was customising clothes for myself, dressing as though I'd come out of an Oxfam shop, mixing maxi skirts and stripey jumpers and prints and wearing platform-heeled boots. Then I had a bad car accident and it took me a year and a half to get going again. I came to London to work for a guy on the course who had become very successful, Adrian Cartmell. I became a freelance illustrator and joined forces with Wendy Dagworthy who was doing exciting avant-garde things, dressing a few "It Girls" and people like Roxy Music. Then I worked for Quorum for six years and finally set up on my own, with my husband, in 1981.

PAULA REGO
artist

When I was four my parents decided I should learn English and arranged for a young girl to come and take walks with me. Her name was Mary Laure Pla. She was 16 and although I didn't realise it at the time, she was my first teacher. She was nice. She told me about *Peter Pan* and about her own life and how she used to have farting competitions with her father – which shocked me. I was an only child brought up to have good manners, and extremely shy.

Then when I was eight I was sent to the local school. In Portugal at that time you only needed to go to school for two years. I was taught to dance and sing and had a wonderful time – but my parents discovered I didn't know how to read or write or do sums. So they hired a local state school teacher to tutor me at home. I had lessons in the playroom three afternoons a week, plus lots of homework.

Doña Violeta was terrifying. She was very dark with a heavy jowl, a moustache and an ample bosom. She taught me all the things I was supposed to know: the kings of Portugal, the rivers of Portugal, how to read and write and do sums. I learned my tables by heart so well that I can recite them even now. She was strict and intimidating and I was very frightened of her. If I wasn't paying attention or got something wrong she'd slap me. One day, I remember I had a dreadful headache and felt too ill to have my lesson. She got a piece of brown paper, soaked it in vinegar, and tied it to my head with a towel and I spent the whole lesson with vinegar dripping into my eyes. I hated her.

From the age of eight I'd decided I wanted to become an artist, but Doña Violeta laughed and told me my work was no good. She made me draw cups and saucers and said I didn't even shade them in properly. Thanks to her, I passed the entrance exam to go to St Julian's, an English school near Estoril, with flying colours – but I never drew cups again for a long time.

At St Julian's my art teacher was Margaret Turnbull who liked my work and encouraged me. I loved her. She did wonderful drawings in Indian ink. She encouraged me to tell stories through my work and showed me how to use oils.

Then when I was 14, Patrick Sarsfield came. He was straight out of art school, very laid back, and he encouraged me to work on a grand scale and fill an entire wall with my pictures. I was very ambitious and he described my talent as "outstanding" which fuelled my delusions of grandeur. He suggested I should come to England to train.

First, however, I was sent to a finishing school near Sevenoaks in Kent to learn to be a young lady. My mother thought it would be a good introduction to English life, rather than going straight into Bohemian art circles. It was a ghastly place, but I liked Mr Bradshaw, who taught art. He got me into the Chelsea School of Art, but somebody told my parents that a girl they knew who went there had got pregnant, so I wasn't allowed to take up my place. Instead, I was to go to the Slade which, being a university, they considered to be more respectable.

But the Slade admissions tutors didn't like my portfolio. They thought it was rubbish. Eventually, they allowed me to study part-time and I was assigned William Townsend as my tutor who was kind and encouraging, even after I left.

At the Slade I met LS Lowry, who was invited to see some of the students' work. He understood my pictures and looked at them for a long time without speaking and then said: "I couldn't do that".

Many people have taught me much over the years, but the teacher whose influence has lasted longest is the one I hated most, Doña Violeta. Thank God I never saw her again after she taught me, but she has stayed with me for ever.

PHILIP GOULD
strategy adviser to Prime Minister Tony Blair

Both my parents were teachers and education was central to their lives. My father was head teacher at the primary school I attended in Knaphill, Woking, and I was intimidated by the ambition placed upon me to do well. I was expected to sail through the 11-plus, but I was dyslexic and struggled in class.

I liked all my teachers, especially Mrs Hockley, who taught me when I was about eight. She was small with sharp features and quite scary. She was very strict, but fair, and had real authority. She really cared about the children in her class and she encouraged me.

Another teacher at that school I really liked was Barry Turner. He and his brother, Peter (who was also a teacher, but at another school), both had charisma and a huge sense of fun. Barry taught with real élan and wit and later he became a great friend of mine and of my dad.

All the time the spectre of the 11-plus, which everyone expected me to pass, was hovering over me. People went on and on about it. On the day of the exam I asked my father for some kind of talisman to hold and he gave me his pen. It was all very emotional.

I went into the examination room and glazed over completely. I thought I could recover the situation in the afternoon but when I went home for lunch I was greeted by my mother in tears and my father looking distressed. They'd seen my papers. I was obviously dead by lunchtime.

If I'd passed, I would have gone to Woking Grammar School. Having failed the exam, standing on my egalitarian instincts and against my father's wishes, I insisted on going to the local secondary modern school. It turned out to be the school from hell.

The head, a man called Barnes, flounced around in his Oxford gown and tried to run the place like a public school. But we learned nothing. There was a lot of corporal punishment. We were streamed and some of the pupils in the A stream could quite comfortably have got into university, but it was never considered. I remember being taken on a school trip to the Royal Aircraft Establishment in Farnborough and being told, as we watched men tooling away: "If you pass your O-levels, this could be your future." I decided to fail my exams.

I did pass one O-level, though – geography which was taught by Mrs Sharpe. She was another teacher who had faith in me and took the trouble to explain things.

Tom Lee, the history master known as the Friday Flogger, tried to persuade me to stay on, but I was anxious to leave. I went to Farnborough Technical College for a bit and, after a while travelling around the country on demonstrations and going to rock concerts, I got involved with Community Service Volunteers, took four A-levels and went to Sussex University to study politics and eventually to the LSE where I met Michael Oakeshott.

Through him I discovered I had some capacity for academic work after all. Suddenly I found I could read Hegel and understand. Oakeshott had a fantastic brain and was an inspirational tutor.

I went into advertising and after ten years, to the London Business School, where I met the most influential teacher I'd ever had, Professor Charles Handy. He was absolutely seminal in giving me the confidence to move from the world of advertising to politics. I became a political consultant, worked with Neil Kinnock and then Tony Blair and was also involved in both of President Clinton's campaigns.

SUSANNAH YORK
actress

I had two special teachers, one taught English and one Latin, and I am very grateful to both because from them I learned the power and the value of language.

Mr Gow, whom we called Gowdie, was the Latin master at Marr College on the west coast of Scotland. He was a magisterial figure in his black gown, with bright red hair and bristling eyebrows. He was tall and slim, looked a bit like [Peter] O'Toole and had a fierce tread as he strode along the school corridors. Even though I got the strap from him on three occasions I never bore a grudge. I was very naughty and I thought he was perfectly entitled to punish me.

Gowdie was strict and had a gift for sarcasm. We were all scared of him but he really loved Latin and loved language and he passed that on. He also loved teaching and responded positively if you'd done your homework well. You really wanted to please him, even though he was so fierce.

Another thing that was rather romantic about him and fascinated me was that according to rumour he had been a prisoner of war in Japan. We never asked him about it, of course; you didn't ask teachers personal questions in those days. I had a feeling that Gowdie liked me because I was an eager pupil and never took it amiss when I was punished. In a strange way, I think he quite enjoyed my cheekiness.

The other teacher I dearly loved was Mrs Lewis who taught English at East Haddon, the boarding school in Northamptonshire where I spent my last couple of school years. She was a wonderful teacher who, like Gowdie, didn't suffer fools and was a great disciplinarian. And, also like him, she had a keen sense of humour.

Mrs Lewis sometimes wore a black gown, but I can see her in a brown suit. She was short and plump with twinkly brown eyes in a strong face, and she walked fast. It was A-level time and she used to teach us individually in her study as well as in class. We were doing *Hamlet* and the romantic poets and she was just excellent.

Mrs Lewis's daughter, Caroline, was in my class and became my best friend. She was naughty, too, so I suppose what's why we gravitated together. We were both good at English and quite competitive.

Mrs Lewis was a playwright and she used to write funny scripts for our end of term productions. I was in everything. I'd started writing plays and producing them when I was at primary school. I remember being heartbroken when Mrs Lewis put on *The Merchant of Venice* one term and I wasn't chosen to play Shylock. Then I was mortified because Caroline got to play Portia and I was stuck with Bassanio. But the next summer I was cast as Puck in *A Midsummer-Night's Dream,* which was fine.

In the school holidays Caroline would come and stay with me and we are still good friends and meet regularly. I am godmother to her daughter and she is godmother to mine. Mrs Lewis, alas, is no longer around, but we kept in touch for many years. We all did well in our A-levels and I went on to RADA and quickly into films. I think Gowdie knew what became of me because even though I changed my name from Susie Fletcher, every now and again people from Marr College pop out of the woodwork.

When I was doing my one-woman show in Australia I got a letter from someone who had heard me talking about Gowdie and they confirmed, all those years later, that he had indeed been a prisoner in a Japanese camp.

PETER USTINOV
actor, writer, director, raconteur

My interest in education has increased enormously since I left school. I didn't enjoy Westminster much, where in my day we were absurdly dressed in tailcoat, striped trousers, top hat and carried a furled umbrella from the age of 13, but I was happy at Mr Gibbs' Preparatory School For Boys in Sloane Street, Chelsea.

Mr Gibbs, the headmaster, had a bristling white moustache and obviously had trouble shaving because he always had tufts of cotton wool on his face where he had cut himself. He used to do up my football boots for me because I couldn't tie knots and he would sing as he did so. He had Boy Scout camps in his garden which I took part in. He was rather vague and when he drove us around in his Austin 12 he would absent-mindedly change gear with my knee and be very surprised when the gear hadn't taken. I think he taught us divinity occasionally, which later on was taken over by Professor FOM Earp – known to us all as Foam.

Foam wasn't really cut out for divinity. He was a man of science. He had invented a bicycle with eight gears, but the trouble was you had to stop the bicycle before you engaged each gear. He attempted to solve Christ's miracles chemically. I remember him saying that water changing into wine was probably due to permanganate of potash deposits in the hills, that had a purple colour, being blown into the water and making it look like wine.

In chemistry lessons his experiments didn't always turn out as expected. He frightened us tremendously on one occasion when he created a colossal explosion and disappeared from sight. Suddenly, very slowly after a dramatic pause, he rose from behind his desk with a completely blackened face and his dress in disarray and demanded:"What did I do wrong?" pointing at the space between me and the next boy. When neither of us answered he told us what he had done, supposedly deliberately. He put me off chemistry completely. I can't bear the smell of sulphuric acid and all those things, which seem to me intrinsically dangerous.

On the whole, I was quiet as a schoolboy and used the fact that I was slightly prematurely corpulent and clumsy as a defence. I learned to survive by making people laugh. And although I hated cricket, I helped the school to win quite a lot of matches by some creative scoring and also distracting the attention of the other school's scorer at vital moments.

I was impatient to grow up and be my own master. School days were something to be got through. I have never quite recovered from the psychological impact of the comment on one report from Mr Gibbs which read:"This boy shows great originality, which must be curbed at all costs."

I was top in English, French, history and geography and bottom in all the other subjects, which made life difficult because the School Certificate in those days required an average in all. So I didn't take the exam. I went to drama school instead.

It wasn't until I was on a discussion show with Melvyn Bragg and two scientists many, many years later that I realised how interesting science could be. I wished then I had spent less time at school gazing out of the window. Now I am frightfully interested in education. Since I was elected Chancellor of Durham University I have learned a great deal more than most students can have done. I learned none of the languages I now speak when I was a child, apart from French.

I regret I didn't know my teachers better because when I met one of them on my *This is Your Life* TV programme I liked him very much and got on well with him. Mr Gomme, who I think taught English, surprised me by suddenly talking to my wife in perfect French and saying:"My great ambition was to be a French master, but nobody ever allowed me to."

PRUE LEITH
cookery guru, restaurateur and businesswoman

I was quite naughty at school. I was inattentive and bad at most things, especially arithmetic. I just couldn't understand the concept of units. Then when I was six or seven my parents got me a tutor: a charismatic young man called Jacky Ralfs, who taught me at the kitchen table and made learning so much fun I actually looked forward to his lessons.

Jacky Ralfs was an actor, working part time as an English teacher at a boys' school in Cheltenham to supplement his income. He was a family friend. My mother, who had her own theatre company when we lived in South Africa, and was South Africa's Edith Evans, had given him his first job.

He started off trying the classic route of two plus two, but instead of shaking his head when I didn't understand, he'd try a different technique. I remember him drawing little bags containing apples with three in one and four in another and saying: "If I gave you this bag of apples and that bag of apples, how many apples would you have?" I knew immediately. I understood perfectly when the sum was shown in practical terms.

Even at six I was interested in food. Even the geography and history I remember concerns food. I think about the vegetarian culture and how southern India is dry and people are poor so they eat rice and vegetables, but in the north where it is lush and there are cattle they get rich food.

The other thing that attracted me to Jacky Ralfs was that he was glamorous and exciting and fun. I don't think teachers realise what an influence they have on children by their own personality and charm. Jacky was good-looking, tall and dark with curly hair, twinkling eyes and a friendly, round, impish face.

He dressed as he obviously thought a teacher should look if he was playing the part on stage, in a smart tweedy jacket with a yellow waistcoat. He was good company. As well as tutoring me in maths I remember him reading poetry to me. But the most important thing I learned from him was dogged determination. We had a swingball in the garden and I wasn't very good at hitting the thing, but he encouraged me to keep on trying over and over again until I got the hang of it.

Years later when I was at a very sporty school (St Mary's, Johannesburg) and relegated to the 14th of 14 tennis courts – the one where the weeds grew and the net had holes in it – I remembered him saying: "You'd be surprised what happens if you just keep going". I resolved to run for every ball in the Jacky Ralfs manner and it paid off. I didn't end up in the top group, but I got into the second team.

In my last year at school I finally decided I had better do some work. I had long since been banned from the Afrikaans class but found I couldn't get matric without passing Afrikaans as well as the other subjects I was studying. Without Afrikaans all the effort I was putting into everything else was for naught. So I taught myself in the school library. Because the school was run by nuns we weren't allowed any girly stuff to read, but there were Afrikaans magazines about farming in the library and they had love stories in them. I learned Afrikaans from reading these rather moral stories about the romances of farmers' boys.

I followed Jacky's theatrical career for a while and I remember going to see him in *The Browning Version*. We lost touch, but all through my career I have kept a photograph of him with my mother in *The Winslow Boy* on my office wall to remind me of his wise advice.

PATRICK MOORE
astronomer

My name was down for Eton and Cambridge, but I never made either. I was ill throughout my boyhood with heart trouble and only managed one term at Dulwich College Preparatory School. In my second term I was there for one day, and that was the end of my schooldays. Then, when I was 17, war broke out. I said I was 18, manipulated the medical and joined the RAF's bomber command.

As a boy, I had a number of private tutors, but the one who stands out was the Reverend John Nissen. He was a great chap. He gave me a tremendous hand. He was the vicar at Coleman's Hatch, not far from East Grinstead, where I lived. He taught me maths, which was my weak link. I have a more or less photographic memory, so English and history were no problem, but I was never any good at maths, and I'm not now. I had to work like blazes.

Mr Nissen taught me enough to enable me to get by in the equivalent of O-level and A-level – in those days school certificate and matric. You had to pass maths, English, another language, history and one more subject – all at once. If you got five distinctions, which I did, they gave you matric on a plate. I never had to take any more exams. They gave me my Cambridge entrance by the same method.

Mr Nissen had been a science master at Lancing College, and gone into the church on his retirement. He had an infectious sense of humour and we had great fun. I was ill, and in and out of bed all through my childhood, but I managed to cycle over to the vicarage for lessons a couple of times a week. By the time I was about 15, just before I went in for the exam, I remember sitting with him in the study and he fished out an old tobacco pouch and we both filled our pipes and lit them.

I kept in touch with Mr Nissen after he stopped teaching me. He became a friend of the family. He knew what became of me, although he died many years ago. However, it wasn't due to his encouragement that I went on to write or broadcast or do any of the things I've done since. I didn't need any encouragement. My interest in astronomy was not due to his influence either. Physics was his subject. I'd been fascinated by astronomy, in which I am entirely self-taught, since the age of six, and had actually published a few papers about the surface of the moon as a boy, based on observations made with a three-inch refracting telescope I had acquired second-hand for £7 10s.

My mother, who was the greatest influence on me, was interested in astronomy and I picked up and read some of her books. The first one, which I still have, was called *The Story of the Solar System* by GF Chambers. It was an adult's book, but by the age of six I could cope with it. Then I found the companion volume, *The Story of the Stars,* which I also still have. I searched the second-hand bookshops and went on from there. I was elected to the British Astronomical Association at the age of 11.

Opposite my home in East Grinstead was a big estate built by a chap named Hanley, a multi millionaire. In his garden he had a little observatory run for him by a man called WS Franks, and when he died suddenly, Hanley asked me to run the observatory for him. So from the age of 14 I was running an observatory on my own.

Coincidentally, not long ago I gave a lecture to the British Astronomical Association in London, where I had given my first paper at the age of 13, and the subject I chose for my talk was WS Franks.

SIAN PHILLIPS
actress

Miss Joan Inkin was my first-form mistress at Pontardawe Grammar School in South Wales. She seemed very exotic because she was the only teacher in the school who wasn't Welsh. She was English, taught PE and had been trained at a terribly smart college in Denmark. Miss Inkin was attractive to me because she was so different. She looked different, she spoke differently and as well as teaching physical education, she formed my taste. She taught me not to conform to fashion, as young girls tend to do.

I didn't go to school at all for the first ten years of my life because I was ill. My mother was a brilliant teacher. She could mug up on any subject and get you through an exam. In those days if you married you had to leave the profession, so she only taught privately. At home, education was regarded above everything else.

I was something of an oddity because I got no marks in my maths paper and 100 per cent in my English paper for the grammar school entrance exams – but they gave me a scholarship. Like all the other pupils, Welsh was my first language and although all our books were in English and we had to write our essays in English, the staff often taught in Welsh, and we slipped easily between the two languages.

Miss Inkin, a middle-class Englishwoman who didn't speak Welsh, was a curiosity in this environment. Most of the teachers lived nearby but her home was some distance from the school. She spoke French and was very sophisticated and refined. She became great friends with my mother. After I left she married Brinley Rees, a gifted Welsh scholar, and we were invited to the wedding.

I worked as a child actress with the BBC and performed in many private concerts. Miss Inkin took me under her wing and changed my wardrobe. This was the age of curly perms, high-heeled shoes and tailored suits but Miss Inkin had a straight Vidal Sassoon-style haircut and always wore exquisite flat shoes and wonderful clothes. Under her influence I dressed in black ballet pumps for my concert appearances, wore my hair straight, and instead of floral frocks, had a plain navy dress with a white silk collar and cuffs.

I was incredibly busy. As well as working for the BBC and doing concerts, I stayed behind at school for choir practice, dance practice and action song practice to compete in eisteddfodau and trained for exhibition gymnastics. We also had a lot of homework. My mother insisted I stayed in the top three of the A-stream or the acting would have to stop. The staff knew the deal and helped me. Several teachers gave me private coaching during the lunch break to make up for lessons I'd missed.

It was a co-educational grammar school but the sexes weren't allowed to fraternise. Boys and girls were divided within the classroom and the playground. The staff lavished us with care and attention and put in a phenomenal amount of work on preparation and follow-up.

I had several other good teachers apart from Miss Inkin. My Latin teacher, Miss Daniels, who was very shy and rather dry, was wonderful too. She taught me for six years and I loved every lesson.

Another favourite was Miss Vivien Williams, who taught French, which I enjoyed and spoke quite fluently. She was very glamorous and wore make-up, which was unusual then. Her clothes were always up to the minute and her hair beautifully styled.

Miss Agnes Thomas, who taught biology and botany, was the pivot of my social life because she ran the Welsh youth movement, Urdd.

I wanted to go to RADA, but my mother insisted I did a degree first. I went to the University of Wales in Cardiff and wound up reading philosophy. It turned out to be a blessing – the university was just across the road from the BBC studios so I was able to have a proper job there and study at the same time. My mother always hoped I'd go off the idea of being an actress and become a teacher.

MICHAEL FISH
former weather forecaster

I was a day boy at Eastbourne College and before that at Ascham, the college's preparatory school. I had to be at school from 8am until 9pm, six days a week and I had to go in twice on Sundays. I had all the advantages of being a boarder. I was able to join in activities like debating and so forth. The only thing I missed out on was being around to take regular 6am readings for the meteorological society. But I had my own little weather station in the garden at home.

Rivers Currie, a tall, hairy Scotsman who sometimes wore a kilt, taught geography at Ascham. Probably because he was such a good teacher, it became my favourite subject. He made lessons interesting by bringing in props and he was friendly, outgoing and enthusiastic. I looked forward to his classes. I suppose weather and the climate must have been part of the syllabus, but not meteorology as I know it.

Rivers Currie was less strict than some of the masters, who frightened the life out of me. In the senior school, particularly, some were absolute terrors. As a result I failed certain subjects when it came to O-level and A-level. Caning was quite routine in both the junior and the senior schools.

At Eastbourne College the teacher I remember best is Donald Perrins, the physics master. He was ex-RAF and was head of the RAF section of the school's CCF of which I was a member. He was dark-haired, of medium build and clean-shaven.

Donald Perrins managed to keep discipline firmly but pleasantly, without having to resort to the gym shoe or the cane or the flying blackboard duster. He, too, was enthusiastic about his subject and had a way of putting things across so you remembered them.

I was interested in science and needed good A-levels in maths, physics and chemistry to get into university and join the Met Office which had become my goal in my early teens. I wanted to be an ordinary meteorologist and research scientist. There were TV weather presenters in those days, but I had no plans at all to become one. I was a reluctant TV personality; I considered myself to be a civil servant. Eastbourne College has produced several illustrious old boys – Sir Hugh Casson, for example – much better-known than I am.

Donald Perrins was an inspirational teacher and without him I would not have got the grades I needed to progress further. I was a keen student as far as maths and science were concerned because they were a means to an end. I didn't do very well in arts subjects. I studied physics at City University.

The only time I touched on meteorology at school was in CCF exercises when it was part of the background training, along with navigation, physics of flight and that sort of thing.

I bumped into Rivers Currie not long ago and I still hear of Donald Perrins because I became friendly with his daughter and her husband. He has retired now, as have most of my former teachers. Until recently I was heavily involved in the college old boys' association, organising reunions. I still keep in touch with my old prep school, too.

Looking back, however, I think my schooldays were the worst, not the best days of my life. In term time there wasn't time for anything else apart from school. We weren't allowed even to look at girls – being caught looking at or, even worse, touching a member of the opposite sex was considered a reason for a beating.

Things have changed now. The school has gone co-educational. I don't approve. I think being at a single-sex school meant I got on with my studies because there were few distractions. We were disciplined and worked hard. We had fun, but not to extremes. Eastbourne College gave me a good education, confidence, an ability to speak in public and write well, several lifelong friends and an old-boy network that is extremely useful on occasion.

COLLEEN McCULLOUGH
novelist

The best thing about being taught by nuns was that they encouraged you to do something, rather than aim solely for marriage and children. I was a child of the Depression, when university wasn't the norm, especially in Australia. But the nuns encouraged all of us to go to university.

My parents were station hands in New South Wales and I moved from one rural convent school to another until I was 12 and went to High Cross College in Sydney. It was an intellectual school and I was a bluestocking. The school was in one of the ritziest areas of the city and was fee-paying. I was there on a scholarship. I was in a class of 21, all of whom went on to become Somebodies. One became a doctor, one a veterinarian, one a violinist, another the chief archivist of the Commonwealth Bank of Australia.

My school years contained a number of good teachers and several were memorable, if only for their own personal hang-ups.

Old Sister Benedict, for example, who taught maths, hated the idea of any of us wearing trousers and would say: "If you wear slacks, I'll give you smacks." She was a holy terror, very irascible, short-tempered and would jump up and down and yell and scream at the drop of a hat.

Sister Immaculata, who taught chemistry, was a jolly person, but impossible to please. Even when three of us in the class came first, second and third in the state in our matriculation exams, she didn't seem impressed. She had whiskers, which fascinated me, and was very good at basketball.

Sister Teresa, who also taught chemistry, and I think, physics as well, was very beautiful. She was much younger than the other nuns and had a sweet nature. She was very dark, perhaps of Italian origin.

Then there was Sister Ignatius who was very old and the head of the school. She taught English and warned us: "Woe betide the girl I catch reading Georgette Heyer. She is utterly immoral." At the time I remember I was reading a banned novel called *Love Me, Sailor* – replete with four-letter obscenities and graphic descriptions of sex. She thought we should stick to respectable Jane Austen, Dickens and Hardy and such writers.

The nuns were Sisters of Mary so they all wore black habits with a traditional wimple. The school uniform was quite attractive. The tunic was well-cut with pleats at the side and was a beautiful shade of pinkish brown. We wore fawn shirts and a brown tie with a red and fawn stripe, and panama hats, fawn lisle stockings and brown lace-up shoes.

In our final year we had to go to school on Saturdays and were allowed to wear our home clothes, but there were strict rules about what was appropriate. Dresses must never be low cut and always had to have sleeves. One Saturday the glamour puss of the class arrived in a dress which was by no means low cut, but the nuns sewed crêpe paper round the neck and put in crêpe paper sleeves.

I was never top of the class because I refused to do well in religion and that irritated the nuns. I could score close to 100 per cent in every other subject, but in religion I always got 50 per cent. My family were atheists and I went home from suffocating religion to an atheistic household. I succeeded at school despite my teachers and became a neurophysiologist.

I don't look back fondly on my schooldays, but the nuns did give me a valuable piece of advice. Catherine Gaskin, who had been a few classes ahead of me, wrote *This Other Eden* when she was 16 and knowing I also wrote, they advised me not to attempt to publish until I was into my thirties, otherwise I would not be able to cope with success. My first novel, *Tim*, came out when I was 34 and *The Thorn Birds* when I was 40.

NIGEL PLANER
actor

I had two special teachers and interestingly one taught art and English, which were my favourite subjects, and one, maths which was my least favourite.

Lenny – John Leonard had a goatee beard and mad hair, was tall and bony and had patches on the elbows of his baggy tweed jackets. He was a real Mr Chalkdust. He was also an inspirational teacher. He taught me art, English and Latin up to the age of 13 at King's House School in Richmond, Surrey. I forgave him the Latin, which I don't think he enjoyed any more than we did, because of his enthusiasm and encouragement in the other subjects.

He loved murals and had decorated the school with his frescoes of Tuscan landscapes. In art lessons he would give you a brief and if you wanted to do something different, far from repress you, he would become very excited about it. I remember once drawing a huge picture of Galileo and his telescope, which was much larger than life-size, and Lenny mounted it on a board and got it put up in the school hall where it remained for years, until it was destroyed in a fire.

I'd been acting in the local amateur group since the age of eight and Lenny encouraged me to take part in school drama productions and puppet shows. In English lessons he had a clever technique for encouraging us to read. He'd pick up a book and start reading to us then, just as it was getting interesting, he would close the book and move on to something else so we were motivated to finish the book for ourselves.

At my next school – Westminster – the teacher whom I remember fondly taught maths, my worst subject. I was in the bottom stream and the moment they got onto calculus I was lost. Mr Fox was a young chap with a bushy moustache, probably in his first teaching post, who took the top grade maths people and because he was just starting out, they had given him the bottom group as well. He was a maths genius and he achieved something brilliant – he got me through maths O-level.

At our first lesson he announced: "I know you don't like this subject, so tell me what you do like." I said I liked painting and drama and somebody else said football. Then he explained that he was as passionate about maths as we were about the things we'd chosen and he would set aside the first 25 minutes of the double maths lesson every Monday for us to try to convince him what was so special about what interested us. The deal was that in return he demanded our 100 per cent undivided attention and effort while he explained what was so amazing about maths.

He was incredibly patient. If we didn't understand when he explained one way, he would try a different route. It wasn't just blackboard and bookwork. I remember him taking us out into the playground to demonstrate, by standing us in various positions, how angles worked.

I didn't keep in touch with Mr Fox when I left the school, but Lenny came to see me in a play once. Both Lenny and Mr Fox gave me empowerment, instilled in me the sense of "I can do this." One other teacher gave me that feeling and I am still in touch with him and we have become friends. Christopher Martin taught French at Westminster and I was in a production of *Waiting for Godot* in French, which he directed. I remember him particularly because of the way he inspired me on the sports field.

I was a fat child and dreaded athletics. I was always at the back of every race, with the asthmatic boys. In one 440 yard race, Christopher Martin, who was very fit, ran round the field just ahead of me, encouraging me by insisting: "You can do it. You can do a personal best." I have never forgotten that.

DOWAGER DUCHESS OF DEVONSHIRE

My five sisters and I were educated at home by a succession of governesses to whom we behaved very badly. We were absolutely insufferable. They were all perfectly nice young women, but we ganged up against them. There was a formal list of things we were to be taught, based on PNEU (Parents National Educational Union), but as far as I remember most of the time we played cards. It was good fun and made me very good at *Racing Demon*, but wasn't what we were supposed to be doing.

I remember one of these governesses – Miss Hussey – because she stayed two years, which was a record. She was an anonymous-looking woman with brown hair and a beige face. She wore no make-up because it was against the rules and she dressed in tweeds. She had been in India and used to tell us about it until we yawned with boredom.

My mother was my first teacher. She taught us all to read and spell and then when we were seven we went into the schoolroom to be taught by the governess. I did go to boarding school in Oxford for two wickedly awful days, but I didn't like it. I fainted in geometry and was sent home, thank God.

I learned much more from my family and people like the groom, the blacksmith, the cowman and the gardener, than I ever learned in the schoolroom.

My best friend and one of my best teachers was Charles Hooper, our groom. He had suffered terribly from shell shock in the First World War and he used to lose his temper with my sisters who weren't good riders, but he was always very kind to me because I adored the horses and everything to do with them. I learned from him about life and death and the seasons; he showed great patience with me. I suppose I was his favourite because I was the youngest and I was interested in what he was interested in.

I also adored the blacksmith, though I'm afraid I can't now remember his name. He was a lay preacher and very clever. He wasn't educated in the conventional sense, but he knew everything. From him I learned patience as I watched him work with the iron, shoeing the horses. He would try to talk to me about religion sometimes, but I'm afraid I was only interested in the animals.

Constable, the cowman, taught me how to milk cows and I was allowed to put my finger in the cream in the dairy – something that is absolutely taboo now. My mother kept some beautiful cows and I was fascinated by the cowshed and everything that went on there.

Most of my sisters' friends turned out to be intellectuals, such as Waugh, Acton and Betjeman. The two men with the best manners I have ever seen were Harold Macmillan and Sir Oswald Mosley, my sister, Diana's husband. You could learn a lot just by watching them. My husband was incredibly clever. His great interest was politics and he was completely brilliant at it and always ten jumps ahead. I learned a lot from him. And my father [Lord Redesdale] taught me a certain amount about running an estate, which has been useful at Chatsworth. He was a real countryman and understood the people who worked the land.

These days I think children's lives are ruined by exams. They are such a cause of unhappiness. I suppose there has to be a system of employing people by exam results, but all they tell you is what has been bunged into their heads. They don't tell you if they are honest, can get on with people, are truthful, show discretion, cheerfulness and punctuality. You don't learn those things from exams. Look at somebody entirely self-taught such as Joseph Paxton who was the son of a gardener. He was made head gardener here at 23, went on to be a railway engineer, built the Crystal Palace and became an MP. I consider people like him to be clever, not people who have passed exams.

RANULPH FIENNES
explorer

One of my first French masters at Eton was a man called David Cornwell who became a writer, changed his name to John le Carré and left. Then David Callender took over. He became my appointed senior teacher and had the unenviable job of trying to help me to get the five O-levels and two A-levels I needed to get into Sandhurst. The only thing I ever wanted to do was to be a regular army officer.

Eventually it was realised that I was very badly designed for understanding maths or sciences so I was switched to languages and David Callender taught me French, English and German after school in a small group at his home. Occasionally his wife would give us tea.

Mr Callender was so good at his job that I actually found for the first time that I was competent at something. I enjoyed German and was good at it and I discovered I had a talent for writing.

One project he set was to select a book and précis the whole thing in a certain number of words. I chose the autobiography of a Russian Englishman,

Serge Obolensky, called *One Man in his Time* and I had about a week to reduce around 100,000 words to 2,000, keeping in all the salient points and cutting out the less relevant ones. I found it challenging and satisfying and being used to teachers being honest, and therefore rude about things I did, I bathed in the obviously genuine praise I got for this particular project. It gave me confidence and I thought, "Gosh, I'm going to be good at English" and I realised I could write. Everything I have done since has been thanks to David Callender's inspiration.

Before I came under his tuition, I had a sense of failure at school. I didn't think I was ever going to get one O-level, never mind five. In fact I eventually got four. Even though I went to a crammers, I didn't manage to pass any A-levels. So I didn't get to Sandhurst. Instead I took a short service commission and joined the Royal Scots Greys and later, the SAS.

About a year after I left Eton I went back to the school with some friends and disrupted the Fourth of June celebrations. The night before the famous fireworks and procession of boats, using underwater equipment, we laid ropes and hooks. Then, when the Eights stood up in their narrow boats to throw their hats into the air, we livened up the proceedings by overturning their craft.

Unfortunately, my diving equipment went wrong and I shot to the surface and was chased by couple of motor boats driven by the Etonian river masters – one of whom was Dave Callender. I headed for the bank and some overhanging trees where I got rid of the air cylinder. I found it difficult to run in a frog suit, so when a group of senior boys was put ashore to chase me, I lay in a puddle, with my nose just above the water level. Eventually I got back to the car and changed.

Unfortunately, the abandoned air cylinder, which I had borrowed from my then girlfriend (later my wife), had a number on it and I thought I would be in serious trouble from prospective father-in-law and others if it was found. I fooled one of the boys into giving me a lift to pick it up by saying I was an Eton boy and I'd seen some hoodlums with an air bottle on the other bank and I was going to take it back to Mr Callender. Because I was able to mention his name, they believed me and I got away with it.

About 15 years later I told this story in one of my books and some years after that when another of my books became a best seller, Mr Callender wrote to me and invited me to visit. He was very friendly and charming and we laughed about the incident with the boats, but I'm not sure he had always found it amusing.

MARSHA HUNT
singer, actress and writer

There have been three special people in my life and each of them represented a new beginning in my education. Ruth Pchelkin taught me in ninth grade at school, Thom Gunn was one of my lecturers at university and David Toguri was the dance master when I was in *Hair*.

Ruth taught English at Oakland High, California, and was the first teacher to appreciate that I was different. Instead of wanting me to conform, she encouraged me to be different. I grew up in Philadelphia and coming from the East Coast made me stand out. I had a different accent, came from an all-girls' school, was less relaxed than my peers and was one of only 25 Negroes among 3,000 students. I became president of my class and was very involved, but at the same time I was very separate. I didn't move with the crowd.

My father was a psychiatrist who'd been to Harvard and my mother was one of the first black librarians in Philadelphia. I was a diligent student and was expected to be. At that time if you came from a Negro family the way to succeed was to sing, tap dance or box, or become a doctor or a lawyer. High achieving at school was what I was supposed to do. My brother and sister and I were all expected to become doctors.

Ruth Pchelkin was divine and I use that word in its religious sense. She was quiet and stern, but generous with her time and she was constantly trying to expand the world for me. I would write essays for her and instead of grading them by grammar and spelling, she always looked for content and creativity. It was she who got me writing. A few years ago I tried to find her because I wanted to tell her I'd become a professional writer and ask her if she would like to read some of my books, but I couldn't find her.

Thom Gunn, the poet, lectured at the University of California when I was there and seemed to me a very exotic creature. He came to school on a motorbike in his black leather gear and was fabulously good-looking. He was the first Englishman I met. He was also gay, though I didn't know it at the time. He taught a course on TS Eliot's *Notes Towards the Definition of Culture* and I was fascinated and hung on his every word. I was attracted by Thom's difference from all the other tutors just as I was attracted to Ruth because of the different way she taught me.

I never finished my degree because I got caught up with the Free Speech movement and student sit-ins and took a term off to come to England. I figured I'd wash dishes, wait tables or babysit to work my way around the country, but I met another American student who told me about a job going for a singer in a band at £5 a week. I went along for an audition and ended up joining Alexis Korner's trio. I was spotted by Long John Baldry and joined his group (which included Reg Dwight, later known as Elton John). Then, when I was unsuccessfully searching for an au pair job to earn the money to pay my fare home to go back to university, I heard about auditions for *Hair* and joined the show.

David Toguri was the dance master. He was Japanese-Canadian and came from a family of doctors. Most of us in the show weren't actors; we'd been recruited from the music business, and it was his job to train us. David was the person who taught me what some people describe as confidence, but I think of as self-awareness. His rehearsals weren't just about movement and dancing; he wanted to understand your motivation as a performer, to know why you moved in a particular way. It was an awakening. I'd been singing in bands for nearly two years, but when I left *Hair* after six months to go solo I'd learned from David how to project myself from a stage. I am very competitive and on stage with 25 people I was still that child who thought she had to get A grades and who wanted to get A grades.

NED SHERRIN
producer, performer, writer, director,

My school days were the happiest days of my life. I went to Sexey's in Somerset as a weekly boarder and enjoyed it enormously. My father was a farmer but I didn't like getting my hands dirty and found it easier to be a swot. I was a goody-goody at school, and pushy. When I reached the sixth form I thought I'd have to study chemistry, physics and biology like everyone else because there was no arts sixth at Sexey's. After one term I realised this was counter-productive – I was never going to get anywhere if I was restricted to these appalling subjects. A conspiracy with three teachers, Messrs Brockhouse, Morgan and Williams, led to a successful coup and the establishment of an arts sixth form with one pupil. Me.

Manipulating my divorce from science was not easy. The school, which had been founded in 1898 as Sexey's Trade School, had never taught arts subjects beyond School Certificate and the headmaster, Mr Page, a physicist himself, was reluctant. I shudder to think what would have become of me without my three allies.

The only aspect of science I was interested in was botany. Pressing flowers had always been something of a passion, so I did botany and Latin as subsidiary subjects, and history and English as my major ones for Higher School Certificate.

Eric Brockhouse taught history in a spirited and lively manner. He was keen on cricket and football, as I was. He was English. The other two teachers in the conspiracy were Welsh. EA Morgan taught Latin and DJ Williams, English. Later in life when he had retired to Bournemouth, Mr Williams used to write me rather pained and disappointed letters because he thought *That Was the Week* was subversive. More in sorrow than in anger, he suggested it was a pity how I had turned out.

Mr Williams had a Welsh freedom with words. He was a dapper little man who wore striped suits and a gown. He was a great chapel-goer and a bachelor. I think his sentiments were more left-wing than mine. I was a stern unbending Tory even then and we used to tease each other a bit.

There was no dramatic tradition at Sexey's in my time. The nearest we got to it was an annual end-of-term concert. I was particularly proud of a platinum blond wig made out of binder twine from the farm which I wore in productions. I thought it was the last word in realism.

We had school outings to the Bristol Old Vic and to the Shakespeare Memorial Theatre at Stratford-upon-Avon. I remember seeing Godfrey Tearle and Diana Wynyard in *Macbeth*. With a party of Sexey boys, I also saw Peter Brook's production of *The Winter's Tale* with a young Paul Schofield as the shepherd.

English and history came easily to me. I had no natural aptitude for languages, but I needed Latin to go to Oxford – which I arrogantly expected to do. EA Morgan got me through. I was terribly behind, so I sometimes had extra tuition outside school hours. Mr Morgan was tall and bald, and dressed in sports coats and flannels. He, too, was a chapel man. I think he relished the chance to teach Latin; I was the only pupil studying the subject at that time.

My older brother, Alfred, was three years ahead of me and at first I was given the nickname Trailer because I followed him around. Alfred wasn't interested in school and at weekends was keen to get home to the farm whereas I would have been happy to have stayed over.

Thanks to Messrs. Brockhouse, Morgan and Williams I passed Higher School Certificate and got a county scholarship and a state scholarship to Oxford to read history or English or both.

Then my father found out there was a thing called a means test and unfortunately he would have to pay anyway. He thought that studying history and English would inevitably lead me to becoming a schoolmaster and he had a profound contempt for schoolmasters. So I said I'd read law instead. That was all right.

ANNA MASSEY
actress

spent most of my school life at a little school in Chelsea run by two sisters, Dorothea and Lillian Mitford-Colmer. Dorothea taught arithmetic and Lillian geometry and algebra. Lillian made the quest of what "x" was and the shape of the triangle and the parallelogram so exciting that I excelled in these subjects and often came top of the form. Her lessons were always fun and never seemed like hard work. She taught me to think logically, which has been tremendously useful in the hard times in my life.

She was a big woman but she thought she was rather elegant, so moved like a sort of hefty gazelle. She had masses of hair swept up at different angles with hairpins which kept falling out, and terrible teeth. Her sister, as I remember, looked like a kindly witch and always had a drip on the end of her nose.

Both women were probably in their sixties and although Lillian was younger, she was the headmistress, so we were rather in awe of her. Algebra was her favourite subject and she made it a lot of people's favourite, too. She had a phenomenally beautiful smile which she flashed if you found out that $x = 9$ or whatever. She and I had a good rapport because I worked hard and always conformed.

I was a shy and anxious child, but with a terrible temper which never came out at school, only at home with my beloved nanny, Gertrude Burbidge, who was the mainstay of my life and stayed with me until her death in 1968. My only fault at school was that I never stopped talking. I was often put in the corner or given a detention mark. At my first school, Miss Betts' nursery, I can remember spending much of my time under a table in the corner of the room, which was the punishment for talking in class.

Most of the children at the Mitford-Colmers' school were the sons and daughters of diplomats. There were never more than ten in a class and later on, only about five. It was multi-racial and multi-religious. I was in a class with girls from China, India and Japan. My parents had separated when I was a baby and both remarried. I had breaks in my education when I went to school in America or had governesses, but I spent most of my time with the Mitford-Colmers from the age of six until I was 15.

I spent one term at Brillamont in Lausanne where I was desperately unhappy. I was so miserable mother got Dirk Bogarde to write to me to try to cheer me up. But nothing would have cheered me up; I just wanted to be at home. We had to speak French all the time at Brillamont and I made little progress – but I did learn the facts of life from other girls in the dormitory, something I would never have been taught at school.

After I left the Mitford-Colmers I was sent to be "finished" in Paris and Rome. In Paris I stayed with Madame Verlet, whom I hated. She was stern and cold and snobbish. I had lessons at the Alliance Française in the mornings and in the afternoons went to the theatre. In Rome I stayed with the Grossi family and had a good tutor in Mary Cavaletti who took me on tours of the city and taught me about architecture and paintings.

It was always assumed that I would act, but there was never any plan to send me to drama school. Acting was in my blood. I sat at the table at home and saw plenty of actors acting all the bloody time. I was going into repertory, but then I was offered the leading role in William Douglas-Home's new play, The Reluctant Debutante.

I had a number of voice teachers who couldn't teach before Iris Warren came into my life when I was 18 or 19 and showed me how to release my vocal capacity, liberate my imagination and alleviate the terrible panic and fear of stage fright. Her lessons were invigorating. Rather like an analyst, Iris dealt with all her pupils slightly differently and I use the exercises she taught me to this day.

TOM PARKER BOWLES
restaurant critic and food writer

My memories of schooldays are based almost entirely around food. My abiding memory of prep school is of hunger. The food was crap, but we each had a patch of land and I remember growing carrots and cress and radishes and lots of things that I could eat.

The head of gardening at Summerfields was the Rev Willie Pryor, a classic eccentric who also taught divinity, geography and science in my first two years at the school. He had a shock of white hair, dressed in tweeds and rode everywhere on his bicycle. He started a group called the Wombles and had us going round Oxford picking up litter. He taught by telling stories. When we learned about condensation and precipitation, for instance, he talked about Captain Raindrop and Cirrus the Wisp. To illustrate what happens when heat rises, he smoked his pipe in the classroom. Occasionally he would lose his temper and scream and shout, but he was never scary and was an incredibly nice man.

At Eton I was lucky because my housemaster, Dr Atkinson, was a foodie so on Sundays instead of being served those awful vacuum packed slices of unidentifiable grey meat, he'd make sure we had a roast.

I floated through most of my schooldays with absolutely no record of any merit whatsoever, ether academic or sporting. I passed my exams but I was awful at maths and science. I became more confident as I grew older and the more I specialised, the easier life became. But I always enjoyed English and I had a very good teacher at A-level called Angus Graham-Campbell. He was the first teacher I met who treated you as an adult and spoke to you naturally and honestly. The first book we did with him was *Emma*. It was the first Jane Austen novel I had studied in depth and it became one of my favourite books.

Mr Graham-Campbell was one of the younger brigade of masters at Eton and he stood out as an individual as well as a teacher. He had grey curly hair and there was a rumour that he had been a bit of a hippie in his youth. He'd been at Eton in the Sixties and Seventies and had a broader outlook than most of the masters. He wrote plays for radio, and being a dramatist made him more interesting.

He had a relaxed, university style of teaching. He would sit in the middle of the room tipping back on his chair, probably take off his tie, and encourage us to give our opinion of a particular piece of writing. He never preached, never told you what you should or shouldn't think. He would gently push you, explaining: "This is what some people think and this is what other people think. Tell me what you think." He was full of wonderful theories. I remember, for instance, him explaining why he thought Prince Eddy was Jack the Ripper.

On one occasion he arranged an Austenesque banquet where we ate and drank the sort of things they would have had in Regency times. We had lots of different courses, based on a picnic at Box Hill.

In my final school year we had to choose one extra curricular activity, which could be anything from mechanics to Chinese. I picked cookery, which was taught by Mrs Noakes who was young and blonde and pretty. It was a good gig and a great escape from the formality of the classroom. Mrs Noakes was married to one of the English masters and we went to their house where she taught us how to chop onions and to make classic dishes – everything from soufflés to coq au vin and fresh pasta. We cooked these delicious things and then ate what we had made. It was great fun.

My mother had taught me basic cooking skills and a love of food. She is very good at roasts; not so good at pastries and cakes. As a child I watched and stirred and ate. We lived in the country on a farm so enjoyed seasonal meat and vegetables and always had home made bread. My favourite dish was my mother's speciality: chicken roasted with a lemon shoved up its arse.

CANDIDA LYCETT GREEN
author and journalist

My first influential teacher was Mrs Taylor who taught me read and to knit and do cross-stitch. I was five and I can still remember the excitement of reading about Mr Lobb who did pretty dull things like going to the shops and having tea, in words of about four letters. There were only nine of us in the class at the little village school in Farnborough in the Berkshire Downs. Mrs Taylor was tall and thin and stood with her back to the huge stove in the corner of the classroom. She was very enthusiastic and her lessons were jolly. We sang a lot of songs. I remember one that went: *"Down in the valley grandma used to tell there was a chalet with a quaint old wishing well..."*

My next special teacher was Sister Sylvia, the sprightly art mistress at a convent school called Great Oaks in Goring and Streatley. She was incredibly patient and gave me confidence that I could paint. I remember when I was about 11 taking a whole term to produce an oil painting of a geranium in a terracotta pot. She was a brilliant artist herself. I still have a wonderful drawing she did in my autograph book of rabbits dressed up in clothes under a tree, as good as anything by Beatrix Potter.

At St Mary's, Wantage, there was a history teacher called Miss Phillips who fired me up about history to the extent that I am still fascinated by every aspect of the 18th century. She was an enormous woman with a theatrical delivery who made stories of battles come to life. Her animated teaching style was in sharp contrast to 90 per cent of the other teachers, who were deadly dull. Judith Keppell, who won the jackpot on *Who wants to be a Millionaire?*, was in my class and I think the reason she got that important final history question right was because Miss Phillips imbued it into her.

There was also a very good art mistress at St Mary's called Miss Wimperis who once wrote on one of my reports: "Candida works quickly and well." My dad [John Betjeman] was so proud of that comment, he repeated it forever more. My school reports were always terrible. I was sacked from St Mary's in the end. I went off with a boy at the school dance and didn't return until midnight and the school closed at 11 o'clock. I was a bad influence in class. I enjoyed breaking rules. My father was a school governor which was useful because we got butter instead of margarine after I complained to him. He hated margarine himself. He was quite famous when I was at St Mary's and a lot of the teachers were in love with him so they sucked up to me, hoping to get to him through me.

In general, my memories of school are of wonderful friends and general evasion of everything else, though I was quite good at French and games. I was in the first lacrosse team. After O-levels I was packed off to a tutorial in London which was disastrous because I didn't turn up to lessons. I took a secretarial course and worked for Richard Ingrams at *Private Eye* where I stapled together the first copy of the magazine. Richard still reads all the books I write and corrects them for me like a schoolmaster. Mark Boxer, for whom I wrote my first book, *English Cottages,* was another fantastic teacher. He was a perfectionist who made me rewrite and rewrite until I got it exactly right.

All these people have been inspirational, but I have learned most from my parents. My father taught me to be confident in doing my own thing and to trust my eye, that it was important, for instance, to know that you liked a painting, not who it was by. He was constantly saying: "Well done", and I believed him. My mother taught me about wild flowers and to cook and passed on to me her love and understanding of horses. She took me on art tours of Italy as a grumpy teenager. They both stood up for what they believed in and taught me to be brave in my convictions and I'm not a herd follower as a result.

MICHAEL HOLROYD
biographer

Peter Spanoghe was an extraordinary, intuitive teacher in what I think was a non-vintage period in teaching in Britain, shortly after the War. Unfortunately I didn't encounter him until towards the end of my school career at Eton which can best be described as "discreet".

Peter Spanoghe taught languages, but he brought in history and literature as well. He told a story and you wanted to know what happened next. From having not been very distinguished in class, suddenly I was top in French. Normally I was bored in lessons, but he made them sing. I don't know how he did it; it was like a conjuring trick. He pared back the cuticle of boredom.

His subjects were German, French and English and he slipped easily between them depending on what happened during the lessons, what people responded to. Lessons didn't seem to be pre-planned in a didactic way; they had an evolutionary quality.

Until I was taught by Peter Spanoghe, I didn't know I had a talent for languages. I had been somewhat paralysed with shyness because my mother spoke seven languages and danced on tables and exchanged jokes with waiters with a glass of champagne in her hand, and did all the things that make a 14 or 15-year-old acutely embarrassed. Mr. Spanoghe released me from my shyness. It was as if he had a magic key. He was quick-witted and made lessons fun. I wasn't frightened of making a fool of myself. He made you laugh, so it didn't matter if you said something incorrect because that was part of the trial and error of the lesson.

Although he walked with a pronounced limp, he was nevertheless one of the most active people in the school. His whole body was full of vitality. He would lean forward and look you straight in the eye. He was married to a beautiful woman in a wheelchair. He left the school soon after I did. I learned some years later that he had had an operation and his leg worked again.

I saw him once in the street in Chelsea and I wanted to go up and say thank you, but that old shyness that he had once allowed me to get rid of, returned and I very much regret that I didn't speak to him. Some years later I thought I'd check to see if his name was in the London telephone book. It was and I rang but there was no answer, so I wrote. His widow got in touch with me and said he had died three or four months before, so I'd missed him a second time.

As well as his teaching, I should like to have thanked him for a letter he wrote to my housemaster, RJN Parr, known as Purple Parr, in which he described me as "a promising tortoise ....not nearly at his peak." Previous reports had emphasised rather less appealing aspects of my "doubtful temperament."

Purple Parr, a portly, well-waistcoated and bespectacled man with a very red face, taught mathematics. He was discouraging. Even when he said something which was intended as praise, it turned out disparaging. He couldn't help himself. He'd say things like: "You did rather well – but of course it was a particularly easy paper this year."

Even worse, though, was Bloody Bill, (HK Marsden), a tall, bent grim- visaged, churlish, prying mathematics teacher with a relish for power and a devotion to the theory and practice of corporal punishment. I didn't see much of him, thank God.

Another teacher I admired and who brought his subject to life, was Sydney Watson. He ran the Eton College Musical Society. He, too, made things fun, and was encouraging. If something wasn't very good, he'd say: "That's not at all bad, but we can do better." And you felt, "Yes, I can do better." Like Peter Spanoghe, he also leapt around a lot.

I had two places at university to study science on the recommendation of my father who thought that was where the future lay, but I turned away from doing something in which I had no natural interest. Instead, I continued my education at Maidenhead Public Library, while pursuing careers in law, the military, and eventually, writing.

JOSEPHINE COX
novelist

Miss Jackson was very prim and proper. She was a spinster who didn't have a sense of humour or a huge personality and didn't really know how to handle children. But somehow she and I were on the same wavelength. She had an uncanny way of knowing if you were worried or frightened or were itching to ask a question. I felt myself drawn to her and where I might be terrified of asking questions of some of the other teachers without being invited to, I wouldn't hesitate to ask Miss Jackson.

She was my English teacher from the age of seven to nine at St Anne's School on the outskirts of Blackburn. She was painstakingly thorough and very patient. She wasn't a sweet old lady, although she looked like one. She was small and wore long panelled tweed skirts and hand-knitted jumpers. Her short, permed hair was pushed behind her ears, and she had vivid blue eyes that would pick you out right across the room. When you least expected it, she would pounce on you and ask: "What did I just say?" and you would freeze. She was known as Snake-tongued Jackson because she could cut you in half with her tongue.

Miss Jackson instilled in me a love of literature and words. We had no books at home because it was all mum could do to shoe us and clothe us (I was one of ten children). One day after school Miss Jackson called me over and asked if I would like to borrow some of her books. She took me to her home, a tiny little house down a little back alley and everything in the house was just like her, all in perfect order, absolutely pristine.

I think the first book I borrowed was a collection of Wordsworth's poetry – carefully covered in brown paper. My great favourite was Charles Dickens' *Oliver Twist*. Some of the books she lent me were a bit above me and when I took them back she always asked me to tell her honestly what I thought of them and she was sympathetic if I said I didn't like something.

One Friday she asked us all to collect jam jars over the weekend and told us we would get a halfpenny for small ones and a penny for big ones. Being naïve I spent my entire weekend collecting jam jars in my little brother's pram, thinking I was going to be rich. I had so many jars the conductor wouldn't let me on the bus with them on the Monday morning, so I walked the four miles to school, dragging two sacks full of jam jars along. Miss Jackson took me up on stage in assembly and proudly told everyone how much money I had raised – for charity!

I used to write stories about my granddad and his little Scots terrier, Monty, telling of their imaginary adventures. When I was about nine I won a competition for one of these stories and in assembly Miss Jackson handed me my prize and told everyone: "One day the whole world will read Josephine's stories."

Thirty-five years later when my first novel was published I was sitting in WH Smith's in Blackburn signing books when I heard a voice say: "Hello Josephine." I looked up and there was Miss Jackson, looking exactly the same as I remembered her. I had mentioned her by her nickname in the book, thinking she was no longer around, and she was absolutely furious.

What had enraged her most was being mentioned without her permission. I felt like a nine-year-old again, trying to hide behind the desk. Eventually my brother, Bernard, who was with me, managed to calm her down by telling her: "If it wasn't for you, our Josie wouldn't be a writer." A smile crossed her mouth and after we took her for a cup of tea and a slice of cake, everything was fine.

DICKIE BIRD
umpire

Arthur "Pop" Hudson did more than anyone to encourage my interest in sport. He was the games master at Raley Secondary Modern School in Barnsley, south Yorkshire, but he also took us for English and, if I remember correctly, for geography.

He was a tall man, over 6ft, and a fitness fanatic. He played a lot of cricket himself. He was in a team called Wombwell Main in the Yorkshire league known as the Yorkshire Council. Every day at lunchtime, and sometimes even in the breaks between lessons, whatever the weather, Arthur Hudson would be in the playground with a bat and ball in the summer and a football in the winter, organising practice sessions. He gave us so much encouragement; I think that's how he got the nickname Pop, because he was like a father figure to us.

Tommy Taylor, who went on to become a Manchester United and England centre-forward, was at school with me and also received a lot of support from Pop Hudson. Sadly, Tommy was one of the Busby Babes who lost their lives in the 1958 Munich air disaster. He was the best centre-forward I've ever seen. He played 19 times for England and scored 18 goals.

Another well-known sportsman, Arthur Rowe, was at Raley with us. He went on to represent England in the shot putt in the Rome Olympics. I definitely think it was due to the encouragement of Pop Hudson that so many of us were keen on sport.

I wasn't very good at other things at school, but I became captain of both cricket and football. I was probably actually better at football but I damaged my right knee and after that stuck to cricket. I was a star batsman and bowler at schoolboy level. When I was 15 I played for Barnsley Cricket Club (alongside Geoff Boycott and Michael Parkinson) in the summer and Barnsley Football Club in the winter, but for a Yorkshireman cricket always has to come first. It's the ambition of every schoolboy in Yorkshire to play for his county at cricket. I've kept every newspaper cutting that mentioned my matches.

Another teacher I remember well was Harold Rushworth, who joined the school towards the end of my time there, and helped Pop Hudson on the sports field. Both men gave me, and the other boys, the enthusiasm and willpower to want to succeed and a belief in ourselves.

I'll remember them both as long as I live. I kept in touch with them after I'd left school, but they are both dead now. I will always be grateful to them. If it hadn't been for their encouragement, I could have ended up down a coal mine like my father.

The only prizes I ever won at school were for sport. In lessons I was always thinking about football or cricket and longing for the time when I could go out and join Pop Hudson in the playground or on the sports field. I once got six of the best from the headmaster, Henry Bird (no relation), for playing truant when a group of us went to watch England play Australia at Headingley.

The day before I left school, the head sent for me and said: "I've got some advice for you, Dickie. If I were you, I'd stick to sport and try to make a living out if it. You're not much good at anything else." It was good advice. And who would have guessed that my autobiography would have sold a million copies and become the best-selling sports book? That's not bad for a lad from a secondary modern school who wasn't much good at his lessons.

PENNY VINCENZI
novelist

I dangled in disgrace face down over Miss Crumpler's knee many a time. I was always getting into trouble at school for talking and the punishment for being naughty was very simple – you were hung over Miss Crumpler's lap for the whole lesson and she carried on teaching as if you didn't exist.

She was a very large lady with twinkly eyes who wore stout shoes and long skirts and her grey hair in a bun. She ruled us with a rod of iron. She was my first teacher when I arrived at a little dame school called The Haven in Parkstone, near Bournemouth, at the age of five.

At the end of term, and I think at half term, every child went individually to see the headmistress, Miss Lawrence, to be tested in reading, sums and spelling. She had a stop watch with which she timed how many difficult words you could read in a minute.

Miss Lawrence was dark and thin and seemed very tall, but when you're five everyone seems very tall. She was frightening, but she was a genius. She ran the school on totally unconventional lines.

The principle was that children proceeded at their own pace. You had structured lessons, but if you were good at English, for instance, as I was, you went into whichever class was right for you. So when I was six I did English with the nine-year-olds. If you were bad at sums you stayed where you were, or even went down. Each class had a shifting population.

The classes were called blue, yellow, white or green not one, two, three, four. Although everyone knew white was the top class, it wasn't labelled as such.

The uniform was lovely. We wore the most beautiful pale blue tunic, the old-fashioned sort with box pleats, and a most heavenly colour green blouse, and the tie was blue and green stripes.

I stayed at the school until I was nine and then we moved to Devon where I went to a convent. I hated all the nuns; they were horrible. For the first and only time in my life I was hit, only on the hand, but it was with a ruler and it hurt a lot. I think I was well taught though because from there I passed my 11-plus.

I was only nine when I produced my first magazine, called *Stories*, which I copied with carbon paper and sold for tuppence — though very few people actually agreed to pay. The stories were all serials so people would want the next issue. I obviously already knew about page-turners as a nine-year-old.

Next I went to Totnes High School for three years until we moved again, to London, and I went to Notting Hill and Ealing High School where I met my other favourite teacher, the English mistress, Margaret Crane.

She was just brilliant. I absolutely adored her and had a terrific crush on her. She was inspiring and great fun and she made reading and English literature fun. Miss Crane let me develop my own writing style, she wasn't pedantic and grammary and rule bound, though she'd say: "This is much too long," as people have been saying to me ever since. She would have been a terrific copy editor. She had a wonderful sense of humour as well and she used to giggle, which was very rare in a teacher.

We became friends and met occasionally after I left school, but lost touch. She went on to become headmistress of Shrewsbury High and must have retired by now.

I was an only child, and education was important to my parents, especially my father who was a bank manager and a talented writer. He always used to tell me: "You can do anything if you want to", an attitude that was reinforced by that first little school.

RHONA CAMERON
comedienne and author

I had a hard time at school. I was badly bullied and ostracised by other kids because I was sexually confused and promiscuous and also because I was adopted. But I had several teachers who made life bearable and by the time I was in my late teens I adored school.

Lawrence Randak at Campie Primary School in Musselburgh was in his early twenties and had spent some years in America. He was full of passion and energy and enthusiasm which we found fascinating and refreshing having been taught mainly by elderly teachers who were Victorian in their attitude and technique. Lawrence Randak taught us to play basketball and cooked us Chinese food and offered us an escape from our small Scottish fishing town where everything was homogenous. I was a lonely, only child and he found me an American pen friend in Boston. I'm still in touch with Lawrence and he comes to see me perform the odd gig.

When I moved on to Musselburgh Grammar School (which was by then a comprehensive) I found I polarised teachers. They either liked me and encouraged me or – like the domestic science mistress, Mrs Fairclough – they loathed me. I already knew how to cook, but Mrs Fairclough consistently gave me poor marks for what I made in class. To test her out one day I swapped my dish of macaroni cheese with one made by the most popular girl in the class.

She got full marks (for my dish) and I got bad marks (for hers). I challenged the teacher and she hated that. I challenged quite a lot of people when I was at school. I was only really interested in drawing, writing, reading and sport.

I'd already shown a talent for writing at primary school where I won a prize for an essay entitled "The day I got my hair cut", written from the point of view of a dog, and Alison Reid encouraged me further. After a bad beginning when she would send me out for being disruptive, we became friends and I babysat for her kids at the weekends. I showed Alison all my poems and writing and she helped me and told me what books to read and introduced me to culture. She was in charge of the debating society, which I ran with my mate, Alistair. I won public speaking awards and other extra-curricular awards and in my last year Alistair and I were made head boy and girl.

I was obsessed with the science teacher, Joan Carlisle, who came into my life around the time my father died. She taught biology, anatomy and physiology, which I wasn't interested in, but I signed up for because of her. She was about 27, blonde, short and athletic with a big bust and I was in love with her and followed her around, sent her poems and rang her up at home. Many years later she came to one of my shows in Edinburgh with her husband and their kids.

Mrs Taylor, who taught drama, was great. She was the first teacher to let us call her by her first name, Judy. She wore smocks and chunky jewellery and was very passionate and volatile and she had an English accent, which was very unusual. We didn't often meet English people in Musselburgh.

But the teacher who was really special was Ian Patterson who taught art. He was a father figure to me after my father died. He was one of those teachers you didn't cross the line with and he commanded respect, even from some of the harder characters. He had a walrus moustache, was very tall and balding. Ian Patterson didn't just influence my work, I went to see all the films he saw and read the books he read. I was brilliant at art and he got me into art school – but I mucked it all up by not getting enough Highers to take up my conditional place. Ian Patterson was devastated because he saw that I had wasted my talent, and I subsequently wasted my life for the next 15 years in drink. I let him down and I let myself down and sadly he's dead now. Strangely, he died in the location of his favourite film, *Death in Venice*.

ROGER GRAEF
criminologist and documentary film maker

Norwood Hinkel was the music teacher at Putney School, a progressive co-ed boarding school in Vermont. No marks were given and there were no formal examinations. It was founded by Carmelita Hinton, one of the most progressive educationalists in the United States. The theory was that teenage competitiveness was enough; a combination of curiosity and wanting to impress our peers would drive us. I was there from 15 to 17.

For the previous seven or eight years I'd been at a very good and highly competitive day school in New York City, the Horace Mann School for Boys, which was a factory producing future lawyers and Wall Street bankers. I'd planned to move on from there to a grander establishment, but I changed my mind when I went to Putney to see a friend graduate.

To their credit, my parents didn't try to influence my choice and it was only after I went to Putney that I discovered that that was what they had always wanted. My father was a doctor, but Putney made a real attempt to mix social classes. There were lots of scholarships, lots of foreign students and working class farmers' boys and girls.

I was passionate about jazz and from the age of 14 had used false ID to get into Birdland on Broadway to listen to the greats like Dave Brubeck, Thelonious Monk and Charlie Mingus.

I disliked classical music because my mother had dragged me to concerts I didn't much enjoy, and suddenly I found myself at a school which was really serious about it. Norwood Hinkel insisted that everyone at Putney sang on Friday nights: Bach cantatas, oratorios, and chorales – really serious stuff – and the standard was high.

I soon got into all this because I was keen on sport and one of the footballers I admired persuaded me to go to a concert given by Rudolph Serkin, one of the greatest pianists in the world, who lived next door to the school. I sat about 10ft away from Serkin playing *Hammerklavier* and suddenly the point of the whole thing hit me like a bulldozer. Within three months I had switched from playing trombone to flute and had changed from being a jazz fan who hated classical music, to trying to get into the choir.

Norwood Hinkel just said "Look fellas, when you come to this school you're going to sing and you're going to play and you're going to do it properly." And we did. He only taught music. He was middle-aged and looked a bit like the dormouse in *Alice in Wonderland*. He spoke with a slight accent and was probably German. He was incredibly serious and very bossy. He treated us all as if we had signed up for the Berlin Philharmonic. The competition worked. I was one of those smart-arse New Yorkers who thought I was able to have opinions about everything, but I rose above my prejudices. We sang madrigals in the football locker room the way other teenagers would sing pop songs – I'm not kidding.

Another great teacher was Charlie Brinkley who taught history. He was charming, aged 45 or 50, thinner than Norwood Hinkel but like Norwood, losing his hair. He had a kind of salon, very much in the Oxbridge tutorial manner, in which his irony and wit were famous. I absolutely loved it.

Charlie Brinkley could cut you off at the knees. Those of us who liked his sense of humour adored him, though some students didn't get the joke. I have to admit that in a way both men were a bit cruel, but having come from a tough school where everybody achieved, I was able to cope.

Going to Putney changed my life. If I hadn't gone there I would have been a lawyer. When I went on to Harvard I planned on becoming a campaigning lawyer but having learned at Putney to try anything, I got involved with the dramatic society and started acting and then directing. I was about 19 and I suddenly realised what I wanted to do for the rest of my life.

SUSIE DENT
word expert on 'Countdown' on ITV

Mrs Briscoe was formidable. She was very strict – there was absolutely no chattering in her lessons and no laughter – and I was rather frightened of her. But she was so passionate about her subject that I loved the German language from the moment I first heard her speak it. She taught me from the age of 13 at the Marist Convent in Ascot and it was because of Mrs Briscoe that I did German at A-level, went on to study German and French at Oxford and then to do an MA in German at Princeton University in America, and to teach.

She was a striking, well-groomed woman, probably in her early forties then, with a lovely face and she wore bright red lipstick. I remember her as a slightly plump Miss Jean Brodie. She invested a lot of time with pupils who were enthusiastic, but didn't have much truck with those who weren't keeping up.

Lessons with Mrs Briscoe were intense, which suited me because I was very quiet and quite studious. My parents got divorced when I was 13 and my way of dealing with the split was to dive into my work. I was ripe for learning.

By the time it got to A-levels a lot of pupils had dropped out, finding German too difficult, and there were just three of us in the class, which worked in our favour because we had hothouse attention. Mrs Briscoe chose some beautiful books for our set texts, such as the lyrical writings of Theodor Storm. I thought his work about nature and love so romantic. I find German much more powerful than any of the Romance languages. There's a wonderful quote which compares French with a park, English with a country garden and German with a deep wood.

Mrs Briscoe was a brilliant teacher and it was she who triggered my passion for the German language, but it was my professor at Princeton, Eric Santner, who was my greatest inspiration.

When I first went to America to study I didn't know anybody and wasn't sure what I wanted to do with my life. Princeton is a very preppy Ivy League university and all the students seemed certain they wanted to become academics. With my English accent, pale complexion and usually dressed in black, I looked and felt very different. Eric was a soulmate without knowing it because he was also slightly different. He didn't fit into the whole preppiness of the place. He was a free spirit; an urban, slightly alternative individual and one of the most thoughtful, inspiring and inspired people I have ever met. He was Jewish, dark and handsome with deep dark eyes. He wore little round glasses and dressed stylishly. I think he came from Chicago, but he'd lived in Germany for a long time.

I did my dissertation on madness in German literature and he was very interested in the use of psychology in studying literature. We both loved the Germany that emerged after all the horrors of the War. I remember seminars outside on sunny days sitting on the grass listening to him and thinking how privileged I was to be there. He has had a phenomenally successful career, has written lots of books and is hugely respected – and rightly so.

I'd gone to Princeton to do a PhD, but changed to an MA and without Eric wouldn't have stayed the course at all. I realised that academia wasn't for me though I taught freshmen for a year and loved that. Eric completely supported my decision to change direction. I came home, joined the Oxford University Press, first working on bi-lingual dictionaries, then English dictionaries, and many years ago joined *Countdown*. I've made hundreds of appearances on the programme now.

I've kept in sporadic touch with Eric Santer, but not with Mrs Briscoe –though I did once bump into her in a library in Oxford and still felt rather awkward in her presence.

HAZEL IRVINE
TV sports presenter

Robert Pullin was my enigmatic music teacher at Hermitage Academy, a comprehensive secondary school in Helensburgh on the River Clyde about 25 miles north-west of Glasgow. I played in the school orchestra, which Mr Pullin conducted with unbelievable gusto, his mop of black hair flopping into his eyes. Sometimes when we got through a particularly difficult piece he'd throw his baton across the room in celebration.

He was very ambitious with his choice of music for us. We had a go at everything, even, I kid you not, the *1812 Overture*. I was in the violin section and eventually moved up from third to first and we had a huge woodwind section and a large number of strings and brass. Mr. Pullin organised us to play public concerts and we did the usual stuff like Strauss and Stravinsky, and our party piece at the end was always the *1812 Overture*, which we played at a considerably slower pace than professional orchestras.

Music practice with Mr Pullin was always great fun. He was a fantastic guy, everybody used to laugh and joke with him. He got the best out of us by the force of his personality and when we finished a piece his eyes would bulge and he'd look around the room with his right hand outstretched. His sheer pride in our achievement came shining out of his face. When we started on a new piece he would have us sight read very slowly through it and I'll never forget the sense of accomplishment we felt when we got to the end. He would look at us as if to say, "You did it. Fantastic." He was a real inspiration.

He was very forward thinking in teaching us an appreciation of music. He was very hot on the stories behind the music; it wasn't just a question of playing the right notes. In our second year he asked each member of the class to bring in an album of our choice and give a 20-minute lecture on it. People chose anything from Bob Marley to AC/DC. I picked Barbra Streisand's *Guilty*, the one she did with the Bee Gees. Mr Pullin was pretty clued up about pop as well as classical music. He was a huge Beatles fan. I was in class the day John Lennon was killed and he talked about Lennon's legacy and played us Beatle songs.

I was also very keen on sport at school, and Mrs Waudby who taught PE was inspiring. She was a very gentle woman who was able to get her message across with great calmness and authority and she, too, showed the enjoyment she got from our achievement. Mrs Waudby was instrumental in my career as a hurdler; she spotted my talent and nurtured it. I represented the school in athletics and was in the hockey and netball and trampoline teams and Mrs Waudby drove us to matches in a white mini bus with the school crest on it. She also encouraged me to write reports of how we'd done for the school magazine and the local paper, the *Helensburgh Advertiser*.

Mr Swanson, who taught me geography for my Highers, was very dapper and quick-witted and had a lot of fun with us. He was probably one of the first teachers who treated us as adults, but he still managed to command a great deal of authority. There is a smarty pants in every class who tries to pull up the teacher and Mr Swanson always had a quick, funny put down that made everyone laugh, even the person who made the remark. He was very good on human geography, which I considered doing at university, but finally chose English – and came home with a degree in art history. Mr Swanson loved his subject and he was passionate about it and, like Mr Pullin and Mrs Waudby, got real pleasure from seeing us achieve.

I kept in touch with all three teachers and have been back to the school several times.

WAYNE SLEEP
dancer

All through my early school years I was teased by both pupils and teachers alike. I was teased because of my name – one teacher used to call me Arthur Sleep because I was always half asleep in class. I was teased because I had a Devon accent, because I was a dancer and because of my height. I was very much an outsider.

My reports were average. I was in the C stream at West Hartlepool Technical School, where I remember making a model theatre in woodwork class which fell apart because I'd stuck it together with bits of chewing gum.

The first teacher I met who I really liked was the headmistress of the Royal Ballet Junior School which I joined at 13, Lady Agnew. She was great. She taught Greek mythology and geography. My geography wasn't so good, but I loved Greek mythology because it involved acting.

Lady Agnew was very grand, very eccentric; an elegant, statuesque lady with auburn hair which she wore in a plait wrapped right round her head. She was always immaculately turned out in tailored tweedy costumes. Her first name was very unusual – she was called Swansea – and she'd taught in Africa for a while. She liked me.

Lady Agnew took us on outings to the Royal Ballet and she would watch me throw myself round the salon afterwards trying to do the steps I'd just seen the professionals doing on stage. Other teachers thought I was showing off, but she encouraged me to extend my range. When I reached the sixth form Lady Agnew took us to art exhibitions on a Friday morning. We saw the first pop art exhibition in London and the first Goya exhibition.

Graham Bowles was the English literature teacher at the school and I loved him because I loved English literature. I remember he only had one arm, but I never found out why this was. Every week Mr Bowles got us to recite a poem and I excelled at that. I loved verse and he encouraged me. He knew all about the personal lives of the writers we studied as well as their work, which made lessons much more interesting. I got three 0-levels and one of them was in English literature. I also passed history and art.

Molly Zambra, the art teacher, inspired us all. She had time for every single person in the class. Some of the other kids were brilliant at art and I felt inferior because my work was just OK, but she gave me confidence and nurtured my talent and brought me right up to the standard to pass the exam.

Mrs Zambra was as wide as she was tall. She waddled as she walked and breathed heavily because of her weight. I was really fond of her and gave her a stool I'd made in woodwork as a present. I kept in touch with all three teachers after I left.

My most formidable teacher, however, and my mentor, was Dame Ninette de Valois, who had just retired from directing the Royal Ballet and become director of the upper ballet school when I was there. She and I bonded right away. She invited me round for lunch and we talked a lot.

When it became obvious that I wasn't going to reach the required height for a dancer I got very depressed. I stopped growing at 5ft 2in at the age of 17 and was going to take a pill that I hoped would make me taller. Dame Nina wouldn't hear of it. She thought I was destined to be a dancer and assured me I had a future and said: "You're just going to have to jump twice and high and spin twice as fast as anybody else." Not long before she died, at the age of 101, she was a studio guest when I was on the television show, This is your Life and described me as "The greatest virtuoso dancer the Royal Ballet has ever produced." I was so proud.

RASSHIED DIN

designer of the Diana, Princess of Wales, memorial at Althorp

For me school was a battle zone. I went to Ordsall Secondary Modern, which was in the docklands area of Salford, and there was a lot of violence and bullying. Even the teachers were beaten up.

My father was Pakistani and couldn't read or write and my mother, who was English, had had a very poor education. It was important to them that their children did well at school. There were 10 of us who survived of a total of 13 born and I was the seventh son, which is supposed to be lucky. My parents ran a chip shop and my two favourite teachers, Miss Stevens and Mrs Taylor, went there regularly to buy their lunch.

Lesley Stevens taught art, which was my favourite subject. She was a tough character – you had to be to survive at that school – but very enthusiastic. She looked a bit like Suzi Quatro. She was very attractive and wore short skirts with a man's shirt which was always covered in paint.

Quite often I would bunk off other lessons to carry on with the piece of work I was doing in the art class and she would cover for me. During lunch breaks, when you were not allowed in the school, she would lock me in the stockroom so I could carry on working, and she would let me work on after school.

At weekends she took me and a couple of other favoured pupils to art galleries. She was friendly with my parents and sometimes popped round for tea. She saw a talent in me and encouraged it. I was a cautious student. I didn't want to stand out by being too good or too bad, but I was ambitious. By the time I was 15 I knew I wanted to be an interior designer. At home we took it in turns to have the one single bedroom and when it was my turn, I painted it completely white – floors, walls, ceiling, everything – and took down the curtains.

When I told the school's so-called careers officer I wanted to do interior design his response was: "We haven't got anything like that here, lad," as he read through his list. He offered me the chance to become an electrician or a clerk in the dockyards.

When I insisted on something artistic, he suggested painting and decorating and enrolled me at the local college of technology. While I was there I went into the art department and suddenly my eyes were opened. I did a foundation course at Salford Tech at the same time as O-levels and went back to Miss Stevens for help with the coursework.

Mrs Taylor taught English at Ordsall and she, too, had a fantastic sense of humour. She made English easy and great fun. She was a real Sixties woman, skinny and very stylish in her mini skirts and boots.

Mrs Taylor lived in Failsworth, near Manchester, and I remember going round with a couple of other pupils to help decorate her house. She gave us lasagne, which I'd never eaten before and thought was very exotic. After that she introduced me to other new food and occasionally we would all go out to a restaurant as a treat.

When I was in my fifth year the school became a comprehensive so I didn't, as had been planned, become head boy. I won a number of prizes for art and English and was good at sport, not because I particularly enjoyed it, but it was a way of not getting bullied. School was a survival course and holds few good memories. The happiest day of my life was the day I left.

Things were much better at Salford College of Technology and there I met Muriel Valf, who taught English literature and language. She taught Shakespeare in such a way it was a real pleasure going to her lessons. Like my other two special teachers, she was young and attractive.

She had long blonde hair and sparkling eyes. She didn't become a friend in the way the others did, but she was great in supporting me and encouraging me to get out of Salford and she helped me to get into Birmingham Polytechnic, as it then was.

JILL PATON WALSH
novelist and children's writer

Sister Mary Philomena was beefy, red-faced, Welsh, short-tempered and had very bad teeth. She taught singing at St Michael's convent in north Finchley.

Music was a compulsory part of the curriculum and Sister Philomena's attitude was that God gave everybody a voice and although sometimes she couldn't imagine why He wanted to hear some of the sounds people made, if it was the voice God gave you, then that's what He wanted to hear. You raised it and you sang, and you damn well sang in tune. She'd play a phrase on the piano and make you sing it, and use the ruler on your knuckles if you didn't get it right.

She would take a whole class and enter them in north London choral competitions and sometimes win, which was amazing since there was no selection and the choir included people like me who were tone deaf.

In spite of the ruler and the harshness if we sang out of tune, we all adored her. Even though I don't have a voice, I learned to listen to music and to sing in tune. But more than that, she taught me how to handle talent and the lack of talent. She was inspirational. I have remembered her attitude when I am teaching myself. It's easy to say: "You can't really do this," but the best teachers don't give up.

I learned when I was teaching what is now called creative writing, that those who have no natural talent must not be allowed to opt out. Everybody can do in the end what they want or need to do, to a much greater extent than we give them credit for – if they keep trying and if someone has faith in them.

The main difference between Sister Philomena and other teachers was that she was in love not only with her God and with her vocation, but also with her subject. She adored music. She had a lovely voice, deep, vibrant, powerful, mezzo perhaps. I remember she loved to sing Schubert's ode to music, *Du Holde Kunst*. In class we sang rather fusty folk songs and pop classics and a great deal of plainsong because we sang a mass every week.

I didn't keep in touch with Sister Philomena after I left. She was in late middle age when I was a child and will long since have gone to sing in the heavenly choirs.

Two of my contemporaries and I were the first girls from the school to get into university for at least 10 years. There was a feeling that it was a dangerous thing to be clever; thinking might cause you to question your faith. And worse than being ungodly, it was unmaidenly. When I got into Oxford they offered a mass for my soul. They were quite right; I got into difficulties at once and left the church.

I went to St Anne's to read English and became a teacher for a while. In those days women stopped work when they had a family and I stopped teaching to have my three children. I began writing almost immediately because I found being at home boring and I desperately missed the children I had been teaching. In particular, I missed the less able ones, those who needed careful handling and who had been very rewarding to teach. I wanted to write for children like them. The result was *Hengest's Tale*, the first of 30 children's books I have written.

Sister Philomena hasn't crept into any of my books in person, but in attitude I think she has – this feeling that a thing is always worth doing. If you do something well, you get lots of satisfaction, but if you can't do it well, it's worth doing it as well as you can.

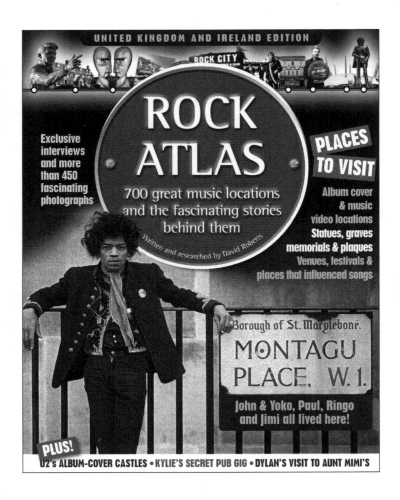

UNITED KINGDOM AND IRELAND EDITION

ROCK ATLAS

700 great music locations
and the fascinating stories
behind them

Written and researched by David Roberts

Exclusive
interviews
and more
than 450
fascinating
photographs

PLACES
TO VISIT

Album cover
& music
video locations
Statues, graves
memorials & plaques
Venues, festivals &
places that influenced songs

Borough of St. Marylebone.

MONTAGU
PLACE, W.1.

John & Yoko, Paul, Ringo
and Jimi all lived here!

PLUS!
U2's ALBUM-COVER CASTLES • KYLIE'S SECRET PUB GIG • DYLAN'S VISIT TO AUNT MIMI'S

256